Comments on the first edition of *Futurewise*:
'I was eager to see how your predictions compared with reality. Therefore I read once more [the first edition] of *Futurewise*. Result: continuous astonishment at how much of what you predicted has become true – in many cases at an even more accelerated pace than originally assumed. This result merits a huge bravo and encouragement.'

Werner Augstburger, former Senior Vice-President, UBS

Comments after Futurewise presentations:
'Superb. One of the most interesting and entertaining presentations I've ever heard.' 'A real "out there" thinker.' 'He challenged many of our business beliefs.' 'Top performance.' 'Energetic, interesting.' 'Very entertaining.'

Evaluation forms of partners, Accenture

'Please express our deepest gratitude for participating in the Microsoft Global Accounts Summit last week in the Hague. Your session was very well received. Every person in that room was glued to what you had to say.'

Stephanie Rowland, Global Accounts, Microsoft

'Your presentation was one of the most striking "events" I ever experienced.'

W. Mul, Director, Corporate Human Resources, Anthos

Comments on 'Building a Better Business':
'A really helpful guide to success.'

Brent Hoberman, Co-founder and former CEO of lastminute.com

'A perfect summary of all important factors that contribute to success in business and private life.'

Robert Salzl, CEO, Arabella Hotel Holding International

'Excellent management books should spur you into action. This one does!'

Lord Leitch, Chairman of the Employment Panel, formerly CEO of Zurich Financial Services in UK and AsiaSEN, Aria Foods

DR PATRICK DIXON advises senior teams of many of the world's largest corporations on a wide variety of global trends and their impact on risk exposure, customer behaviour, product innovation, competitor activity, marketing, management processes, motivation, leadership and public policy. He has been ranked as one of the 20 most influential thinkers alive today,* is author of 12 books, chairman of Global Change Ltd and Fellow, Centre for Management Development, London Business School.

His multimedia presentations on the future are experienced by up to 2,000 people a time in up to four countries a week. His clients include HSBC, BP, Siemens, GSK, Google, Microsoft, UBS, Credit Suisse, ABN AMRO, Aviva, Allianz, MunichRe, Infosys, Shell, 3i, BBC, Fedex, PricewaterhouseCoopers and the World Bank. He has also presented at the World Economic Forum.

He is often described in the media as Europe's leading futurist, and has appeared on hundreds of TV and radio broadcasts for CNN, CNBC, Sky News, BBC and ITV. He has written for many publications including the *Financial Times* and *Time* magazine. His own WebTV site has had over 10 million unique visitors.

He is also heavily involved in humanitarian projects in the poorest nations. In 1988 he founded the international AIDS agency ACET, now a rapidly growing federation of community-based prevention and care programmes in 22 countries, which he continues to lead. Dr Dixon trained as a physician at Kings College Cambridge and Charing Cross Hospital, London. In 1979 he began his own IT start-up in artificial intelligence and medical computing, before going on to specialise in the care of those dying of cancer. He was born in 1957 and is married with four children.

patrickdixon@globalchange.com
+44 7768 511 390
www.globalchange.com
(articles, presentations, videos, free books)

*Thinkers 50 global executive survey (2005).

ALSO BY PATRICK DIXON

Building a Better Business
The Genetic Revolution
The Truth about Drugs
The Truth about Westminster
The Truth about AIDS
AIDS and You
The Island of Bolay
Cyberchurch
Out of the Ghetto
Signs of Revival
The Rising Price of Love

FUTUREWISE

To Sheila, my best friend, closest adviser and source of endless encouragement for over 30 years.

FUTUREWISE

Six Faces of Global change

*A personal and corporate guide
to survival and success
in the third millennium*

PATRICK DIXON

PROFILE BOOKS

This fourth edition published in Great Britain in 2007 by
Profile Books Ltd
3A Exmouth House
Pine Street
Exmouth Market
London EC1R OJH
www.profilebooks.co.uk

3 5 7 9 10 8 6 4 2

Typeset in New Baskerville by MacGuru Ltd
info@macguru.org.uk

Printed in the UK by CPI Bookmarque, Croydon, CR0 4TD

A CIP catalogue record for this book is available from the
British Library.

ISBN 978 1 86197 814 1

Contents

Introduction

Life in the third millennium

You cannot fight against the future. Time is on our side.

W. E. Gladstone 1809–98

Either we take hold of the future or the future will take hold of us. Your company may have a reputation for brilliant leadership, outstanding innovation, clever branding and effective change management, but the business could fail if the world changes and you are unprepared. The larger the corporation, the greater the risk that you are flying blind, misled by old data.

Such institutional blindness is common, which is one reason why so many organisations use futurists and scenario planners to analyse future trends. Trends can pose threats as well as opportunities. We urgently need the big picture, to plot the longer-term sweep of future history, or lose focus and direction.

We need to be futurewise. That means planning to change tomorrow, future-thinking at every level, taking a broad view to out-plot the opposition. Being futurewise is about shaping the future, making history, having contingencies, staying one step ahead.

This millennium will witness the greatest challenges to human survival that we have ever seen, and many of them will face us in the early years of its first century. It will also provide us with science and technology beyond our greatest imaginings, and the greatest shift in values for over 50 years.

The future is about emotion. As history shows us, and more recently in reactions to terror attacks, SARS, the threat of bird flu and in food health scares, reactions to events are usually far more significant than the events themselves. Therefore we need to give close attention to how fast the emotional climate is changing and why. This can be unfamiliar territory for those analysts who prefer historic numbers, graphs and tables as their basis for future strategy. As we will see, small activist groups, many influenced by religion, will learn how to wield vast influence, driven by a passion for a better world.

This fourth edition of *Futurewise* has been altered very little from the twenty-year vision first set out in 1998 but has been stretched a decade further into the future. Many of the things that I expected are already history, such as: rapid growth of tribe and state-sponsored terrorism, loss of civil liberties as a result, new viral threats, growing protests against globalisation, Internet replacing phones, the rapid rise of China, growth of London, rise of single issue activism, demand for stronger corporate ethics, recycling as a way of life, growth of Islam as a political force, the online retail revolution, economic and commodity price instability, growth of 'reality' TV shows, chips fused with brain tissue, advances in human cloning, designer babies, global agreement on carbon trading as a response to growing anxiety about climate change, rioting in France over pensions and strains in Europe following the euro, prior to enlargement.

Very few of the many expectations listed in earlier editions have been removed, unless they have now become history, although some timings have been adjusted forwards. We may debate about dates but the trends on which *Futurewise* is based are clearer than ever. So what is coming next? While no one can predict the future, there are fundamental processes at work which have many consequences. From these we can plot out reasonable expectations – things that could happen which need to be considered and prepared for. That is the futurewise challenge.

SIX FACES OF THE FUTURE

The future has six faces, each of which will have a dramatic effect on all of us in the third millennium. Each is important but not equally so, depending on who you are and where you are positioned on this globe and on the social scale. It is impossible to keep them all in view at once: some are related, others are opposites. Together they form the faces of a cube which is constantly turning. The faces spell the word 'FUTURE'.

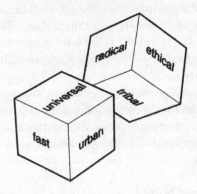

Fast and Urban sit together on one side, Radical and Ethical on the other. On top is Universal, and beneath at the opposite extreme is Tribal. Most executives spend their lives looking at the cube from above, at a world which is fast, urban and universal. However, one twist through 180 degrees presents us with a very different view: a world which is tribal, radical and ethical. Understanding the tension between these two dominant views is essential to understanding life in the third millennium. As we have seen, a tiny minority who are strongly radical, ethical and tribal can affect the rest of us profoundly.

Expectations, predictions and challenges to management

Out of these six faces cascade over 500 key expectations, specific issues and opportunities as logical workings-out of these important global trends. These range from inevitability to high to low probability – but still significant enough to require strategic planning and personal preparation. There are more than 200 challenges to management – key questions which demand answers. There are more than 100 futurewise issues for individuals. However, there is one single overriding factor which is central to understanding tomorrow: the Millennium Factor.

THE M FACTOR

Few people have woken up so far to the impact of the millennium. My children are the M generation. Their entire adult existence is being lived in the third millennium. Children born today will have little understanding of the second millennium. The M Factor will not be instant but profound, far-reaching and very long lasting. Expect to see the M Factor affect every aspect of life on earth over the next 150 years.

We are seeing it already in many countries, as a radical rethink about values. Indeed, whenever I talk to people about the future, they talk to me of their concerns for themselves, their families, their communities and the whole world.

Making sense of our history

The human brain makes sense of the past by dividing it into intervals: the day marked by the sun, month originally by the moon, year by season. Then there are decades and centuries. So the nineteenth century becomes the Victorian era, and is seen as a single defining period with its own distinct culture and traditions. But unlike the sun or moon cycles, these time-stones are entirely artificial, set in concrete only by the diary of humankind. They are entirely the product of a human need to pigeonhole events into neat time-frames. And four time-events were to hit us in the same instant: new year, decade, century and millennium.

Every decade has a character

Every decade has its character. Only a millisecond of eternity separated the 1960s from the 1970s yet we all recognise instantly the music, style and architecture of the 1960s. The same could be said for every decade in the past 100 years. It is totally irrational to think that whole periods of human existence can be neatly framed by decades, centuries or even millennia dated from the hypothetical birth date of Jesus Christ, but they are. We all know what we mean when we say that a building is nineteenth-century. By the year 1904 people recognised that the old century was dead.

Get into the third millennium

In the latter half of the twentieth century if you wanted to insult your boss you would have said that he or she was still stuck in the 1970s or 1980s – or perhaps even the nineteenth century. However, the insult has changed: 'You're still stuck in a late twentieth-century time warp. Get real, this is the third millennium!' or 'That's so last century'.

No architect wants to design a late twentieth-century building. At Greenwich in London, a huge millennium dome, designed by Richard Rogers, was built to celebrate 2000. Imagine a group of Japanese tourists being shown round in 2050. What will the guide say?

There is only one accolade that is likely to satisfy architects of the large number of great buildings opened in 2000–20 that is: 'Ladies and gentlemen, here is an outstanding example of early third millennium architecture, expressing as it does the hopes, aspirations, dreams, anxieties and fears of the new millennium.'

Expect to see hundreds of millennium structures around the world, all curiosities by 2015, many decaying and an embarrassment by 2025, all competing to be the defining image of a truly third millennial building. Expect more Eiffel Towers: big white elephants criticised at the time that people grow to love and then fight to save.

Expect third millennial fashion, clothes, radio, television, culture, music, art and social codes. The real winners will be those who tap into this huge shift – and help define it. What television producer wants to produce second millennial TV? What clothes designer dare risk his or her annual collection being labelled as a rehash of tired late twentieth-century fashions? Every creative talent will be focused on trying to interpret what the third millennium means. Expect to see radical shifts by 2020 in every aspect of art and culture with eccentricity pushed to the limits of every extreme, before settling down into a third millennial rhythm of life.

Changes can be dramatic – look at the shifts in social customs and dress from the eighteenth to nineteenth to twentieth centuries. Do we really believe the globalised dark suit and tie will still be standard male uniform in 2050? Expect not only major shifts in fashion but also revolutionary new fabrics.

So what does third millennial life look like? Faster, more technology-dominated, data-obsessed but more intuitive, sensitive, spiritual and environmentally aware.

If you are a pre-millennialist ...

Pre-millennialists tend to see 2000 to 2020 as just another couple of decades. The trends of the 1980s and 1990s continue, just more of the same. Post-millennialists are very different. They are products of the third millennium. They live in it. They are twenty-first century people, a new age. Expect to see one of the greatest generation gaps in recent history between pre- and post-millennialists. The trouble with trends is that we always look forward. We look back to find the line of the curve but our perspective is blocked by the patterns of the past. Looking ahead is progress.

However, the lesson of history is that the pendulum always swings. It is never still except for a millisecond at the outer limit of each swing. It is true that at extremes the pendulum moves relatively slowly and it is far harder to tell the current direction. It never swings true, but always twists somewhere new.

Trends and countertrends

To every trend there is a countertrend, which is why media pundits are able at once to describe, for example, trends to greater liberalism and greater conservatism. Both are true – of different tribes in the same society. So gay rights movements continue to make advances at the same time as America is becoming gripped by cultural conservatism, with ideas such as marriage, religion and civil society seen as the answer for the future.

Drug use soars, with growing calls for decriminalisation, at the same time as a neo-prohibitionist movement seeks to make it all but impossible to smoke a cigarette in a public place. Expect to see millennial culture clashes between opposing trends, a world increasingly of extremes with tendencies to intolerance as groups fight to dominate the future. But not driven merely by *culture* clashes, the greatest forces will be unleashed by clashes of *conscience* influenced by strong religious conviction, or lack of it.

Which trends will be dominant?

The big question is this: if trend and countertrend coexist, which will be dominant in the new millennium? The truth is that in a pluralistic, multitrack society there are a number of pendulums operating and each creates new business opportunities. Dominance is less important with the emergence of micro-communities, micro-markets where all that matters is being able to target every trend with a package of products and services.

Expect to see whole industries built around micro-marketing techniques, micro-advertising, micro-distribution networks, micro-affinity groups.

Trend 'wild cards' – managing risk

Expect trend 'wild cards' over the next 20 years and plan for them with rapid-reaction capability and streamlined decision-making. Most business time is spent managing high probability, low impact events, which are usually extensions of existing business activity. But the really interesting areas to watch are the small blips on the outer edge of the radar screen, some of which are moving rapidly. These low probability, high impact events or 'wild cards' can strike rapidly and transform your world. It's easy to dismiss them as improbable and therefore insignificant. However, there are a great number of them. A large business may be able to list several hundred potential wild cards, each with a probability of happening of 1 per cent or less in any year. However, on closer inspection, such lists usually turn out to contain risks which are more likely to happen than first thought. Therefore the risk of such a business being hit by such a low probability, high impact wild card is far higher than boards usually realise. And in every risk there is also opportunity for fast-moving companies to respond in innovative ways. Wild cards can be clustered into types of event to plan common responses. At the outer edge, wild cards include catastrophic events such as viral pandemics, dirty bombs, nuclear accidents, vast volcanic eruptions and climatic disasters.

Sustainability – major driver of change

The key to understanding the post-millennialist is one word: sustainability. The reason is simple: current trends are unsustainable, or seem to be. We have never before had the means to view an entire century and the effect is extraordinary. One hundred years of film – still and moving – has charted almost every detail of our lives. We began with horses and carts and ended with people living in space. We began with books of paper and card and ended up with cyber-reality. Can we survive another hundred years of increasingly rapid change? What about another thousand years? Could this be the last millennium?

Economic growth is at the centre of every government strategy, yet in the third millennium expect that rapid economic growth as a universal goal will be increasingly questioned by activist groups in the wealthiest nations. Growth means more things, greater wealth, but does it mean greater happiness? If quality of life means being happy and fulfilled, what is the secret of it all? Since the very wealthy show little or no sign of being any happier than lesser mortals on modest incomes, this is a fundamental question.

Economic growth is clearly vital to the poorest nations, to provide food, clean water, education, better health care and other things. However, the real human need for relentless growth in material wealth of those in the most affluent nations will be increasingly debated, especially in terms of costs to future generations from overconsumption and environmental damage.

We can divide every nation into hundreds of social groups. Each is a market sector. Each has its own set of pendulums. Each will react to the events described in this book in different ways.

You may be an optimist or a pessimist. The future is uncertain and many possibilities are alarming, but I am an optimist, convinced by the potential of science, medicine and technology, and the capacity of human beings to build a better kind of world. But the way ahead will not be easy, being beset with moral challenges, economic and geopolitical instability, resource limitations and consequences of climate change.

Radar screen and road map

So here is a radar screen and a road map. The radar screen is a grid you can place over any organisation, a structure for thinking about the future. It will help you scan your own world for emerging trends.

The road map? You will find in this book not only a way to make sense of new blips on the radar screen but also a guide to how they may behave in the general frame of the future.

CHAPTER 1

Fast

Speed will be everything

HISTORY IS ACCELERATING

The first face of the future is FAST: speed will be everything. Never before has the future so rapidly become the past for so many people. History is changing faster than you can calculate a risk or exploit an opportunity, whether you look at trends in the economy, global events, industry, social factors, politics, or share prices.

Who wants to wait?
The developed world is cash-rich, time-poor and intensely impatient. Up to 30 per cent of web sales can be lost if a page takes more than 30 seconds to load. Expect even less tolerance tomorrow in an increasingly instant age. The impact on the way we buy, sell and live will be huge. Holidays will get shorter, more focused and more frequent, often interrupted by messaging from around the world. Expect rapid growth of stress-busting weekends, indulgent experiences, and exotic activity bursts.

No time for Do-It-Yourself (DIY) and materials
Expect falls in sales of DIY tools in all developed countries over the next decade, as time-poor, stressed-out people opt to hire in expert help, rather than risk their health, time, property and money. Losses will be offset by dramatic growth of DIY sales in emerging nations such as Poland, Slovakia, Slovenia, Belarus, Russia, India, Brazil, Indonesia, Thailand and China.

Expect outbreaks of irrational behaviour caused by minor delays – as we see when busy executives gather around a hotel lift, repeatedly punching the call button in a foolish attempt to make it arrive faster.

Political whirlwinds affect whole continents
Look at the speed with which the Soviet Union collapsed in 1990.

When the Iron Curtain fell, people thought the reunification of Germany would take five years. It took five months – although with huge longer-term problems. Expect further rapid realignments, with North Korea top of the list as the last outpost of Stalinism, a country bankrupted and starving after three decades of mismanaged central planning and its intense suspicion of all neighbouring countries. North Korea could crash at any moment, spilling thousands of starving refugees into China, South Korea and Japan. Expect, too, increasing signs of regional pressure for change in China.

Look too at the rapid creation of the global alliance against terrorism, formed in less than a month in 2001, with unheard of co-operation and international consensus. Russia and the US stood shoulder to shoulder in warm solidarity – until the Iraq war, disagreements about how to respond to Iran's nuclear programme and further Israeli-Palestinian conflict.

Trends are becoming more unpredictable
Take Mexico's financial crisis in 1995, dubbed the first financial crisis of the twenty-first century. It hit with ferocious speed, as global investors fled. Then came Thailand's devaluation of more than 23 per cent in 1997, following huge exchange rate fluctuations. Thai authorities wasted more than $30 million propping up failing financial institutions exposed to bad loans, before shutting down 42 companies. The Bank of Thailand lent 10 per cent of the country's entire gross national product to 91 finance companies. Then came the sudden collapse in the currencies of the Philippines (70 per cent fall), South Korea and Malaysia, Indonesia and

Turkey. Expect further runs on currency in emerging economies
and a rush into protective alliances which will also be overpowered
by market forces, driving both inflation and deflation in different
sectors.

Expect contagious forces: events in one area will impact globally
as we saw in the dioxin panic in Belgium when contamination of
animal feed led to a ban on entire food lines from Europe.

Expect growing uncertainty about what the Chinese government will do with its foreign currency reserves – more than 1
trillion in dollars alone by early 2007, most of which was still in US
government bonds. Expect these reserves to be used more creatively in future, to buy entire corporations, invest in real estate and
to buy other strategic assets such as energy supplies. Just 10 per
cent of China's dollar reserves could be leveraged to make a $600
billion investment fund.

Tigers turn to lion cubs
The so-called 'tiger economies' of South East Asia grew fast on the
back of cheap labour and cheap exports but now have the whole
of China to compete with, while the expectations of their own
labour forces have risen.

New contingencies, IMF and inter-bank co-operation, better
investor information and better government communication, are
not going to be enough to prevent more speculative attacks on
one currency after another. Global money flows are just too big
to control, as the Bank of England found when it was forced out
of the Exchange Rate Mechanism. Expect the UK to remain out
of the euro until at least 2012, observing the agonies that some
other nations experience in managing their economies with zero
control over domestic interest rates, their own exchange rates or
rates of inflation. In the meantime the ongoing US budget deficit
and trade deficits will raise growing numbers of questions about
US long-term economic stability.

Expect increasing North–South tension as emerging economies
come to realise that abolishing all trade and currency restrictions
in a rush for growth also places their countries at the mercy of
rumours, hunches and market opinion. Expect an even greater

backlash against globalisation, with some nations reduced to 'economic slavery' by massive, destabilising currency flows. Expect large institutions to continue to make (and lose) huge fortunes trying to outguess volatile markets in these countries. Expect countries to rally round to help stabilise each other's currencies, as seen in Thailand where China, Japan, Australia, Singapore and Malaysia were among those contributing emergency loans. Expect far more countries to see rioting in the streets as workers, students, wealthy intellectuals and the retired all unite to vent their various angers and frustrations at leaders, global institutions, wealthy, 'arrogant' nations and ethnic minorities.

World markets will be seen more in the future for what they are already: a great global gambling den, using hunch, intuition, guesses about how other investors will feel, detailed analysis, inside knowledge, a host of other factors – and a dose of good fortune.

Instability of basic commodities

Basic commodity prices will also continue to fluctuate wildly at times. Take zinc, for example, whose price fell 18 per cent in an hour on 29 July 1997, catching on the hop Chinese producers who had pre-sold what they did not own, or the meteoric rise of copper prices which had a similar impact in 2005. Expect increasingly complex investment instruments to be developed, so that a commodity sometimes rises or falls dramatically as a large market intervention is made, linked to a completely different and apparently unrelated event. Expect growing worries about these poorly understood derivatives and about the activities of ever more powerful but lightly regulated hedge funds.

These rapidly growing so-called funds will eventually be seen for what they are: insurers against future price movements, organisations that place large bets that the value of a share or commodity will rise or fall by a particular date, rather than managers of real assets. Expect many more hedge fund scandals, some with losses of many billions of dollars, and consolidation of more than 9,000 funds, with greater emphasis on transparency, risk management, integrity and control.

Inflation and deflation
While hyper-inflation will continue to threaten failed economies such as Zimbabwe, in most developed economies, inflationary problems are already beyond the memory of most under 30-year-olds. The majority of young adults have no experience of inflation above 5–10 per cent. Their world for the past decade and a half has been one of deflation in retail prices of almost all manufactured goods and many services – with the major exceptions of health and education.

Despite popular opinion, even oil prices were still below their mid-1970s peak in early 2007, when allowing for inflation. The net result of all this has been that consumers have been able to spend more money on things like housing, further contributing to rising real estate prices (see pages 68–70).

In future decades the current obsession of central banks with targeted inflation rates of 2–3 per cent may look strange, and dangerously close at times to deflationary risks given a sudden economic shock.

Retail outlets will react to falling prices by pushing their products up-market to try to maintain profit margins – for example, by replacing UHT fruit-juice with freshly squeezed product, or replacing robotic car washes with teams of low-wage immigrants.

Management gurus are the high priests of confusion
Every week there are more books on management. Each one often contradicts what has gone before, struggling to find a fresh view. Insecure managers will continue to gobble up the latest fads, kissing common sense and their own experience goodbye. Expert, confident managers will continue as before to dismiss management fads in favour of their own intuition and intelligence, working out their own solutions, adapting and borrowing as they go from a wide variety of sources.

However, the speed of change will guarantee an almost permanent supply of semi-neurotic managers who are constantly on the lookout for some new, comprehensive solution to their day-to-day problems. But where is the real evidence? Anecdotes, one-off case studies and personal opinions are not enough to run a business with. They are no substitute for rigorous analysis.

Management theory is still an immature, inexact and unproven semi-science. Expect that to gradually change over the next two decades as rigorous statistical and analytical tools are devised to try to prove or disprove the key elements of success in management methods.

Expect 'management historians' to become sought after, analysing industrial successes and failures during the previous Industrial Revolution and at the turn of the twentieth century. At the same time the traditional case-study approach to business school training will come under pressure from those who question its relevance to new situations today and the validity of firm conclusions based on a series of anecdotes from a unique company at a particular stage in the unfolding global economy.

Better 'early warning systems'

The interval between early signs and a full-blown new trend is shorter than ever and long-range forecasting is becoming more difficult. The narrower the field, the harder it is. So, for example, while the trend towards global networking is undisputed, the exact year in which the value of online share trades will overtake traditional brokerage is not.

This means that corporations need to have far more sophisticated early warning systems, able to tell the difference between 'background noise' (minor changes) and the first sight of a major new trend. The trouble is that most decision makers tend to be cocooned by people in the same industry or even the same company. Corporate blindness and industry blindness are real dangers. The most important new trends may be most obvious to experts outside the work and culture of the institution. An example is online banking, where banks, very wisely, drew heavily on consultants from high-tech companies rather than just financial services.

The problem with large institutions is the time lag between a board decision and the mobilising of the entire company in a new direction. Just drawing up plans for approval can take months. But today's world requires a different approach. Multitrack scenario planning is needed, with strategies laid out for several options and some investment in each. The extra cost is offset by the extra profitability gained through being able to move faster than the rest.

Smaller companies will have a competitive advantage. Take, for example, North Island Credit Union in San Diego, which had an entire new IT system running less than ten months after agreeing the contract. A global bank would have taken at least two years.

The future will not be more of the same

Tomorrow's technology is next week's dinosaur. The trouble is that most companies are obsessed with pushing accepted technology to the limits, when the greatest long-term threat or opportunity could come from a technology or innovation which is so different that very few take it seriously today. Most managers struggle to keep up with technology they already have, and are unable to grasp the full impact of the future. They stumble from one new software application or online tool to the next. Success means fast integration of today's new technologies and preparation for the next generation of tools.

History shows that most companies fail to cross the bridge from old to new: they just shrivel and die, driven by people who are future blind. Media companies become software houses. Food retailers become banks. Phone companies become entertainment providers. It can be a confusing world for people who have spent an entire decade or more in a single industry.

Don't (always) believe market research

Listen to your customers carefully – but don't always believe what they say. Business tends to see through the lens of what it thinks it can sell and customers only know what they are used to. But teams and customers don't understand enough, nor are they visionary enough to be able to guess what they might want from totally unknown possibilities in future. Market research only tells you how people think and feel today. It tells you little about life beyond the next year or two.

If a bank had asked its customers in 1995 whether they would want to spend hours at home staring at a computer screen, managing their own accounts, and buying books or food, most would have said no. The 25 per cent of UK web users who now write web diaries (blogs) would not have told researchers they wanted to do so if asked two years before they started.

Expect consumer surveys and market research to be sidelined by scenario-based customer profiles. Market research is non-exclusive data. Anyone can go out and ask the same questions, so where's the competitive edge? Everyone has to do it for feedback on what's happening today, but the faster the world changes, the less relevant market research becomes for planning.

Trust will often be your greatest asset

Trust can be rapidly lost. In many industries such as banking or insurance, trust is your only real asset – without it the business is over. But in a digital age, trust can be lost in a day, yet take decades to rebuild. Therefore expect particular attention in future to be given to reputational risk. And that means more than staff management or clever public relations.

The future is not about hype, but about revelation and information. Most people searching online believe blogs (web diaries) and other consumer comments far more than official corporate websites. Traditional advertising will be a waste of time in future if the online community is condemning a product as dangerous or rubbish. Good products and services on the other hand will increasingly sell themselves through community networking at the speed of light, supported by sensitive campaigns, rather than with most sales driven by them.

At conferences, I frequently ask delegates who they believe the most, when searching for a hotel online: the official online advertisements or sites like www.tripadvisor.com which contains tens of thousands of comments by recent hotel visitors? The vast majority of delegates vote every time for trip advisor, which is why these kinds of sites will often be more important than any advertising campaigns in the future.

Expect many marketers to add false client entries to such sites, to boost popularity or destroy a competitor. These sites will fight to retain their own reputations for independence and accuracy by trying to verify that those posting reviews are genuine customers.

THE TELEPHONE REVOLUTION

As I predicted a decade ago, we are now seeing widespread availability of global calls for a flat rate, regardless of distance. High-quality multichannel interactive TV, video links and data streams will alter social behaviour and family relationships. When travelling I have connected my hotel room to my home for days at a time – with sound and video – using broadband net connection. I sit virtually in my office at home. Our children are able to walk virtually into my hotel room. Hotel charges range from zero to $10 a day.

Tens of millions in the poorest nations have already abandoned landlines for mobiles in most circumstances. More than half of all adults in the world already owned a mobile by 2006 (3 billion active handsets). Export more than 4 billion by 2010. Developing countries have leapfrogged over old copper networks with mobile technology which allows a developing city to install instant city-wide 4G networks with just a few masts on buildings.Expect a continued boom in wireless technology in all the poorest nations. Expect office switchboards to use any landline or mobile as extensions, creating virtual global telephone exchanges. Expect all except disposable mobiles to have cameras and colour video screens. Expect explosive growth of community-based wireless networks, where home users of wireless broadband allow free access to millions of other people, on a reciprocal basis, while also being paid a small fee if non-users sign on.

The ideal phone
The ideal phone weighs almost nothing, has batteries that never need charging (methanol fuel cells), accepts voice commands and works anywhere – even in a 20-mile tunnel. The next decade will see universal use of ultra-low-cost mobile devices which can use landline, satellite or local wireless networks.

Expect phones to get larger and smaller. Larger for those wanting full integration with personal organisers, videostreaming and web surfing. Smaller for those in a voice-activated wireless world. Expect some manufacturers to lose their way as old-style mobiles are swept away by micro and macro devices, as well as mobile cards for laptops, most with inbuilt global positioning. Location-sensitive technology will unleash new innovations to direct users to local services.

Call centres are the new sweatshops or workhouses

As I predicted a decade ago, we have seen a massive push in international call-centres. But accent is key. Expect many businesses to move customer service call centres back from countries like India after worries about losing customer confidence, and as India's labour costs rise.

Wherever based, this is high-pressure, chicken-coop work with 90 per cent of employees' time spent on calls, crammed into little boxes in front of computer screens. Expect new regulations in Europe and North America concerning the working environment of these humans working in battery-hen conditions.

Expect a big reaction against companies that go on forcing callers to push buttons in response to endless choices and a return to human beings on the end of the line. People need more contact not less in a virtual world. Voice recognition allows key words to be understood from near-continuous speech, regardless of accent, but the technology will continue to make customers angry, with a strong preference for real human contact.

Expect the universal implementation of intelligent call answering, with incoming lines switched automatically to the person or department which last dealt with calls from that number. Operators will expect to have complete data on the customer on-screen as they answer the call, as well as automated suggestions on products to cross-sell.

Cross-selling makes the margin

Expect high-volume cross-selling operations in every large business, with loss leaders used to sell higher-margin products. Expect cross-selling to diversify. For example, an insurance quote will be followed with 50 per cent discounts on weekend breaks and 10 per cent off car dealer prices.

You will find companies have an uncanny ability to tell exactly what you want just before you realise you need it. It's already started online, with adverts prompted by your interests and recent page requests.

THE NEXT DIGITAL REVOLUTION

More microprocessors than people

We live in a world where there are now many billions more micro-processors than people on earth. At that rate it means we will see machines in 2030 with multiple processors that are 10,000 times more powerful than the fastest chips we have today, continuing the pattern of doubling in power every 18 months. Expect break-throughs with nanotechnology within 20 years, allowing chips to shrink massively to microscopic levels as well as providing revolution-ary new coatings for use in clothing, engineering and medicine.

Convergence and divergence

Expect manufacturers to pack ever more digital gadgets in single devices in the race to the top on capability and to the bottom on price and distinctiveness. Expect big confusion as to what tomor-row's consumers will actually want and about how younger and older people will behave. The end result will be loss of focus about strategy, design and innovation. The real winners will be those who can beat competition on price with identical multifunction products, or those who innovate in creative ways to be different.

Expect more ipod-style innovation with products that diverge from everything else on the market, doing one of two things superbly well with brilliant design, becoming lifestyle or fashion accessories.

Convergence is all about co-packaging and economies of scale, but all true innovation is by definition about divergence. Doing things differently to serve customers better. Low cost will mean we will all own more devices, each of which is used mainly for one or two things only. An ongoing challenge will be for large flat screen manufacturers to keep pace with ever greater requirements for low-cost high resolution TV and movies. Expect a huge battle between rival next-generation DVD formats, and confusion among consumers with delays in purchasing equipment.

Software will always be full of bugs

Portable computers today are so powerful that even if technology stands still it will take programmers at least 50 years to exploit their capability. The trouble is that they have less than 20 months before a new generation arrives, upwards-compatible, but total compatibility is a myth.

The bugs never get sorted out in old versions and bugs in new ones never will be either, for the same reason.

The situation is made far worse by the general culture of the industry. Car manufacturers would never get away with launching vehicles they knew were completely unreliable. But that is normal practice throughout the computer industry, and will continue to be so until software becomes fully self-repairing. Even then, expect problems. I often speak at IT conferences and find that most of every audience is struggling with basic tasks like synchronising their computers to their personal organisers. But these are computer experts. It is a scandal that such poor quality and unreliable systems are sold at all.

Virus attacks will continue to soar. Expect many more dangerous viruses to emerge and expenditure on anti-virus software to increase rapidly, with daily updates for vulnerable high-value systems.

And then there is junk e-mail – now more than 90 per cent of all mail sent globally, with 7 billion messages a month by early 2007, doubling every six months. A few dollars will buy 100 million addresses, generating billions of adverts a month, all sent at zero cost; 30 per cent of this junk is pornographic – some containing obscene images illegal in many countries. Yet children with e-mail addresses are also targeted. Junk wastes time, violates personal values and corrupts the innocent. Expect legal controls on a global scale backed by new technologies. National laws are ineffective.

Google Adsense – democratic ads
- Live auction 24 hours a day for every key word
- Free placement using Google intelligence onto relevant pages
- Customers click on free ads, marketers pay per click
- Each click is a vote which can improve positioning
- Hundreds of trial campaigns can run at once
- Instant results and revenue calculations
- Long-term tracking of behaviour of those who respond to ads
- Vulnerable to fraud-software attacks – creating millions of fictitious clicks to earn revenue or run up massive bills for competitors

Expect Google to challenge the universal presence of Microsoft applications for e-mail, word-processing, image manipulation, web-building and database creation with bundles of free software both fast and reliable paid for by advertising.

Disaster recovery will be a major headache
A growing number of people have experienced appalling loss of time, productivity and original work by computer failure and backup nightmares. I have lost count of friends of mine who have lost several years of e-mails or hundreds of contacts, or entire drafts of books or a life's work of research and lecture notes. Computer sales have increased exponentially. Therefore the majority of such personal stories of catastrophe are around the corner. And most of them will hit small to medium-sized companies the hardest together with many workers – all of whom thought that it would never happen to them. Since they comprise most of the economy, this is a big time-bomb waiting to go off.

Half of all companies fold following a major loss of data. Expect PC disaster recovery to become a key issue, with lawsuits taken out against companies for selling backup systems which fail to restore a complete working system at the touch of a button.

If companies are vulnerable, then many teleworked executives at home are especially at risk. How many backup every day? How many would survive a burglary or fire? One professor recently left his laptop on a train – losing several years of research data, because his only backup was on a removable disk inside the same machine. Expect a whole new support industry for home workers and small businesses including telephone support, remote PC configuration and software repair and (rarely) same-day site visits. Expect home workers to back up data online to computers in other cities.

THE FUTURE OF NETWORKING

Continued share price speculation will be irrelevant to the relentless march of the online revolution. People don't check the Google price before deciding to buy a holiday online. By 2015 more than 1.5 billion people will have some access to the online world.

Every home in most developed countries will be networked with global intelligence. Lowest income groups will find the web wandering in through the front door, in every phone and video recorder and in other devices.

It will take at least another 20 years of mega-fast technology before the online world even begins to deliver some of its greatest impacts. Life beyond the Net is a world where everything, everywhere is totally, wirelessly connected, all the time.

The next stage of online development (so-called web 2.0) will be dominated by community-building: projects like the Wikipedia encyclopaedia that anyone can add to or edit, blogs or web diaries which are written by 5–20 per cent of different countries' online community. eBay is just one example of successful businesses built on communities, itself creating many millions of new businesses, each exploiting gaps in what the ever-larger retail giants are able to provide. MySpace, Facebook, the Google Adsense system, tagging webpages for others to look at – all these are examples of this rapidly growing dimension.

The spirit of the online community will continue to be a passionate belief that information should wherever possible be given away for the benefit of humankind as a whole. This ethic will have a profound effect on many businesses, on the debate about intellectual property, and on attitudes to copyright and digital theft.

Wireless tagging

This is the world of radio-frequency identification devices (RFIDs). Already 10 billion intelligent devices are released into the environment every year, each one the size of a grain of sand. Each with hardware, software, microprocessor, memory, able to send and receive data, needing no battery and able to last for up to 100 years. These devices are powered by electro-magnetic radiation in their own environment.

If Wal-Mart tags just the warehouse boxes going into their stores, they alone will need 10 billion a year, while Carrefour will need a further 2 billion and Tesco 1 billion.

We can expect over 100 billion RFID tags a year to enter the environment by 2015. This will jump to many trillions if big retailers follow the example of Metro in Germany, which has started tagging each item in shopping trolleys. While Metro gains check-out speed, expect big concerns about privacy as we have seen in reactions to tagging of razor blades by Gillette and trousers by Benetton. Electronic tagging will revolutionise manufacturing, wholesale and distribution, reducing theft by up to 70 per cent and warehousing costs by up to 40 per cent. These tags will be in universal use for tracking airline luggage, freight containers, courier packages, car tyres, clothing and other higher-value items by 2015.

Expect concerns not only about loss of privacy but also about counterfeiting, hacking, eavesdropping and denial of service attacks. People will be worried that strangers will be able to learn about clothes they wear, jewellery they buy and credit cards they own using scanners hidden away in a briefcase or a pocket.

Watch out for next-generation clinical monitoring and biometric devices, many of which will be using related technologies. This will develop into a $230 billion market by 2020, with ultra-low-cost retinal scanners and fingerprint recognition in every computer.

Expect rapid growth of electronic ticketing for all modes of travel, using mobile phones for payment. We will see an end to paper travel documents, including passports, made irrelevant by iris and fingerprint scanning, together with instant access to visa information at ports of entry, except in the poorest nations, where passports will still be needed.

Biochips and bionic people

Salmon, cows, sheep and other animals are already being labelled with chips under their skin, and the same is happening with pets. Fish devices transmit their identity to monitoring stations as they travel up and down rivers.

Expect widespread tagging of people by 2010. Probation teams and other 'control' groups are already using this technology to track convicted criminals. Expect social or voluntary tagging to become more accepted, such as the skin chips used by members of a nightclub in London to allow instant admission. Biology will drive many computers. Expect DNA computers, taking advantage of miniaturisation in every cell, where a blueprint for an entire human can be packed in a nucleus – 20–30 years away perhaps, possibly less. In the meantime brain cells are being grown on chips to create intelligent biodigital devices.

Electromagnetic radiation – growing concerns

Expect growing consumer worries about exposure to electromagnetic radiation from mobile phones, masts, wireless networking and wireless tagging. There is already strong evidence that such radiation in high doses has a direct effect on living tissue. There have also been other research reports suggesting that heavy use can increase the risk of an acoustic neuroma (tumour of the nerve supplying the ear). Expect many more research papers suggesting a wide range of effects (or no effects) to add to the confusion. Eventually it is likely that there will be enough evidence to provoke the first class-action lawsuits by people convinced that their health has been damaged in some way. But they will find it very hard to prove a case.

In the meantime the UK government has already issued repeated warnings to parents about restricting mobile use by young children, and has banned the building of new homes near overhead high-voltage power lines. Expect science to prove a slight effect from phone use but a very low risk in normal use compared with the benefits of use to millions of people. Expect research to confirm that a very small proportion of the general population are particularly sensitive to electromagnetic radiation.

Net threat to tax collection and national sovereignty

Recently I decided to add to my website a bookshop offering for sale 1.5 million titles. It took less than 30 minutes to create this virtual branch of an existing online store, earning me 8 per cent commission on every sale. My company is in the UK, the web server in the US, and the online store is owned by a US company. So where is the business to be taxed?

As international regulation tightens, expect to see some countries emerge as cyber-havens with a policy of non-co-operation. Expect other countries to create free zones or semi-states, geographic areas where companies can relocate as online enterprise high-tech villages, immune from normal taxes. Expect many nation states to retaliate by seeking to punish information service providers who handle content from these non-regulated sites.

At present the location of the sale is determined by the address of the credit card user, but future e-payment systems and false registrations will make these tracking processes more difficult.

Companies will relocate to avoid not only tax but also decency and gambling laws. Pornography sales account for perhaps 10–15 per cent of all Internet retail turnover; 10 per cent of all web search requests yield adult sites and 1 per cent of all searchable web content is adult-rated. The sex industry will be a significant driving force in online commerce throughout the next 30 years, pushing out the boundaries of new technologies such as video phones, interactive TV and virtual reality. Another online driver will be gambling. Americans bet $6 billion online in 2006 – almost half the global total, before Congress voted to ban credit card payments by US residents for such services.

The web has the power to distort national economies, to control government policies and to redesign national frontiers. The e-world may mean the end of income tax as we know it and complex e-transactions are making audits of company finances more difficult. Already it is relatively easy to switch unlimited amounts of money online without trace, and send virtual cash in attachments.

Homes of the future are intelligent and resource saving

Expect your washing machine to alert an engineer when it starts overheating and the garage doors to open as you approach, the lights to go on and the coffee machine to begin pouring a fresh cup of coffee.

Expect all new homes in Western countries to have some intelligence by 2015. With sensitive people-responsive temperature control in every room, light controls and other features, smart houses will boast 15–20 per cent energy savings. However, expect some household name companies to suffer huge losses on 'intelligent home' technologies that few want – such things as fridges with touch sensitive panels for e-mail and web on the doors.

Expect intelligence to be coupled with local background power generation in many homes from solar cells, and from wind. Expect growing numbers of new homes to feature local sewage treatment, with methane gas recovery for heat and cooking, together with recycling of 'grey water' from rain, bath water and washing machines for use in the garden.

Expect other energy saving technologies at home, such as geothermal heating, which reduces costs by up to 75 per cent, using a heat pump connected to a long coiled pipe buried deep in the garden. As the pipe cools, the house radiator gets hot. Solar energy warms the earth and the pipe, allowing more heat to be sucked out of the ground. The process can be reversed in summer, cooling the house and warming up the rock/earth. This heat can be stored for use in winter.

Telecom will be dominated by owners of the biggest networks

Telecom requires huge economies of scale for survival and global domination. Therefore expect more rapid mergers and new alliances as large companies join in a frantic bid to carve up the world. Many smaller companies will be wiped out. Expect widespread concerns about monopoly power to be offset by rapidly falling telecom prices, and by lack of effective regulatory mechanisms for global predators. Expect speeds of more than 20 megabytes a second on mobile networks – more than ten times faster than the fastest broadband most people had in 2006 and 400 times faster than an old phone line.

The impact of broadband/3G/4G/5G

What happens when phones are always online and transmitting data at up to 20 megabits per second?

◆ Book download 0.025 seconds
◆ 20,000 e-mails 12 seconds
◆ 110 minute film 8 minutes

Two hour videoconference is equivalent to

◆ 12 million e-mails and attachments

Conclusions: Telecom companies charging for data flow, not connection time, will push the market towards video as the only way of maximising bandwidth use and revenue. Internet traffic will be totally dominated by video by 2012. Video-enabled phones will change how people live as price per call falls dramatically. As reporting in the Iraq war showed, video is about entering someone else's world and experience, showing them what's going on.

Internet replaces phones

Internet calls will pose a major threat to traditional telecom companies by 2010, although few will develop an adequate response by 2012 or even recognise their degree of exposure. Skype alone will be used for voice or video calls by more than 200 million people a year by 2010 while others will offer free conference calls for up to 500 a time and free multiway video conferences for more than 20 people in a session.

Information apartheid

Every nation will divide into information haves and information have-nots. The privileged will accelerate ahead leaving a digital underclass far behind. But some in wealthy countries will totally reject the digital world – refusing mobile phones or e-mail. A nation's future prosperity will be determined by the proportion of haves and have-nots, something which will change fast in many poorer nations by 2012.

Keeping information secure will be a major headache. Intellectual property, copyright and patents will be increasingly difficult to protect, and will be challenged from many different directions.

The future of the music industry

The old music industry will be cut down to size following huge losses from music copying. Extra revenue from official music downloads will not be enough to prevent major restructuring. It will be almost impossible for the largest companies to launch medium-sized bands and we will see a smaller number of bets on new talent. Despite this, the numbers of albums released each year will explode, mostly made in musicians' own homes, using their own equipment and marketed themselves to communities like MySpace. Some of these self-made promotions will become global fashion icons.

Homeworkers will gain power

Many people already have greater bandwidth and more powerful software at home or in their pockets than at work. This is partly due to last-century thinking by chief technology officers particularly in their failure to take advantage of free productivity tools like Skype or Google Desktop. Companies that find ways to integrate these kinds of tools into their corporate systems without security risk will see a jump in productivity of their senior teams.

Expect the gap to widen with personal innovation and creativity happening mainly at home. As every boss knows, it is almost impossible to write a report in a busy office and allowing people to do such things at home can boost productivity by more than five times.

Lifestyle electronics

Expect intelligent clothes, wireless monitoring, for example of blood pressure and pulse by your watch with automatic alerts to hospital teams. Expect common standards for plug-in-and-go additions to what you wear.

The end of books?

Non-fiction books work well on-screen, but reading fiction usually requires a long linear read and paper is likely to remain popular for decades to come. Paper is convenient, faster to read, more comfortable on the eye, has higher resolution and you can write on it.

Aesthetics will be important in physical publishing: the smell, feel, weight and binding of a 'real book', the quality of the paper and the kind of ink. Expect publishers to continue to integrate with other media companies to form complete information corporations. Expect severe online competition for all non-fiction reference works, with users expecting to pay little or nothing per page. Expect digital books with more than 100 double-sided paper-thin electronic pages. But 'real' books will remain popular, partly because of publishers' paranoia about digital theft and partly because of speed of access and convenience. An example is a flight timetable – it is faster to open a page than to type in a query.

FUTURE OF THE WEB

I already have easy access to over 10 million web TV channels, which is just a few of the websites already broadcasting video on demand, mostly brief promotional clips. People say they have no need for that many channels, but that's because they have no vision. I don't watch much TV – but I want at least 100 million channels. That means that I can watch whatever I search for. It could be a page about new cars, with a video of the latest design. It could be a domestic version of the 'Big Brother' TV show.

I launched my own TV station online in 1998. It takes less than five minutes to record a comment on today's news and add it to a server the other side of the world. My site has been used by 10 million different people (globalchange.com). Web TV for most people is still poor quality but it will rapidly improve as the cost of bandwidth falls. Several million personal sites already offer sound or videoclips using MySpace and other free platforms. YouTube users alone were posting more than 65,000 video clips every day in 2006. Expect huge efforts by business to tap these kinds of communities for new products and services. Expect the web to overtake newspapers for news access in all developed countries for the majority of people by 2012.

Expect thousands of larger churches and mosques regularly broadcasting live services, and hundreds of academic institutions, parliaments and law courts, all pumping out a mixture of live and pre-recorded sound for those that click on their sites.

Mainstream TV companies lose audience

One thing is certain: mainstream TV companies are in for a severe hammering. Traditional stations will fight back with endless rehashes of sitcoms, reality shows, game shows and repeat movies but it won't reverse the rapid slide. But there will be a demand for live shows, especially where the audience at home feels involved, for example in voting. Expect experiments with live drama and comedy shows and other interactive formats.

Television shows shaped by instant audience feedback

Live shows of all kinds will be greatly influenced by an entirely new broadcasting concept: audience scoping, or instant analysis of how viewers are feeling. Traditional audience shows rely on a studio audience to create feedback through laughter or signs of boredom. But studio audiences are completely atypical. They have chosen to be there as enthusiasts and can't leave. They have all the benefits of live performance and are dangerously unrepresentative of what is happening in living rooms across a nation.

Expect TV companies to be able to see what is happening, using the web and interactive TV controls. Every few seconds a screen will show them whether the last joke caused the audience to fall 2 per cent or rise 2 per cent. Fast audience falls are the result of channel zapping within two to three seconds of mild boredom or offence, while audiences soar if a percentage can be persuaded to hang on for a few minutes before zapping somewhere else or turning the TV off. Audiences are built by collecting and keeping viewers who zap into programmes, adding to faithful regulars. Desperate fights for increasingly bored audiences will create bizarre behaviour when presenters can literally watch millions of people walk away or sit glued to their seats. Sensationalism is very effective in the short term (15 seconds to 15 minutes) but it won't arrest the overall slide. Great shows will build audiences in seconds as viewers alert friends by text messaging. It's already happening.

E-voting systems will not only allow shaping of live TV shows, but will also be powerful enough to trigger the resignation of public officials during interviews. Next generation e-voting in every home will enable instant referenda on important issues and will be used in national elections. The result will be that higher percentages of both young and old vote regularly – and in ageing societies the net effect will be that people over 75 will be more likely to decide the future of their nations.

Desperate TV companies pay people to watch

The situation is so desperate that ABC announced it would actually pay viewers to watch programmes, offering air miles in return for questionnaires proving they had watched certain broadcasts. While advertising revenue is under threat the costs of quality TV productions continue to rise. The latest gimmick is to try to claim that although a station has few viewers, they are the right kind for your product. Individual channels in future won't have audience size or cash to make high-quality, high-cost programmes.

Advertising will change from fast clips sent out to people who don't want them to interactive adverts for people looking for information, coupled with ambient advertising – such as a product on a shelf in view of the camera during a show. Advertising breaks are already far less effective as millions zap other channels instantly, or robots do advert cuts for them. TV ads will work in the future only if they are entertaining or informative.

Passive viewing is being replaced by much more inventive searching for what to watch. That's where web TV will score highest of all: total choice. Instant access to 500,000 programmes on TV in high definition will soon be a reality as the BBC digitises its entire archive.

Expect TV, movies, music, words and software to be pirated at an unprecedented scale despite every effort of copyright holders. This will affect revenues and profits.

Expect TV browsing on mobiles to soar as charges fall – whether the latest goal, a news bulletin, a short comedy show or a greeting from friends. Expect news networks to use live instant news feeds most days from mobile video phone users who happen to be in the right place at the right time – and who get paid for their amateur journalism.

CYBER-MEDICINE

Telemedicine works

Telemedicine saves costs and lives. Why go to see a specialist when she can give you an instant interview in your own home?

- home monitoring of high-risk babies after birth
- remote advice from experts to home or hospital
- immediate access to patient records in emergency admissions
- reduction in hospital stay
- lower ambulance costs
- surgical procedure by a surgeon the other side of the world using robotic equipment

Virtually inside hearts and lungs

Next-generation imaging machines build virtual three dimensional models of life inside the patient. A surgeon can 'travel' up a
blood vessel, or down the windpipe right inside the lungs and can
practise complex operations using the 3D model.

Expect dramatic advances in three dimensional medical imaging
over the next five years. Because the machines are so expensive,
expect a further stimulus to telemedicine as world-class specialists
gather in global conference calls to decide on treatment in rare
and difficult cases, and then bring in a remote surgeon, assisted by
a local team, to oversee the procedure.

Let robots treat the sick

Medical students in future will need to know more about talking to
people and less about treatments. What's the point in a head full
of knowledge when most of it is soon out of date? When care plans
are created by robots, personal attention matters more than ever:
touch, feel, empathy and understanding from real human beings,
selected for their ability to understand.

Computer-assisted diagnosis will become universal in some
countries by 2010 before beginning a wide range of treatments, with doctors forced to use it not by law but by insurance
companies. The database will represent the collective experience
of tens of thousands of physicians. A doctor will take a huge
risk in insisting in court that his or her judgement is superior
to the computer's when the patient has died in unfortunate
circumstances.

The first universal diagnostic systems are already online. Capsule is a British programme designed to advise doctors on prescribing. Decisions using the system are 70 per cent more accurate.

Computer diagnostics will never replace clinicians' judgement, and treatment will still be heavily influenced by a patient's own views. However, computer diagnostics will help doctors practise safely for decades after qualifying.

Surgeons measured by the numbers their operations kill

Surgeons in the future will be measured by numbers they treat successfully, numbers their operations kill, complication rates after operations and length of hospital stay. Expect a rethink. These crude measures encourage bad practice – for example, early discharge, which may be safe but is stressful, painful and unpleasant. A doctor may refuse to operate on someone at risk of dying in surgery even though the patient accepts that risk. Such life dilemmas as these will dominate medical practice throughout the next three decades.

Within ten years we will have mastered the art of fusing micro-chips with living cells. Muscles driven by implanted devices or skin electrodes are no longer rare. Expect other experiments such as sight for the blind, using chips inside the head to generate nerve patterns. Brain cells in rats have already been grown on the surface of digital processors. By 2015 expect the first cyber-brains in experimental animals, where crude data is directly accessed and stored. Cochlear implants are already giving hearing to the deaf, and chips implanted into the retina are already improving sight. But these biodigital enhancers will look very crude compared with spectacular advances in tissue regeneration using stem cells from a person's own body. These are likely to be repairing sight in the blind by 2020 (see pages 111–12).

VIRTUAL CAMPUS – FUTURE OF EDUCATION

Virtual campuses are springing up everywhere. Tens of thousands of people already attend college online. Many executives are already refusing to attend on-site training, insisting on remote learning wherever possible. In future students will be charged for courses by hours online. Many campuses will provide lecture videos and notes for free and charge only for 'live contact', e-mail replies, or for marking course work.

Live video broadcasts from lecture rooms could be visited by thousands, with response by e-mail or chat, voice or video links (a few at a time).

Handwritten exams are so last-century. It is wrong to determine the future of students by how fast they can form letters on bits of paper, when their employability will be determined by how well they can express themselves on a screen, and how well they can use online tools. Expect a complete rethink about giving students online access during exams and about allowing them access to their own computer files.

Education never stops

The only way to adapt to a changing world is to keep learning. Expect people to take several graduate or postgraduate courses in a lifetime. However, as a countertrend expect a backlash against paper qualifications, as employers realise that leadership, energy, dynamism, initiative and organisational skills are not created by studying books or going to lectures. Expect a rethink about the content of MBA courses, with far more emphasis on leadership and analysis, as well as on world class communication and advocacy skills, with more practical insights from people who are actually running businesses and fewer lectures from academics.

Expect governments to set increasingly ambitious targets for adult literacy, numeracy and computing skills, and for schools to be increasingly called to account for bad performance, not only by parents but also by past pupils. Expect lawsuits by ex-pupils who feel their entire adult lives have been wrecked by poor teaching, failure to recognise special needs, failure to prevent cases of bullying or sexual abuse, or failure to stretch bright pupils to their full potential.

Expect fresh thinking about what high school is for: preparation for a fulfilled life. Today's system can churn out dysfunctional young adults who are unable to form long-term stable relationships and have little idea about the secret of personal happiness.

Expect a new emphasis on developing a broad world view as part of education. Insight as well as foresight. Cultural sensitivity as well as historical data.

Expect a return to single-sex schools in many areas where co-education has resulted in tens of thousands of boys dropping out or for religious and cultural reasons. Expect persuasive arguments that single-sex education for both sexes means sharper concentration and fewer distractions or less showing off, especially with the age of puberty falling to eight in girls (see page 92).

Expect a complete rethink about punishment and discipline, with the recognition that a no-touch policy isn't working. Expect growing intolerance of playground culture that takes threats, beatings and stabbings for granted, with strident calls for teachers to be able to teach without fear of attack from pupils or parents. Expect changes to come in steps, following particularly awful and well-publicised events such as the death of another teacher or the death of a pupil after savage bullying.

Expect tough new sanctions, including greater freedom to suspend or expel pupils for anti-social behaviour. Expect growing expenditure on special needs schools for very disruptive pupils. Mainstream schools will not be able to risk keeping disruptive pupils as the emphasis on getting results grows.

Expect continued ghettoisation in schools, with people choosing a school and then working out where they need to live. Expect the final collapse of bussing and artificial attempts at black-white integration in US cities.

Expect college libraries to become fossils of little or no importance to students except those who want to physically handle an important book.

Data location and rapid analysis are survival skills
In a world of information overload there are some basic skills that third millennial students will need. None of them are difficult to master. The greatest skill is text scanning, which is quite different from reading and requires no technology.

Faster data entry to human brain
◆ Sound via ears: 112 kbps
◆ Light via eyes: 3,000,000 kbps
◆ Lesson: Reading is faster than listening for data acquisition.
   One picture = 1,000 words, one video clip = 10,000 words.
   Phone calls are very slow compared to e-mails for information.

Most senior executives can scan 5,000 words per minute. On the phone they understand 100 words per minute.

Text scanning: a third millennial skill
◆ Primary skill will rely on plagiarism
◆ Rapid location of other people's work using search engine
◆ Ability to scan text fast – a page in 15 seconds, an entire printed book in 20 minutes
◆ Ability to assess authenticity and reliability using other online reference points
◆ Ability to write a world-class executive summary on a company or product that you know nothing about in less than 30 minutes.

In the past a top scientific adviser of a multinational giant might have received a phone call asking for a briefing on a new product just launched by a competitor. The adviser would have been expected to provide such a brief from memory. Today's world is changing so fast that a brief will always be unsafe without an up-to-the-minute data search. Human memory for facts becomes irrelevant. But wider knowledge, understanding and experience become even more important.

New ways to manage knowledge

The key competitive challenge for larger organisations in the first years of the twenty-first century will be this: can the organisation learn, or does it stay ignorant as each person's knowledge remains inside that person's brain, a situation made worse by staff turnover? Loss of corporate memory is a particular issue when downscaling or reorganising. Knowledge management can prevent some of that. Knowledge management will be a key survival issue in all large organisations over the next two decades, together with reducing turnover. Part of the answer lies in technology, but the rest depends on developing a co-operative team culture that encourages collaboration across business units, and that encourages experienced people to stay.

Training in future will be multidimensional

Lecturers will be judged not just by content but by technology and the way they use it. People need to taste the future, reach out and touch it with their hands. 'In your face' experience is worth hundreds of hours of private study.

Expect a huge emphasis on multimedia in corporate presentations, with the routine use of rich multimedia formats in portable executive presentations to clients. Designing these new art forms will be a completely new industry, drawing on experience gained in making corporate videos.

Expect an anti-reaction by 'eccentrics' who make a deliberate point of not using any technology to present, relying entirely on person-to-person interaction using flip charts or non-digitised dry-wipe boards.

Just dropping by – 5,000 miles away

I was setting up a three-hour workshop in Zurich for 30 executives from all over the world – and was also online. I was just about to return to my first slide when I heard someone say 'Hello' behind me. I turned to see a smiling face up on the wall.

'Hi there,' he said.

'Hello,' I replied. 'Where did you just spring from?'

'Durban,' came the reply. 'I was just wandering about to see who was around.' By now a stack of others were gathering around his PC. My own small camera gave him a nice view of everything.

I explained that we were in Zurich and invited him to sit in on our workshop. He did, sitting unobserved as a distant partici- pant for the first half an hour, before I flipped him back up on the screen to say hello to everyone and participate in discus- sions. His spontaneous arrival said more about virtual working than any number of PowerPoint slides. Of course he was able to call by only because I had told my computer to be friendly to cyber-callers.

It was the digital equivalent of a member of the public walking past the building and poking their head round the door to ask what all the high-tech displays were for. We enjoyed informal immediacy with someone more than 5,000 miles away. It happened in 1997. Then, such an event was a novelty; today, it's part of the air we breathe.

By 2010, mobile video phones will be everywhere and by 2012 calls will cost the same as ordinary phone calls today. Holo-phones will be interesting when they come: producing three-dimen- sional images right in front of you of the person at the other end. However, live video calls using phones or PCs will be far less popular with image-conscious youth and many executives than short self-promotional video clips on their personal web pages. The future is about emotion – and video is an emotional thing.

VIRTUAL LIFE

Virtual retailing

Virtual reality will be a boom industry, especially in retailing. Expect VR to be used in shop windows to attract attention, inside the store to demonstrate products, and also online. Expect multi- media to pour out of supermarket trolleys in most large stores triggered by products you selected in the past and your where- abouts in the store. Expect utility repeat shopping (bread, milk) to be done from home and the rest to be entertainment-driven as a leisure experience, hence we will see shopping centres turn almost into retail theme parks with wide age-range attractions.

Expect retailing to move, on the one hand, towards low-cost online sales of products with minimal support, and on the other towards price insensitive, highly personalised sales and support packages for people fed up with wasting half their lives trying to sort out problems with what they have just bought.

Expect the big shakeout of retailers to continue in developed nations, with the loss of millions more smaller retailers by 2010, replaced by chains which will increase their own-brand sales from around 10–20 per cent in 2006 to 30 per cent by 2012. However, many small shops will survive, particularly as car-use restrictions begin to bite, as people become more ecology and quality conscious and as a reaction against sameness. Expect huge growth of big retail chains in most emerging economies. Expect 100 million new e-tailers, using platforms like eBay, with combined turnovers larger than some multinational retail chains.

Expect more products individually tailored to suit people's increasingly varied lifestyles. Benchmarking will continue to be popular but will lead to convergence and eventually competition on price alone. One example is food retailing. Benchmarking of new services simply means all supermarket chains are likely to offer loyalty cards and financial services, but then where is the competitive advantage? Where is the customer value? Where is real loyalty to be found? Expect a new emphasis on continuous innovation that will remain attractive to customers – not just price and corporate efficiency, both of which are easily copied and neither of which will produce lasting shareholder value.

Virtual relationships

Despite many people's fears, most e-communication is between friends, family or team members, not with complete strangers. Written e-messages can have intense emotional power, more than voice or video calls, which is one reason why we can expect rapid messaging growth. The other reason is the freedom it gives to read and reply when convenient compared with the total intrusion of an unexpected phone call.

Virtual reality in entertainment

Virtual reality modelling is already used extensively in manu-facturing design, especially in the auto industry. Expect these technologies to be used in the entertainments industry, and also create entire new alternative worlds. Expect VR films and TV, with new tricks to convince each eye of the viewer into thinking it is receiving a different picture – without headsets. It will be the key to large-scale 3D imagery. Expect virtual reality to dominate amusement arcades and theme parks by 2015 with ever larger worlds, body suits and headsets, and vast virtual reality cinemas.

Many VR worlds already exist

Some time ago I walked in cyberspace down a street and into an art gallery. There I met the person who built it and talked to him about his art. He could see me and I could see him. What was unnerving was that we were in different countries, and so were all the others who joined in our conversation. I have also walked into a branch of a virtual bank and watched someone talk to a member of staff and take out a loan. Each of us had a computer-generated body which could walk, bow, wave, jump or whatever.

Expect millions of young people to enter global online worlds with three-dimensional characters based on photographs of their 'real' selves.

Huge numbers of businesses are already selling virtual products and services to those living in these virtual worlds, including real estate. Expect millions of dollars to be made by virtual real estate companies and by people offering upgrades to your own virtual body, including the ability to move more naturally or even to have virtual sex.

Some day I am going to stake out a piece of land in a cyber-world and build myself a house and an office, and a lecture area perhaps, as well as a meeting place.

Speech recognition faster than we can think

Part of this book has been dictated not written, and my portable computer has converted my speech into accurate text at up to 140 words a minute, equivalent to 8,000 words an hour, or an entire book in 12–25 hours – faster than any author can think.

And this is only the first day of a new speech recognition age. The medical and legal costs of repetitive strain injury could mean insurers will insist that some staff speak, not type.

Expect every major chip manufacturer to rush ahead with dedicated speech recognition chips which become built-in features to a vast range of products, ranging from washing machines to vending machines. The best products will win a big slice of a multibillion dollar market, with companies battling over 0.5 per cent improvements in accuracy at speed. There is a huge difference between having to correct every tenth word and only one word in 50. However, keyboards will continue to be heavily used for editing, redrafting and input during meetings or in noisy environments.

Voices take the strain

Expect to see repetitive voice injury as people find the discipline of clear, accurate speech strains the larynx. Expect large claims for compensation where employers failed to train staff to type properly, and were required to type a lot each day. Insurance companies will become reluctant to pay out unless correct training was given. But this is today's technology. Within ten years it will be standard practice to speak rather than type for many who never bothered to master a keyboard.

Have a look around your office – even with 2006 software, anyone you see who is typing large amounts of text is probably costing you money. Expect the economics to shift firmly in favour of speech recognition by 2010, with pressures to redesign open office areas as a result. Speech often needs privacy.

Expect future speech recognition to be silent, detecting facial and tongue movements. By mouthing words in one language you will be able to generate speech in another. The prototypes already exist but commercial application is at least two decades away.

ARTIFICIAL INTELLIGENCE

Expect self-teaching robots, able to form new thoughts, make new suggestions and think creatively – at least they will appear to be doing so.

Some artificial intelligence purists say that true artificial intelligence does not and probably will never exist. They are both right and wrong. Right in that at present we don't understand how to make computers think for themselves in a sophisticated way, wrong in that humans can be tricked into thinking and feeling that they can.

Male and female robots

Expect to hear sophisticated male and female robots at the end of the phone, and the same reaction against them as for primitive Voice Recognition Units today. In a fractured, chaotic and fast-moving world people will willingly pay a premium for human contact. For a single person living on their own and teleworking at home, a genuine human being on the other end of the line may be the only personal contact of any kind that day.

Expect premium pricing when you want to touch another person's life, when you want to know that another human being will take some action as a result of what you have just said. We are already seeing such price differentials in banking, with some banks charging customers a fee every time they use a human being face-to-face to deposit or withdraw money.

Handwriting recognition

Some people who can't stand using keyboards swear by their portable handwriting units, which convert words written with a stylus into text. The trouble is that writing on such devices will always be slower than fast typing, and less accurate.

Expect to see hundreds more 'handwriting to text' products for a generation who still like to scribble. Expect them to fall out of favour within ten years, swept away by speech recognition and other new technologies. Expect many popular palm-sized devices to be larger than they are today; scribbling on a 2-centimetre square space is even more inefficient.

ONLINE THREAT TO THE FINANCE INDUSTRY

The speed of technological change is having a massive impact on the finance industry.

The Internet could destroy traditional banking

Retail banks will be little more than wholesalers of financial services after the big shakeout. Their business is being eaten away step-by-step by food retailers, insurance companies, clothing stores – anything and anyone willing to make the move into selling credit cards, loans, mortgages, current and deposit accounts.

Every high street chain you can think of is ready to gobble up financial services market share. Pensions with potatoes, mortgages with milk and instant access online to high-interest accounts. History will record the death of many smaller traditional banks by attrition, merger and acquisition followed by cannibalisation of the business.

Banking as it is will never survive

The online community will eventually destroy the retail power base of big traditional banks. Some last-century banking services will survive, at a premium, for those prepared to pay or with no access to technology. And many consumers will stick to old ways for a while longer.

But retail banking as it still is will never survive. Banks made their profits by collecting and hoarding cash, and lending at interest. But when cash itself ceases to exist, what then? In an electronic society there is nothing physical to collect or give out. Banking becomes a meaningless concept, used to describe a defunct industry which trades not cash, but electronic impulses.

Virtual money for a virtual world

Money becomes bits of data in a virtual, electronic age. But who needs a physical bank for that? Strongholds and safes disappear, as do security grilles and guarded delivery vans. Trades happen on any computer. The bartering of bits can happen anywhere on the face of the earth, at any time, but the transition will take time. Banks in America, the EU and other developed regions will be lulled into a false sense of security by data which show the growth of cash, until at least 2020 (cash is anonymous and untaxed). They will also be confused by the fact that most people don't like to change their main bank account too often. They will take comfort from new revenues from old branches now being used to offer face-to-face mortgage and small business advice. And even when the greatest changes in retail behaviour start to be seen and when profits start to fall, we can expect that many banks will put up with low returns or losses for a long time. These will be offset by better returns from large commercial deals, high net worth customers, wholesale and investment banking. They will argue that losses on retail banking are worth taking in order to keep the bank in the public eye.

Expect further rapid growth of PayPal and other non-traditional personal e-payment systems. PayPal is likely to have 100 million users by 2010, operating in more than 50 countries, servicing more than 200 thousand sites which use it as their main payment method. Expect innovative mobile phone companies to try to seize market share of electronic payments for things like restaurant meals, ticketing and retail goods which will all be paid for on the mobile phone bill using text messaging.

Any product, any channel

In future you will buy any financial product, via any channel, from just about any source you could imagine.

Most senior bankers I talk to recognise it is only a matter of time before a mortgage will be switched from one lender to another by an authorised broker, at a single mouse click. Once the legality is established, expect such loans to be moved up to several times a day by broker robots constantly looking for better deals on identical terms. It will spell death to traditional lender-borrower relationships.

Old branches and online transactions

Over 80 per cent of European banks and a similar proportion elsewhere had recreated themselves as virtual banks by 2006. They were driven by fear of what their competitors were up to, and by the elusive dream that online transactions could cost them only 1 per cent of the cost of those conducted in the usual way. Unfortunately, there are no real savings to be had without making staff redundant and closing branches. But that takes time, and branches are hard to dispose of – so most branches in future will have other purposes such as face-to-face financial advisory support.

Expect more scams and frauds in e-banking. One offshore bank has already appeared and disappeared again after taking substantial deposits and just one European bank has been losing more than €1 million a day through e-mail scams requesting people to give their personal banking details on a page which looks just like the bank's own. This is despite every effort by the police. Fraudulent sites can appear and disappear in 15 minutes – just long enough to capture 5,000 people who respond to a wave of junk mail messages.

Online investing boom

Stockbrokerage will never be the same again. By 2006 there were already 4.3 million investors trading $187 billion of their own stocks online. Commissions have plummeted, threatening traditional stockbrokerage. So what happens to brokers? If advice is free and you pay for the deal, what is to stop me phoning my broker for advice and then doing the deal online?

Commissions are now so low that people can enter and leave the market during coffee breaks – and make a profit. Even the smallest movement in share prices is worth speculating on when deals are basically free, and online betting means that investors can make money even if markets fall, by predicting price movements. Once deal prices drop to $8 or less as a fixed price, the amount may be too small to be worth the bother of collecting for some banks. So doing the deal for some customers could become a completely cost-free loss leader.

Death of the national stock exchanges

The days of national stock exchanges are coming to an end. The process is starting to happen, though more slowly than I expected ten years ago. Companies don't like them because their global business is greater than a single exchange. Investors don't want them – they want to trade online 24 hours a day. Technology doesn't need them – because servers in one building can handle all the mouse clicks. Expect dozens of new 24-hour virtual markets of which one or two will achieve rapid global influence. In the meantime, 30 traditional exchanges in Europe have begun to react with various degrees of apathy or alarm, and with a range of new alliances and partnerships, some involving counterparts in the US, and others totally new trading platforms created by banks themselves. Expect no more than ten survivors in ten years. Virtual exchanges will cut dealing costs by more than 85 per cent, encouraging risk-taking, growth of volumes and huge liquidity – which will be the most important success factor. But the greatest issue is trust, which in turn will depend on building confidence in effective regulation.

Death of stock exchanges – online dealing
- ◆ $10 for unlimited share volume
- ◆ Small investors get current price data on-screen
- ◆ Buy/sell at work during coffee breaks
- ◆ Zero commission deals will be common
- ◆ Make your own cyber-market
- ◆ Companies sell their own stock online
- ◆ National stock markets begin to die
- ◆ Global stock exchanges – virtual, always open

Many traditional brokers still have their heads in the sand. They imagine that the 'trust' factor will save them, that people will be too scared to do big deals on a PC. That may be true in 2010, but it won't be in the longer term. Anyway, when commissions are low or free a customer can spread the risk across a large number of smaller trades.

Investors are not going to let themselves be charged thousands of dollars a year to have some broker click a button for them on a PC in an office elsewhere. So the future for brokers lies in what they are best at: giving expert advice, making sense of all the data. However, few will pay as much for a call as they would previously have paid in commission on a fat deal.

As I predicted there has been a big shift in charging mechanisms for larger accounts, a relationship which is now often negotiated annually for a fixed price – including unlimited advice and trading. And pressure is growing on performance – it is rare for an investment fund to consistently outperform market tracking funds run by robots, after deducting management charges. It all depends on who is in the team – and that keeps changing as people move to competitors.

Investment funds – future scandal

I have spoken to hundreds of retail fund managers over the years and in most industry-wide conferences the majority admit during my presentations that they are unwilling to invest their own money in their own funds unless forced to do so by their employers, because yields are often low after all the charges (up to 2 per cent a year) compared with online trackers (as little as 0.1 per cent a year). Many tell me that their own products are bought mainly by people who are too foolish to invest elsewhere. The *Financial Times* recently reviewed the performance of 44 actively managed funds over 20 years and only eight out-performed the FTSE All Share Index. Furthermore, analysis of 'tracking errors' revealed that many 'active funds' are not actively managed at all by human beings. Expect a big shake-up of this sector with accusations of miss-selling on a vast scale, especially when the truth emerges that many distributors have boycotted better value products because they pay lower commission.

Service is the name of the game

As in every other industry, service will make the difference in banking. There can be no other route to long-term success, unless you are competing on price alone, and that will be increasingly difficult. Now every executive has instant access to world data, you can guarantee that they will more often be up-to-date on what they want to talk about than their advisers.

Value-added service will include a comprehensive, well worked out world-view, placing every new event into a global frame that makes sense to the client. That's the future. Clients overwhelmed by the background noise of data flows want insight. The more the data, the more the confusion.

HEAVY TECHNO-INVESTMENT

No large corporation is going to make it in good shape without heavy techno-investment. The trouble is that most boards have no IT expertise. How can a company possibly hope to stay competitive if such people are its main source of vision about new technology? So part of techno-investment is buying techno-vision: high-impact communicators who have long-distance vision; people who can help us see beyond the tools we have today.

In most large corporations the Chief Technology Officer or Chief Information Officer is kept out of board meetings, often represented only through the Chief Finance Officer or someone else similarly incompetent to advise on next-generation technology. Expect all kinds of bad decisions as a result of separating technology innovation from business strategy, and a new breed of CTOs with broad business experience, sitting on executive boards.

Demand for futuring

Trend hunting in the future will be a far cry from the 1980s or 1990s, when everything was more certain. In a globalised market there are too many variables and discontinuities for back-projection and forward-projection to work reliably. The people who saw cyberspace before it was born were radical visionaries, boffins playing around with bad modems, crackly lines and missed connections, eccentric hacks who dreamed of the impossible because it would be fun. They were people who weren't burdened by bottom-line profit.

That's why economists don't make good futurists when it comes to new technologies, and why so many boards of large corporations are in such a mess when it comes to quantum leaps in thinking.

Second millennial thinking will never get us there. It will just produce better versions of second millennial products for a dying species of second millennial elderly people. Expect some corporations to throw up their hands in despair and give up the third millennial race altogether. They will accept the inevitability of a dying business, with volumes declining, aiming to remain profitable as long as possible with premium products and niche marketing. Some institutions would prefer to die than change.

A senior board member of a Fortune 1000 company told me: 'I'm glad I'm retiring so I don't have to face these decisions.' The trouble is that he had not retired yet, was responsible for technology, knew almost nothing about it, delayed taking the decisions and prevented others from doing so.

'What can we do?' another senior executive declares. 'We know our industry is basically dying.'

Expect plenty more fatalistic comments: whole boards that try to convince shareholders that the greatest profitability will be to scale down and down and then sell out, rather than take massive risks in unknown areas with fierce competition.

BIG BROTHER IS WATCHING

George Orwell's book *1984* gives a chilling picture of how technology could be used by a dictator to control millions. But the tools available today are already far advanced beyond what Orwell saw.

Using today's technology it would be cheap and practical to place a tiny online camera and microphone in every room of every home that could be dialled up and interrogated by Big Brother. It would add a negligible amount to the cost of any new building.

Privacy died a long time ago. In many countries the security services can track you within 6 metres by the signal of your mobile, your calls are screened, every e-mail is monitored – and all that was before the so-called 'war on terror' began (pages 131–2). All your banking and credit card transactions are seen and every webpage you request is kept on file. Our growing dependence on card-based or picture-based payment systems makes us vulnerable to being locked out by central government action, effectively a non-person unable to live except by using physical cash. But that too may become more difficult if RGID chips are embedded into bank notes.

I recently demonstrated the latest bugging devices to some company executives because they were ignorant and naively vulnerable to attack. High-quality colour cameras hidden in the head of a tiny Philips screw, pens transmitting perfect sound a third of a mile. Little bugs hidden in plugs that can be listened to online the other side of the world. Boxes to decode digital mobile phone calls – said to be secure.

During a lecture, I bugged one of the participants without him even realising. I then gave the receiver to all the others, one by one. The sound was so brilliant that they failed even to work out who was carrying the bug. They were horrified when I told them the bug was so undetectable that it would be carried by that person right back to his hotel room, and that sitting here, a third of a mile away, I would be able to hear every word he said. He started looking in his case but he was walking around with it on his own person. He was unable to find it, even with help.

Relatively cheaply you can buy a laser bug, which can pick up conversations inside an office from up to half a mile away, by bouncing laser light off the window. As the window vibrates it alters the light signals received. With the right equipment you can watch whatever is happening on a flat screen or conventional TV monitor in the next building by tuning into the radio transmission that every PC creates. The only way to prevent this is to ensure that all portables and desktops have special outer packaging.

So you are going to hear a lot more about privacy laws, surveillance, encryption and other related things. But laws will not prevent invasion by people intent on taking your company's best secrets. Market-sensitive information is worth tens of millions of dollars.

Bugs can be hard to detect with machines. They can be turned on or off by radio signals from a listening post on the other side of the world. Five minutes after a meeting is due to start the bug is turned on – for a few seconds. If the room is quiet, the bug is killed again. If the listeners tune in while a meeting is in progress, they begin to listen. When the meeting is winding up the bug is put back to sleep. A sweep of the room before or after the meeting will never detect a transmitter of this kind without very expensive and sophisticated room analysis, looking for frequency echoes that might be coming from a microphone. The sweep might take the best part of a day, and in theory needs to be repeated every time the room is used. Most bugs are placed by staff, so the vetting of visitors is not enough. Anyway, vetting visitors is impossible without stripping them naked – or worse.

Your own staff are the biggest security risk

Few board members have caught up with the implications of all this. They naively rely on security guards and electronic door keys. Cleaners, secretaries, junior and senior staff can be tempted by the offer of money or can be blackmailed. And you will never know how often it happens because your competitors are hardly likely to tell you how many times they have been stung, even assuming that they know themselves. When it comes to markets, share price swings can alert suspicions, but other intelligence is far harder to track.

Expect new, aggressive anti-espionage measures, another name for spying on your own staff. Bugged offices, hidden cameras, secretly recorded phone calls, intercepted mail, networks which routinely explore every last byte on every hard disk. The bugging of staff in their own homes, and clandestine surveillance, will raise the hackles of civil liberty groups. And many other ethical dilemmas will be thrown up when surveillance teams uncover more than they bargained for, say evidence of child abuse and other serious crime or links with terrorism.

In many countries it is not an offence to listen in secretly to a conversation on your own telephone or in your own room. There-fore the bugging of a company office with authorisation from those running the company is perfectly within the law. Bugging of staff in their own homes is more likely to be illegal. Recording telephone conversations of telesales teams, however, is an accepted practice 'for quality control'. Expect this to extend to acceptance that a company paying a worker has every right to observe the person at work to monitor performance, whether that person is aware of it or not.

Foreign spy agencies are being increasingly turned to economic spying, as well as searching for potential terrorists.

Biolock security

Banks, airlines, immigration officers or dictators will know exactly who you are from the pattern of blood vessels in the back of your eye as you stare at a screen – as distinctive as a fingerprint (fingerprints themselves may also be scanned). Tiny iris movements prove you are alive, not a high resolution photo. Sure, there will always be groups of people offering ways to cheat these devices. Expect security measures and attacks to continue a rollercoaster race, with claim and counter-claim by industry experts and packs of anarchistic hackers.

Expect a whole new super-breed of techno-freaks whose entire waking existence is devoted to busting electronic security systems. Some will be terrorists, some just bored ex-students, but others will be earning huge sums from large companies which have recruited them to wage war against their own systems as a means of testing them. Others will be self-employed, in a shadowy world where their discoveries are sold for easy money.

Bank A is rung by anarchist B, who says he can prove that $45,000 was transferred from one person's account to another the previous night and back again. He says he will tell Reuters press agency about it if he isn't rewarded for his efforts in 'testing the bank's security' for them (for free). The bank pays up, rather than risk the embarrassment. Banks also pay hackers to keep quiet when they threatened to publish names and addresses of private banking clients, or even when millions of dollars have been stolen.

Very few people are ever prosecuted for breaches of bank security. In most cases the culprit is a member of staff. He or she is then asked to leave, and is given a wonderful reference to get a job with another bank. Everything is kept quiet. The police are not informed. Six months later history repeats itself. This pattern is very common today. Expect banks to become more open with each other and with police, while trying at all costs to avoid damaging media coverage of their vulnerability.

Whenever I talk about the future, people talk to me about values and concerns they have. Where will it all lead? What kind of world are we creating? We will find the answers in the final chapter.

OTHER CONSEQUENCES OF THE NET SOCIETY

Internet addiction
Online addiction is a recognised and rapidly growing medical problem which can break up marriages and erode workplace productivity. Addiction to pornography and gambling will both grow as a result of unlimited global online access, prompting debate about ways to tighten use, especially by children and teenagers.

Informatics
We will hear a lot more about informatics, combining computer science, artificial intelligence and cognitive science – building robots to clean hospital corridors, mow lawns, vacuum swimming pools, clean carpets or farm the land. Efforts so far have been primitive.

The cars of tomorrow will be computer-driven and steered, with automatic speed regulators, road sensors, radar and cameras to detect vehicles in front and behind. Cars will be fully networked, allowing weather warnings derived from activation of windscreen wipers in cars ahead, or pre-paid tolls, booking of hotel rooms, video links to home and office, and automatic journey progress to others who need to know where you are and when you will arrive.

We will see road trains, large numbers of cars linked with electronic towbars. Studies show that traffic volumes and speeds can be increased. Those who step out of line will be identified electronically and fined before they reach home. But hackers could cause havoc. A single keystroke could throw a national motorway network into chaos.

The big issue will be insurance cover and reliability. The technology for all this already exists, but car manufacturers fear just one motorway pile-up could cause loss of confidence and damaged sales.

So wherever we look the world is getting faster, driven by technology and communication. We need a practical strategy to survive the challenges to management – and to survive as individuals.

Constant rapid change will create demand for things that stay the same: protected buildings, preserved landscapes, traditional products and processes.

CHALLENGES TO MANAGEMENT

How flexible is your organisation?
- Can your organisation adapt and change fast enough to survive?
- What strategies do you have to accelerate the adoption of change?
- Are you using training, seminars, workshops and conferences enough to set in place the new culture across the entire organisation?
- Are you using enough outside visionaries and motivators, world-class communicators able to say some of the tough things that are harder for internal people to say?

Wild-card risks
- Have you recently listed potential risks?
- If you are a small business, have you considered things such as:
  - data loss from disk failure/theft/fire
  - lawsuit
  - failure of telephone switchboard or web server
  - jury service call-up of CEO for long trial

- ❖ multiple bad debts – non-paying customers
- ❖ failure of major suppliers
- ❖ reputation attack in media
- ❖ product failure/recall.
- ◆ List some low probability, high-impact events.
- ◆ What steps should be taken to minimise risk?
- ◆ How can you benefit from possible wild cards?

Parallel planning

- ◆ Since planning takes longer than events to happen, have you invested enough time in parallel planning?
- ◆ Do you know what steps you will take, and by when, if a situation changes rapidly?
- ◆ Will those outcomes be in place fast enough or is more parallel investment needed now?

Telecommunications

- ◆ Are you getting the best value for money in telecommunications?
- ◆ Given the price wars, with the situation changing by the month, and the ease of transferring the same telephone numbers from cable company to cable company, when was your bulk buying last reviewed?
- ◆ What is the corporate policy on mobiles?
- ◆ What is company policy on satellite phones?
- ◆ Have you considered placing telecoms and air travel under the same 'communications' budget heading, to encourage conversion of expensive air travel into high-tech cyberlinks and other communication technologies?

Call-centre subcontracting

- ◆ How much of your incoming telephone traffic could be handled by a subcontract to a highly skilled dedicated call centre?

Cross-selling

- ◆ Are you properly geared up for intelligent cross-selling, combining product data with customer profiles, available at the time of every contact?

Internet access and use

◆ Do you openly monitor activity, and site visits, in order to discourage abuse?

◆ Are you taking advantage of free or low-cost online data?

Website value

◆ Are you as proud of your website (your virtual HQ) as of your real HQ?

◆ Does it promote the company effectively?

◆ How does it benchmark against your immediate competition?

◆ What does it need to steal a significant lead on competitors?

◆ What is your five-year online strategy and are enough options being kept open?

◆ Have you properly explored new partnerships and alliances to keep in the mainstream and block others out?

◆ Do decision makers fully appreciate the urgency of how quickly this global market is being sewn up?

◆ How are you promoting your site?

◆ How are you monitoring site activity?

◆ Do you know which pages are most popular and why, where people arrive and where they get bored or fed up?

Encryption and security

◆ Are you using long enough encryption keys?

◆ Are you using encryption everywhere you should?

Futuring

◆ Who are the visionaries and motivators in the company who can give direction and purpose to the revolution?

◆ Do they have enough profile and platform?

◆ Who is looking beyond mere improvements in today's technology to help prepare you for next-generation technologies on which the future of your whole operation may depend?

Corporate knowledge management

◆ How is your whole organisation's intellectual capital and knowledge base being managed?

◆ Are you harnessing intranet power adequately to keep ahead?

Avoiding overload

- Who is summarising trends and data?
- Do those people understand your priorities?
- Do you have one key publication or summary that keeps you abreast of most important changes?
- Are your key staff trained in skim-reading/rapid scanning?
- Are you keeping up to speed with new technology – do you need help?

Multimedia investment

- Is your company measuring up well in a multimedia age whether at shareholder meetings or in one-to-one presentations?
- Do you have the right technology in the right places, e.g. sufficiently high resolution data projectors with adequate sound capability?
- Do people know how to create world-class multimedia presentations?
- What support do you have in-house?

Virtual reality

- Have you considered the potential of virtual reality – product development, product promotion?

Reaction against robots

- Have you prepared for a growing reaction against automatic switchboard systems with push buttons or voice triggered selections, and against voice mail?

Speech recognition

- Continuous speech recognition is one of the most important office tools ever to emerge. Who is evaluating such systems for your company, and how will your company change its methods of working as a result?

Financial services revolution

- Is your company ready for a complete shift in every area to do with finance and financial management?

Bugging and surveillance
- When did you last have a corporate health check regarding commercial espionage?
- How vulnerable is your business to a competitor listening in to board meetings or other conversations?
- Does your senior team realise how easily their own confidentiality can be compromised?

PERSONAL CHALLENGES

How you cope with constant rapid change?
- If you find continuous change stressful, think now about creating areas of your life that will hardly change, and invest in them. Then you will find the areas that change most are less of a problem. Friends, family, a collection of treasured books, your garden, a regular round of golf – make your own slow-changing area. The greater your personal stability, the faster you can integrate change without stress overload.

Tracking trends
- Do you track early trends?
- What newspapers do you read?
- Are you scanning the content of your 'trade magazines'? They will often help with advance warning of change.
- Have you signed up for hot news – e-mailed every day or hour, just containing items matching your interests? In a fast-changing world, getting vital news half a day ahead of the rest can mean the difference between success and just surviving.

Keep learning
- When did you last learn something new and unrelated to what you 'do'? Stretch your brain, keep fresh, take mental exercise, be interesting. The broader your horizons, the greater your vision of the future.
- Are you spending time with people who stimulate you to think more widely?
- When did you last assign time to think laterally, out of the box,

– outside the office, with people outside your own discipline and area of work?

Make your computers work harder

- ◆ Do computers scare you or get you excited? This is a make-or-break area for future success, so wherever you are on the scale, get in deeper. Learn from others, rather than battling on your own. Make sure your own computer knowledge is at least doubling every year, to catch up with accelerating PC power.
- ◆ Can you touch-type? Keyboard use will be important for the next ten years, so get going faster with a PC-driven typing tutor.
- ◆ Are you using the latest speech recognition systems?
- ◆ Have you given yourself time to adjust your patterns of speech for the greatest accuracy?

Prevent burnout

- ◆ How are you preventing your own burnout?
- ◆ How many quality holidays do you take? Take as many as you can. The faster you run, the more you need recovery time. These spaces are where the real thinking happens.
- ◆ How do you relax? Remember you're planning for the long haul.

Be sceptical about the latest fads

- ◆ Are you over-dependent on new management theories?
- ◆ What is *your* theory of management – does it work?

Break free from the office

- ◆ Why are you still addicted to office activity?
- ◆ Does it really improve your performance every day?
- ◆ How much time would it save if you worked from home at least one day a week?
- ◆ Do you really need a desk of your own?
- ◆ Does your own home have enough bandwidth to make tele-working easy?
- ◆ Are you familiar with the facilities provided by your mobile devices?
- ◆ Have you considered a satellite mobile phone for remote locations?

Enjoy cutting-edge technology
- Is the computer you are using sufficiently new and powerful to keep you focused on cutting-edge technology?
- Does it have all the latest add-ons for multimedia communications?
- In addition, do you have a high specification portable PC – vital for complete virtual working? Buy your own!

Be ready for digital disaster
- Does your computer have powerful and reliable backup facilities and do you use them every day?
- What about your personal organiser?
- Would you be able to survive the theft of all computer equipment in your office and all office backup systems?
- Would your personal work survive a major office fire?
- Are you properly protected against viruses?
- Have you considered using an encryption program when sending e-mail?

Keep surfing
- Do you have a fast enough broadband connection at home?
- Do you spend at least one hour a week online as part of your own professional development?
- Have you explored fully new areas such as a websites, multimedia and always-on video linking?

Wage a war on paper
- How fast are you moving towards a paperless office?
- Has your paper filing capacity reduced or increased over the past three months?
- Have you tried working on shared documents using collaboration programs or made long-distance telephone calls or video links online?

Keep looking at the camera
- Have you tried using a video-conference suite?
- Do you know how to really communicate using this medium?
- Do you know how to fill the screen with your head and shoulders by adjusting your position and the camera?

◆ Do you look directly at the camera when you are speaking to create eye-to-eye contact – or do you spend most of the time looking at the other person or even at your own image? Your eyes are the window of your soul. Use them. Don't expect results from video links if you seem to be spending your entire time looking away. Appearance is everything in a virtual exchange. Arrive early, practise with a friend, and spend time socialising as you would in a face-to-face meeting. Don't be in such a hurry. Enjoy being together. Create shared spaces.

Be vigilant
◆ How secure is your office from bugging and other invasions of your privacy?

TEN STRATEGIES TO DOUBLE PERSONAL PRODUCTIVITY AT ZERO COST

1. Improve typing speeds/use speech recognition
2. Use a good e-mail programme – set up correctly to screen and file automatically.
3. Follow strict e-mail disciplines, e.g. a ban on most attachments – this protects against viruses and speeds opening mail. And get yourself a programme to block spam junk messages.
4. Phone less, teleconference and video-conference more, e-mail more, travel less.
5. Encourage home-working across time-zones and for writing longer documents.
6. Encourage own diary and travel management.
7. Use mobile dataphones for Internet, e-mail, short text messages and video.
8. Use a bureau to take all phone messages and send to your mobile as text.
9. Encourage outsourced personal 24-hour technology support.
10. Use the '80:20 rule' and give more time to the 20 per cent you do which produces 80 per cent of your impact.

CHAPTER 2

Urban

Millions drawn to city lights

The second face of the future is urban – the huge impact of population growth, of urbanisation, ageing and other socio-demographic shifts.

POPULATION GROWTH A MAJOR THREAT

Everyone talks about the population explosion, but the graph is a straight line, likely to level off. Actually, it is two lines added together: an ageing and shrinking population in many wealthy countries and a juvenile, expanding population in the poorest countries. One billion children will become consumers in the next 15 years – the biggest jump in human history; 350 million children in Africa today see glimpses of your lifestyle and compare it with their own on less than \$3 a day. If just 0.1 per cent become politically motivated and organised, the result could be new protest movements that dwarf anything our world has ever seen.

A few years ago I asked executives at one of the world's largest oil companies how many people it would take to totally wreck oil production in Nigeria – the seventh largest oil producing nation. Their answer: less than 50, armed with machine guns and cigarette lighters, firing holes into pipes, escaping on motorbikes or inflatable boats. In February 2006, a small number took out 25 per cent of Nigeria's oil production, while in the same month an attack was threatened in Saudi Arabia which would have knocked out 25 per cent of its output.

Population growth will be a major challenge, a fundamental

and dominant feature of the future, producing major tensions as poorer countries enlarge numerically and economically compared to richer countries with older, dependent communities.

World population, around 6.3 billion in 2006, will increase to more than 8 billion by 2025, with 95 per cent of the growth being in the poorest nations. These extra 2 billion people will accumulate because birth rates are falling less quickly than improvements in health. A huge challenge will be to develop low-cost ways to feed, clothe, shelter, power up and water such vast numbers of people without destroying the planet, especially as economic growth increases personal incomes and lifestyle expectations.

Population growth cannot be arrested suddenly without creating all kinds of other crises, with huge population bulges of elderly people in later generations that will make problems faced in Western countries today seem relatively minor. In many, if not the majority of nations worldwide, up to 50 per cent of the population is under 25 years old. That is a fact which cannot be undone without the catastrophic death of vast numbers of young adults through plague or world war. Even if not a single baby is born in these nations over the next 20 years, this one age-bulge guarantees a boom in the number of potential parents over the same period.

More than half the world's population now lives in cities, many of them vast, primitive and disease-ridden, with poor infrastructure. A large number are megacities – more than 10 million people – with vast sprawling areas of crude hovels, slums with poor water provision, no waste collection, poor sanitation, high pollution, traffic jams, power shortages, disease and low investment. Expect this process of urban drift to accelerate so larger cities grow by 1 million more people every 3–6 years. Expect the largest megacities to plateau in size as infrastructure limitations start making life so unpleasant that for every million who arrive, another million leave to live in smaller cities or towns in nearby areas. Yet for all this, mega-slums have micro-economies which are often thriving, whether it is an entrepreneur who rigs up electric lines from a lamppost and starts selling electricity 'by the line', or a boy with a barrow carting in food from outside the city, or a telephone kiosk with a single mobile phone. Expect many slum areas to improve rapidly.

By 1995 126 million Asians lived in megacities. By 2025 it will be 400 million. By then Asia will contain half the world's population. China alone is planning for 300 million more people to move from rural areas to cities by 2020, boosting its city populations to more than 800 million.

Welcome to the megacity

The contrasts are bizarre, unsustainable and getting worse. Take Mumbai (Bombay), a city twice the size of London, its streets clogged with traffic. Every inch of crumbling tarmac is a weaving chaos of cars belching fumes, taxis, buses, lorries and cycles. The streets are so packed with never-ending streams of people that sometimes the only place left to stand is the gutter. The warm, humid air is thick with sulphurous vapours from power stations and heavy industry, mixed with carbon monoxide, carbon dioxide, dust and the heavy smell of humanity.

Along many roads are humble shacks, stacked against each other, packed any old how as far as the eye can see. Cardboard, planks, blue or black plastic sheets, old car tyres, bits of corrugated metal – and rope to hold it all together. The nearest tap is 100 metres away. Electricity goes as far as the street lamps. A million people every night don't even have a shack to sleep in. They just settle down for the night where their tired bodies collapse on the pavement. They lie as if dead until dawn.

The contrasts are brutal – between the street and the shack on one hand and the rupee millionaire on the other. Flats in Mumbai can fetch more than $1 million with slums almost to the front door. Yet on every street corner you can see CNN in the bars or in the shop windows. However destitute they are, the very poorest always have before them images of a world beyond their wildest hopes, a world of exclusive, unattainable affluence. And it seems unfair. But it also creates a mirage, giving some of the very poorest the hope they need in order to survive.

But we are not just talking about Mumbai: this is the future destiny of cities right across South East Asia. This is life in megacities the world over and it's a challenge. Those not living in megacities are either in other developing urban sprawls or working the fields in subsistence farming, with not much in between.

Gap between rich and poor growing

The gap is getting wider between the richest and the poorest, and many people are falling backwards, particularly in places like central Africa where AIDS, foreign debt and continuous low-grade tribal conflicts and wars continue to cripple many national economies.

In 1965, the income per head of the top 20 per cent of the global population was 30 times that of the poorest. Today the gap is 60-fold. Only a handful of East Asian economies have managed to sustain growth rates fast enough to catch up. Middle income countries – with between 40 and 80 per cent of the income average of all countries – are thinner on the ground than they were.

Sending money home

Expect hundreds of millions of foreign workers from the poorest nations to send growing amounts of cash home. These remittances already make a significant contribution to the foreign earnings of many of these countries but are rarely included in official figures.

African nations alone received $167 billion from workers abroad in 2006 (out of the global total of £232 billion for foreign workers sending money home). Officially recorded remittances alone constitute 1.3 per cent of Sub-Saharan Africa's GDP. If informal cash payments are included, the figure could be 3–4 per cent of GDP in some countries and more than half of all foreign currency earnings.

Expect whole industries to grow around the need to move cash quickly and cheaply from a family member in one country to one in another. Expect growth of Western Union-style outlets, and a boom in informal courier services, all carrying (or smuggling) money home.

Gross inequalities are a new form of domination

To have a quarter of the entire human race deprived of basic necessities, such as clean water or adequate food, is shameful in such a wealthy world. Over 60 per cent of the world's population exists on $3 a day or less. Nearly 1 billion are illiterate. Every day around 840 million are hungry or face food insecurity. Almost one in three of those in the least developed countries die before the age of 40. Over 1 billion people lack access to adequate water supplies. As I say, expect a growing backlash in poorer nations and among activists in wealthy nations. It will be as great as the reaction against every trace of the British Empire seen over the second half of the twentieth century. The debt burden of some of the poorest nations exceeds many times over their entire export value per year, and dealing with this problem continues to be a major challenge to global harmony, despite recent attempts at debt relief. We will look at this issue in more depth later in this chapter.

Foreign aid will be seen as imperialism

Foreign aid can seem a form of imperialism, especially in view of the fact that the donor countries have been extracting billions more in debt interest than is given in aid. Some countries have economies dominated by development programmes. In places like Burundi a large percentage of vehicles on the road belong to organisations such as UNICEF, Save the Children or ActionAid.

It is extremely difficult for charities to operate in cash-strapped countries without distorting local priorities. A community leader has a shopping list of ten items, ranging from roads to water and clinics. An NGO is offering help with literacy. The help is accepted and a new education facility is built. It may be helpful, but was it the most appropriate next step?

The worst poverty can be abolished in many nations with remarkable speed. Take Malaysia. In 1971 the government developed pro-poor growth policies. At that time 60 per cent were considered below the poverty line. By 1993 this had dropped to 13 per cent, but that was before the 1997 currency collapse. These are brittle and vulnerable economies, but economic growth can do miracles.

The overall picture in many of the poorest nations is of positive rapid economic growth, and many of their towns and cities will be unrecognisable within a decade, with new wealth flowing into new business enterprises – most owned by families.

Bottom ten countries in the UN Human Development Report (the country at the top of the list is the poorest):

Burundi

Madagascar

Guinea

Mozambique

Cambodia

Mali

Ethiopia

Burkina Faso

Sierra Leone

Niger

Expect special attention to aid for these countries.

Entering new chaotic markets

A key challenge will be to adapt to megacity culture with its own unique patterns of life and social networks. Expect corporations to penetrate megacities with new products and services aimed at the middle classes and others aimed only at the poor majority. Expect them to develop new models of management. Image building will be important. Expect a new 'developing world' emphasis on corporate responsibility and global citizenship, with more high-profile community action programmes.

Bottom of the pyramid

Expect many multinationals to switch focus from the emerging middle-class minority to the hundreds of millions of poorer people as a huge potential market. Hindustan Lever is just one of the many which are making money from those at the 'bottom of the pyramid' while providing a useful social service at the same time. Expect ranges of micro-products like HL's tiny sachets of shampoo, cheap enough for a woman in a slum to buy and to wash her hair once every two weeks. These 6ml sachets account for 53 per cent of HL's revenues from shampoos and have a higher profit margin. Other examples of 'bottom of the pyramid' business to watch are micro-finance and micro-insurance, both of which will be boom industries over the next two decades, not only in their own right, but also as feeder programmes for higher-value products as clients become more affluent. Micro-loans of $3 or more have already helped lift over a million families out of poverty in India.

Companies operating in the poorest nations will be wise to play down their vast wealth, and to cultivate an image of restraint rather than extravagance, particularly regarding the lifestyles of senior staff. Companies flaunting wealth will invite national criticism, local opposition and labour conflict. Likewise the challenges for wealthy individuals, faced by extreme human need, will be immense. Expect many to turn a blind eye, while others engage in a new wave of intensive humanitarian activity, encouraging sustainable development.

THE FUTURE OF CHINA

A major challenge for business will be to push into China at the right time and in the right way, neither wasting huge resources in an emerging market economy, nor leaving it too late to maintain an early entrant advantage. Hong Kong and Shanghai are doorways.

China will continue to fascinate business leaders, seduced by the potential size of the domestic market and vast manufacturing power for the global community. Foreign direct investment into China was six times that into India in 2005, much of it coming from businesses run by ethnic Chinese in other nations. These projects are likely to be far more successful than those driven by boards of multinationals. Expect many stories of huge disappointment in actually taking money out of China, told by Westerners who never managed to penetrate Chinese culture. China will accept globalisation only in its own way and will not be dictated to.

At some point, China will need to come to terms with its past – the 30-year rule of Chairman Mao and the Gang of Four. During the 'lost decade' of the Cultural Revolution millions of lives were shattered and the impact of this continues today, especially in the lives of those who were then young adults (those in their early 60s today).

China is more than 5,000 years old and yet most outside observers tend to think of it as a new phenomenon. For most of the past millennia, China has been a major world economy. The last 150 years were an unusual period of relative weakness and the current growth spurt is merely a catch-up period to regain China's natural place in the world. China has been isolated for centuries by sea and mountains, and the Chinese people regard their country in many ways as the centre of the earth. Indeed, the very symbol of China in the Chinese language expresses that thought.

Expect China to continue to regard other nations and civilisations with a mixture of curiosity, amusement and contempt at their lack of history and cultural sophistication.

Expect China's GDP per person to rise by at least 8–10 per cent a year on average over the next 15 years, doubling from around $1,400 in 2006 to more than $3,000 by 2014. However, most of this growth in personal wealth will be among city dwellers mainly on the eastern seaboard. This process will drive further waves of rural migration, which in turn may create pressure for political change.

Men in these rapidly growing cities will find a severe shortage of women caused by years of selective action including abortion – 119 boys are born for every 100 girls, compared with a natural ratio of 105 to 100. By 2020 China may contain 30–40 million restless batchelors. However, this is not confined to China. India has a similar problem with ratios as high as 122 boys to 100 girls in some places. Expect Chinese men to import large numbers of women from other countries in the region such as Thailand, Cambodia, Vietnam, Malaysia and the Philippines, creating imbalances in turn in some of these countries.

China's population of 1.3 billion is ageing faster than any other country's in history, but despite this it will increase at roughly 0.5 per cent a year. If the single child policy is abolished, China's population could jump. This policy prevented 300 million births over the past 30 years despite the fact that it was often more relaxed in rural areas.

China will continue to drive commodity prices upwards – imports grew ten-fold from 1990 to 2005. Expect more pressure from China's massive drive for growth despite huge investment by the Chinese government in domestic production, for example of steel and coal.

With over a billion potential consumers, foreign investors rushed in between 1990 and 2000, but many companies are finding problems after the initial euphoria. They can't afford not to be there but making money will be hard. Their theoretical markets may melt away when you analyse the amount of disposable income. It is still a tiny amount per head and there is overcapacity in many industry sectors, but now is the time to learn.

China's future stability depends on delivering economic growth in excess of 7 per cent a year to help create hundreds of millions of new urban jobs for those leaving the countryside.

The boom in next-generation mobile phones and web access means that information will be harder to control in future and there could be serious challenges to totalitarian power. Expect step-wise reforms and increasing populism in regional and national government. Expect leaders to feel increasingly sensitive and insecure about public opinion, with major concessions to pressure groups of various kinds when their grievances are felt to be reasonable, and in line with overall government policy.

Expect further severe crackdowns on illegal political activity (just about any group that meets without registration on a regular basis can be classified as such) and severe restrictions on certain religious groups including the underground church, which has more than 70 million members. The fiercer the persecution, the faster the unofficial churches are likely to grow, based on past Chinese experience. Paradoxically, at the same time as these crackdowns we can also expect the general situation in many other areas to become more relaxed.

But in it all there will remain the ever-present risk of a serious misjudgement of public mood, the risk of too rapid liberalisation or of too severe controls, both of which could destabilise the government. While yet another revolutionary process in China is unlikely, even if it were to happen it is likely that the fundamental principles of economic reform and globalisation will continue.

There is another rapid cultural revolution taking place, which is almost invisible but profoundly life-changing for the nation. China's present leaders went to study in Moscow, but their children, with thousands of others, go to Yale, Chicago or Harvard Business School.

THE FUTURE OF INDIA

India will remain the largest and one of the most stable democracies in the world. Think of India's future as a federation of states rather than a single country, as regional governments mature with their own power, culture and priorities. Take Karnataka state of 52 million people, which contains Bangalore. The Minister for Health oversees 114 medical and pharmaceutical colleges, while the Minister for Education oversees 15 universities, 131 engineering colleges and 600 industrial training institutions.

By 2020, India will have a middle class of 300 million people, many aspiring to buy Western lifestyle products. Expect India's cosmetics market, for example, to grow by at least 6 per cent per year and become a $2 billion a year opportunity. Indian culture will be influenced profoundly over the next 15 years by Bollywood films, with up to 1,000 new releases each year and up to 5 billion tickets sold.

Despite outward signs of busy chaos, India will remain one of the best places in the world to make things happen fast. This is a country that is able to deliver, from an empty concrete shell with no facilities, a complete working call centre with trained staff and 24-hour video links to Europe, less than 12 weeks after signing a contract.

India's 2.2 births per 100 adults a year gives the country a median age of 24 compared with China's 1.3 births per 100 adults and median age of 32. Large families spend to survive hence capital costs are likely to remain higher in India than in China, where small families are able to save harder.

People often ask me how long it will take for markets like India to become mature. A long time. Over the next 15 years more than 450 million under 18 year olds, most of them from extremely poor backgrounds, will become adult workers and consumers. Every year we see another million or two lifting themselves out of absolute poverty and joining the middle class. These aspiring consumers will be a constant source of new market opportunities for large companies.

Expect joint action by China and India on a growing number of issues by 2020, as together they become a powerful force in global politics. Exports to each other's countries will exceed $20 billion by 2020 in each direction as they strengthen both as friends and rivals. While India's growth will be held back by poor infrastructure and China will be burdened by its ageing population, both countries will start experiencing severe shortages of highly trained managers, engineers, scientists and other groups, reflected in salary inflation of more than 20 per cent a year for the fortunate few, and around 14 per cent for a great many more. This will start to be an acute problem by 2010, eroding many economic advantages of outsourcing/offshoring, despite the fact that India alone trains 860,000 IT graduates a year, compared with a mere 8,000 in the UK. Infosys alone trains 25,000 IT workers a year – to feed demand for 1,000 new team members every two weeks. A further 1 million a year across India are also being trained as engineers. In comparison, wage levels will hardly increase for most of the 600 million at the bottom of the pyramid, who will continue to earn less than $5 a day.

THE FUTURE OF AFRICA

Sub-Saharan Africa has been torn apart by war, genocide, AIDS and other health challenges, all made worse by governments that have been ineffective and corrupt. But Africa has great potential for the future. Despite popular perceptions, by 2006 there were fewer conflicts in the region than for decades, and countries like Uganda, Tanzania, Mozambique, Rwanda, Nigeria and South Africa were showing sustained, rapid economic growth. Countries like Uganda had shown they could contain AIDS and grow in both population and economic output, despite historic HIV infection levels of more than 20 per cent.

The future growth centres of Sub-Saharan Africa will include Nigeria, Kenya and South Africa, the latter being seen as a safe haven for foreign investment despite geographic isolation and the ever-present risk of Zimbabwean-style chaos. If Zimbabwe is removed from the picture, the overall situation in Southern Africa looks very promising with the increasing strength of SADC as a trading block.

Zimbabwe's situation is likely to get worse before improving, and longer-term stability is unlikely until President Mugabe dies and a new government becomes established. Expect white farmers and business leaders to be asked to return. Some will do so, bringing with them business links and opportunities from South Africa, which will continue to be the engine for growth in that region.

Countries with great mineral wealth will attract headlines but will struggle to develop in a sustainable way compared with their neighbours. UN studies show that mineral assets are usually associated with increased government corruption, increased military spending (to protect assets) and a higher exchange rate, which makes it harder for small and medium-sized enterprises to export. Thus mineral-wealthy countries tend to deteriorate in other ways.

Dealing with debt

Despite huge protest movements, 30 per cent of all African exports were still used simply to repay debt in 2005. The world's poorest nations pay over $100 million every day to wealthy nations. At the same time only five nations were providing 0.7 per cent of their GNP for official development assistance (ODA). A major drive to settle the worst debts by 2000 or soon after has been only partly successful. The poorest 54 countries still have debts of $300 billion–$400 billion. The poorest 152 countries owe over $2.5 trillion. In some countries a huge proportion of all export income is still spent paying interest on loans. But what were those loans for?

The fact is that donor countries have often disguised foreign aid as a boost to their own industry, to provide credits so poor countries can buy a donor nation's exports. But those goods may not have been top of the priority list in the first place.

The World Bank itself lends $24 billion a year, mainly to the poorest nations. But the bank's own review of 83 projects found that half failed to deliver, and many damaged the environment and displaced millions of the poorest and most marginalised people in the world.

If the debts are fully cancelled, it will have the same effect as trebling the amount given to relief and development programmes, assuming the released money is used in the same way. Expect more debt-swap programmes, where debt is bought at a big discount from a bank by a development agency and cancelled in return for a commitment by a government to spend national currency on approved programmes.

As I have said, if these kinds of problems are not solved quickly, it is not hard to imagine the formation of small groups of economic 'freedom fighters', intent on targeting banks and other large institutions with terrorist attacks as a protest at what they see as nothing less than economic slavery. It is just part of the bigger picture of growing unease about the impact of wealthy nations and corporations on poor nations and vulnerable populations.

As with other terrorist groups, they will feel passionately that their cause is just and their mission will command the sympathy of over 1 billion people, even if they disagree with terrorist methods.

Even 'wealthy' countries like South Africa are affected
At a Southern Africa Economic Summit I listened to an impassioned speech by Nelson Mandela on economic slavery and oppression, 'a greater evil today than 300 years of imperialistic slave trade'. He was bitter about the legacy of debt he inherited on the collapse of apartheid. Countries dependent for decades on the stable prices of raw materials such as minerals, coffee and cocoa beans have also been hard hit by unstable or falling prices, market speculators and 'profit takers'.

Trade rather than aid

In Africa, countries like Tanzania which have changed their attitude to the free market have thrived, while others have wallowed in economic decay. Most governments are chasing each other to embrace low inflation, low budget deficits and the encouragement of private business. But until America and Europe stop blocking their own imports of African goods, and cease dumping their own subsidised farm products, there will be relatively slow progress in most of these countries. Blocking the chance for Africa to export textiles, footwear, leather goods and other labour-intensive products fundamentally undermines the possibility of future prosperity.

There is resentment among some senior African leaders, who object to being lectured and cajoled by Western multinationals into lifting currency controls and other measures. They fear the economic rape of their nations by new imperialists who use money instead of guns to invade, take control and rule, to pay little and take wealth out. They see others exploiting the economy rather than themselves, even though many of them are in highly privileged positions. They particularly resent the fact that they have little choice, it seems, but to allow their economies to become the puppets of globalised power bases. Expect multinationals to form brittle relationships with governments and peoples, which snap at short notice. Currency crises will continue to alarm and frustrate leaders in these countries. Yet despite all this, and other problems such as AIDS, expect rapid economic growth to significantly improve the lives of at least 25 per cent of all those in Sub-Saharan Africa over the next 15 to 20 years.

WATER WARS

One consequence of growing populations, urbanisation and global warming (pages 215–27) is water shortage. Water use will be a major feature of government policy decisions in many parts of the world by 2010, together with carbon trading and energy.

More people and greater spending power mean more pressure on resources, including water. We could see water wars between nations quarrelling over, say, how much water flows into a country's borders down a long river, or how much one country is allowed to pollute another's water supply.

In 2006 the Ugandan government took a sudden decision to cut the flow out of Lake Victoria into the River Nile. This was in open defiance of a 1929 treaty under which Egypt had exclusive rights to 80 per cent of Nile water. Uganda's action also threatened a crisis for Sudan, which also depends on the great river. The decision to block the flow into the Nile was to help restore water levels in Lake Victoria, which had been badly affected by drought and possibly by over extraction in previous years by Uganda's hydroelectric power generators.

Germany and Austria are being sued by the Black Sea states through the EU for polluting the River Danube with more than 100 tons a year of nitrates and large amounts of phosphorus. Algae blooms in the Black Sea have killed millions of fish and wiped out 40 species.

If there is no rain in the Pyrenees, there will be no water in Andorra. If the Caspian Sea dies as a result of one country's pollution, four other nations suffer. Expect many more rows between neighbours up and down river.

Limited fresh water in the world

Only 2.5 per cent of the world's water is fresh and two-thirds of that is frozen in glaciers or on the ice caps. Renewable fresh water on earth (rainfall) is only 0.008 per cent of all global water. Two-thirds of this is lost in evaporation and transpiration. The rest is runoff, available for use. But there is a big mismatch between runoff and population. Asia has 36 per cent of runoff but 60 per cent of the world's people. South America has 26 per cent of the runoff but only 6 per cent of the population. The Amazon river alone carries 15 per cent of the earth's runoff but is accessible to only 0.4 per cent of the world's population. Many other rivers are too remote to be of economic use, resulting in the non-availability of 19 per cent of water.

Globally, people already use 35 per cent of accessible supplies. An extra 19 per cent is used 'instream' to dilute pollution, sustain fisheries and transport goods. Thus the human race already uses around half the total world supply through rainwater. But water use quadrupled between 1950 and 2000 as population soared by more than 3 billion. Population is set to climb the same amount by 2035, a 50 per cent increase, but water supply cannot triple again without severe shortages. Something has to change.

To make matters worse, global warming is likely to dump more rain in some places but rob it from others. The World Meteorological Organisation expects 66 per cent of the world's population to suffer severe constraints on water availability by 2025, on current trends.

Groundwater overpumping and aquifer depletion is occurring in many of the world's most important crop-growing areas, including the western US, large parts of India and north China, where water tables are dropping by 1 metre a year. Expect ever longer and more spectacular water pipelines across countries and continents, balancing supply and population, offering new opportunities for trading, political demands and sabotage by terrorists or protests groups.

Water trade is growing. Singapore, for example, takes water from Malaysia, cleans it and sells it back. Expect many more such inter-nation deals.

Many rivers semi-dead in Asia – more to come

Many rivers already die for part of the year in Asia as a result of over-irrigation. These include most rivers in India, among them the mighty Ganges – a principal water source for south Asia – and China's Yellow River.

With urban dwellers set to reach 5 billion by 2025, steps are being taken to switch water from farms to cities. Expect farms in the majority of countries worldwide to be forced to make severe economies in future – thirsty plants instead of thirsty people. Hundreds of litres of water are required in hot countries to produce just a few litres of orange juice or a few kilograms of vegetables. In California, irrigation fell by 121,000 hectares in the 1980s and a further 162,000 hectares were taken out of the irrigation fields by 2000. In China, water is being switched from food production to supplying Beijing. Three hundred other Chinese cities are now experiencing water shortages.

Expect the 'water factor' to affect every individual in most industrialised cities by 2020, with widespread water metering, 'grey water' systems (for example, bath water stored for watering the garden), and a shift in culture to seeing all water as a limited natural resource. Expect as many regulations on the use of water as on energy conservation.

By 2025 the world becomes thirsty for more

By 2025, virtually all the world's economically accessible rivers could be required to meet the needs of agriculture, industry and households, and to maintain lake and river levels. In other words, the world will nearly have run out of existing water supplies by the mid twenty-first century. This is a social and geopolitical time-bomb, which will force government action. This all assumes no negative impact on useful rainfall, or on demand, resulting from global warming and climate change.

The death of the Aral Sea is described by the government of Uzbekistan as one of the most serious ecological catastrophes in the history of the human race, and it took place in a single generation. Originally one of the world's largest lakes, the shores are now far from the original limits with hugely risen mineral levels.

Across the world, there has been a serious decline in water quality. On current trends South Africa will run out of rainwater resources in 50 years and will have to make fresh water from the ocean. The country is moving from the ownership of local water by landowners to seeing it as a national treasure, while Brazil now sees its vast fresh water resources as one of the country's top priorities for protection.

Coupled with this is coastal pollution. While half the world's population still lacks basic sanitation, 80 per cent of all local sea water pollution is from contaminants carried there by fresh water.

Dams will be bigger and more controversial

Controversy will continue to grow over vast dams like the Three Gorges dam on the Yangtze River completed recently by China, forming a lake 600 kilometres long, drowning a city of 250,000 people and displacing over 1 million. Dams often force massive resettlements. The World Bank recently reported that 300 new large (i.e. over 115 metres high) dams a year force 4 million people a year to leave their homes, and often ancestral lands. Resettlement is usually badly planned and executed.

The Congo River at Inga could supply half the energy needs of the whole of Africa, and only 6 per cent of Africa's potential hydroelectric capacity has so far been harnessed. In theory dams are a wonderful idea: offering free power, irrigation and flood prevention, providing a tourist attraction and water sports, fish farming and drought protection. They create jobs, are national status symbols, and prevent global warming.

But dams also change the environment. Constant irrigation can waterlog the ground. Water brings salts to the surface which are left behind as the moisture evaporates, leaving salinated farmland which is increasingly infertile. Fertile silt which used to be carried by floods now clogs up reservoirs. Plant and animal life is lost in a former river, and fish are blocked from going upstream by the dam wall. A study of the Kainji dam on the Niger found that downstream, rice production was reduced by 18 per cent and fish catches by 65 per cent.

Making more water

So what happens when water runs short? One answer is to recycle sewage directly back into a large reservoir, after treatment. San Diego is preparing to do just that in a scheme modelled on one 20 years old in Virginia. So is a British water authority in East Anglia. Despite public squeamishness, the reuse of water increased by 30 per cent in one year. The aim is to 'get people comfortable with the idea of drinking treated sewage'. Treatment technology means that raw sewage can be converted to water ten times purer than normal tap water. In the meantime, hundreds of other uses are being found for it, such as irrigation and flushing toilets. Expect sewage reuse to become a big industry.

New wells may relieve aquifer problems elsewhere, allowing them to recover to some extent. New dams could increase accessible runoff by more than 20 per cent in some cases.

But reservoirs can also be inefficient, with up to 70 per cent of water lost through evaporation each year in hot countries. Expect some reservoirs in future to be emptied in such a way that water seeps deep underground to replenish natural aquifers, to be extracted perhaps some years later using borehole pumps.

Desalination

Desalination is now a proven technology to turn sea water into freshwater. Saudi Arabia alone accounts for 20 per cent of global desalination. It can afford to use oil energy to make 3.4 million cubic metres of fresh water a day as a gift to the population, who are charged only a fraction of the real cost, but even so it is now running an economy campaign.

Expect further advances in desalination technology using reverse osmosis (pressurised seawater forced through a membrane, leaving salt behind). Expect huge growth in the amount of energy used worldwide to make fresh water, placing further pressure on nations regarding their carbon emissions. Desalination in the Middle East alone can be expected to double in the next 20 years.

Water conservation – a major national expenditure by 2010

Water conservation costs typically 5–50 cents a cubic metre, less than the development of new resources or desalination. Thames Water in London wastes enough water every day through leakage to fill 500 Olympic-sized swimming pools. Every household will be asked to make significant savings – for example, on toilet-flushing technology. Only 3 per cent of a British household's consumption is used for cooking or drinking.

Expect to see a big market in water-friendly devices. Expect the clothing industry to work hard on new easy-clean fabrics, including ones that do not need to be cleaned with either scarce water or toxic solvents. Expect nanotechnology-coated fabrics to be developed for air or surface cleaning by 2015 – processes which dislodge molecules of dirt and grease without conventional wetting.

Because farming uses 66 per cent of the world's water, even small savings have a big impact. Expect new drought-resistant crops made by genetic engineering to be seen as water-saving strategies, in effect almost water production plants. Expect new generations of plants that can grow in salt water marshes.

Expect virtual water trading: wheat, for example, requires 1 cubic metre of water to produce 1 kilogram of grain. So importing 1 ton of wheat is equivalent in theory to importing up to 1 million litres of water in a dry country which is currently growing wheat using irrigation. If Egypt grew all its own cereals, it would require one-sixth of the water in the huge Aswan dam reservoir. The World Bank estimates that a quarter of all the water on the planet used to grow food is traded as 'virtual water'. Expect water-rich nations to gain extra value from their water supply by growing and exporting thirsty crops.

INDUSTRIALISED CITIES NOT DYING

Life in industrialised nations is also becoming increasingly urban-ised. Expect the US population to grow from 300 million to 400 million by the 2040s, with rapid growth of urban overflow devel-opments around larger cities, stretching for many miles.

In the 1970s many were predicting the death of cities in Western nations as the middle classes moved out, helped by faster travel and technology, leaving behind the underclass and ethnic groups in ghettos, which would then fall apart through lack of infrastruc-ture. The reality is a mixed picture. Indeed, the opposite is true in some places.

London alive and kicking

London is an example of a large 'Western' city which is experienc-ing a magnet effect, being firmly placed near the top of the world order in popularity as a place to live. Restaurants and wine bars have multiplied, together with cinemas, hotels and nightclubs. London has become one vast work and leisure complex offering the very best of world-class time out for busy executives, round the clock. Those who really prefer the country had better find a second home, with a London pad for late nights in town. London's population has grown by more than half a million in a decade and will grow a further half million in the next.

Expect London's popularity as a global centre of financial services to be threatened eventually, as the network society makes geography increasingly irrelevant. Expect a fierce fight to stay the main player for foreign exchange, and to consolidate its position as major European banks switch operations rapidly in and out of countries. Despite this, expect London to keep top, or near top, position in crossborder lending (currency 18 per cent of the global $10,000 billion market). Expect a struggle to retain the world's largest collection of foreign banking offices, and increasingly aggressive action by New York to protect its status from further erosion, caused partly by burdensome regulations introduced following high-profile US financial scandals. The City's net overseas invisible earnings are over £25 billion a year. Expect that to rise in real terms, with growth of areas such as carbon trading and derivatives.

Globalised travellers move near airport hubs

Air travel dictates that globalised executives have to be close to a large international airport. The 'hub effect' is also true of high-speed trains. Most of the largest hubs for connections are in or near major cities. Hubs are where profit lies. Control the hub, control the market. Seize landing rights and wipe out the opposition.

Eccentrics drift out but wealthiest keep city base

Once again there is a trend and countertrend. The trend is always for people to drift to cities for the buzz and opportunity of city life: lots of people means money to spend, markets to tap, services to provide. Those who are fed up with city life and are middle class can afford the luxury of being eccentric, going 'back to nature', getting out of cities for a greener life, greater security, lower housing costs, teleworking or pulling whole offices out with them.

However, the wealthiest just live in both. They have two, three, ten or 20 homes. That is the trend. And there are many more of them too. But you can bet most of these homes will be in different cities – one reason why city residential property prices are so high, and why the most fashionable houses and apartments are so rarely occupied. Pre-millennialists have to live in or near cities so that they can carry on their favourite and biggest wealth-creating activity: face-to-face meetings. It will be 2020 before the balance becomes dominated by the post-millennial generation who conduct business differently.

And when pre-millennialists get out of airport buildings having travelled halfway round the world, they expect to be at a meeting within a short taxi ride, not to have to take a train to one over 100 miles away. So life in the green countryside is a middle-class fantasy for middle-income service providers or government officials who are not globalised, and for post-millennialists who can cope with an unending diet of virtual meetings without becoming insecure about competitors 'in town' being able to sell more powerfully face to face. However, an increasing number of the super-wealthy will have the best of all worlds, with private helicopters and planes that link their offices, homes, hotels and holidays direct, or via big airports.

Those who are not so wealthy will find themselves increasingly teleworking from virtual offices, but still needing large numbers of face-to-face meetings. While some will drift out of cities, many will find life still demands that they live close to where the real action is, even if many days a month they work at home.

Post-millennialists will be different: many will succeed, after great effort, in organising themselves, their employers and their clients to run virtual companies using third millennial technology. Face-to-face meetings out – virtual meetings in (page 183).

THE FUTURE OF REAL ESTATE

In uncertain times, investment in real estate provides stability compared with stock markets, and usually reasonable returns. In addition there is the emotional attraction of property – visible, tangible, with history. Expect major investment in real estate in many larger cities driven in part by huge oil money surpluses in producing nations, by continued international insecurity, by worries about traditional investment in equities, by excitement about emerging economies and by the buzz found in influential hubs like London and New York.

Expect cycles of development: overcapacity in downturns, followed by growth and new shortages. Premium prices for corporate real estate will depend on easy access to large airport hubs and the presence of other organisations' HQs.

Expect HQ spending by huge multinationals to grow, with a number of embarrassing mistakes as mergers or sell-offs force relocation or resizing of HQs, even before buildings have been completed. Expect more real estate rich companies to sell off and lease back their properties to release cash for their core businesses. Cities to watch will include Shanghai, Beijing and larger inland cities in China; also Mumbai, Delhi, Hyderabad, Bangalore, Kolkata, Sydney, Munich (major travel hub), Bratislava, Kiev, Parnu (Estonia is a high-tech miracle), Dubai, Dohar, Rio de Janeiro (one of the world's most spectacular cities and undiscovered tourist jewel) and Abuja, the new capital of oil-rich Nigeria.

Post-communist real estate will survive

It will take more than 50 years to rebuild Stalin's world of concrete, identical, low-grade apartment blocks. His influence will continue to be felt in subtle ways in the minds of the older generation, who will continue to find it hard to adjust to a world where nothing happens unless they or their children make it happen themselves.

Before they joined the EU, countries like Poland and Hungary had unemployment of up to 40 per cent. Even with more flexible labour markets and low-cost labour, it will take several decades for some of these countries to reach old EU standards. The greatest challenge will be competition from entrepreneurial, high-energy societies such as Hong Kong, Shanghai, Singapore, Bangkok, Nairobi and Mumbai.

The future of house prices

Real estate price calculations will continue to be complex. Take, for example, predictions about the future of the UK housing market, which many said was severely overheated from 2000 to 2006. While we may see shorter-term fluctuations, there are many factors which are likely to keep prices higher rather than lower in the longer term. For example, the UK is a tiny, crowded island with severe planning restrictions and around 1 million immigrants (official and unofficial) between 2002 and 2006 with a further 1 million expected by 2012. They come mostly from new EU nations – jobs are relatively easy to find, they have friends or relatives already in-country, welfare support is generous, and English is a language they understand or want to learn. Then there is pressure on housing created by marriage break-up and the ageing population who go on living at home, but who are releasing equity from their homes to children and grandchildren to buy their own.

Then there is affordability. In 1993 my wife and I bought a home at 13.5 per cent interest with a loan calculated as a maximum of 3.5 times my salary. Today interest rates remain one-third of this, yet the income multiple calculations used by lenders are often similar to what they were. We can see that lending multiples could be doubled and still be more affordable than mortgages were 15 years earlier. Payments on new mortgages as a percentage of take-home pay were only 40 per cent in 2006 compared with 60 per cent in 1989.

In addition, as we have seen there has been deflation in the prices of almost all goods and services, with the major exceptions of health and education, over the past two decades. This means that people are spending a much smaller proportion of their income on things like phones, cars, washing machines or air travel. This extra income can be used to fund the few remaining things in people's lives which are actually becoming more expensive, without putting much strain on the family purse.

Then there is the impact of loss of confidence in pension funds and the fact that more than one-third of adults are making their own arrangements for at least part of their pension, in most cases relying on capital growth of property. Added to that is zero tax on all capital gains on a home that you live in and further tax benefits exist for some pension funds which hold property as an investment. There is also the 'London factor', with a massive influx of real estate wealth into this very popular city, particularly from Russia and the Middle East.

RICH CITY LIFE

Rich city life creates major problems but of a very different kind to the pattern in emerging nations. Social collapse, family breakdown, unemployment, addiction, rising crime, the 'unofficial' untaxed economy and the development of an unemployable and disaffected underclass are all major challenges for the future.

Family breakdown

Take the so-called sexual revolution of the 1960s. The dream was of sexual freedom, of free love, but what is the reality in the twenty-first century? Fuelled by increasing mobility, urbanisation and the breakdown of traditional society, we now have a crisis in the US, Canada and many parts of Europe, Australia and New Zealand, and a situation where Britain now spends £1.5 billion a year placing children in care, the vast majority as a result of family breakdown.

The cost in cash terms of the sexual revolution in the US is over $100 billion every year – costs of divorce, sexually transmitted diseases and other factors. Nevertheless, something is changing. From 1971 to 1993 the divorce rate in Britain rose from around 75,000 to 180,000 a year, but then fell to 155,000 by 2005, despite the headlines, partly because fewer people got married in the first place. However, the number of marriages is now also rising.

The divorce trend was unsustainable. Despite the rapid growth in births outside of marriage (to 42 per cent), couples with children will continue to be a dominant slice of the national make-up, and a key market for a wide range of products and services. Families provide stability and so, in a society which is fragmenting, will tend to win out in the longer term. This is a very important issue for the future, not only in welfare of children, but also in care of older parents.

Marriage less binding than a joint mortgage

'Quickie' divorce and other reforms meant that by the turn of the millennium a joint mortgage between two people was more binding than a marriage ceremony in places like the UK and the US.

But the pendulum is swinging in an urbanised, fractured, rapidly changing world where stability is being increasingly prized. For example, the state of Louisiana introduced a marital covenant that bans divorce except under dire circumstances (such as wife-beating, child abuse, abandonment, two years' separation or adultery). Under the terms of the covenant couples have to declare that they have chosen 'my mate for life wisely' and must also attend pre-marriage counselling.

Community marriage policies

Many towns in America are also adopting 'community marriage policies' in which religious, civic and business leaders agree to encourage couples to get to know each other better before committing themselves. Adopted by more than 60 towns and cities in 26 states, they claim reductions of up to 40 per cent in divorce rates. Local businesses are asked to sponsor weekend retreats for couples whose marriages are in trouble.

Another sign of the times was a record $1.35 million award by a jury in North Carolina to a woman who lost her husband to his new wife. This was effectively a vast fine, and a huge disincentive to divorce.

Sex everywhere but with a wind of change

Sex is everywhere: the Western media continues to break every remaining sexual taboo. That was the trend, but the countertrend is alive and kicking – and not just in the Islamic community.

The 'True Love Waits' movement in the US has more than 2.5 million young people who have signed a pledge at public rallies to remain sexually abstinent until marriage 'from this day forth'. The number of women having premarital sex is now falling for the first time since records began – 5 per cent down. One follower said recently: 'Sexual liberation is as much about the right to say no. I'm a feminist and I think I'm a lot more liberated in choosing not to have sex.' The movement began in 1993 and has taken off in 76 other countries, including South Africa, where it has become the 'fastest growing fad among young people', with 380,000 members increasing at 5,000 a month – mainly church-linked.

It's not just the AIDS factor. There's something far deeper here, a profound rethink one generation on from the 1960s dream.

Pro-family – a key government issue

Governments cannot afford to care for societies where conventional families have become rare, regardless of their own philosophies. A sign of the times has been the conversion of left-wing parties in European countries to 'pro-family' rhetoric. The alternative is impossibly expensive. Expect 'family' to become a central issue in the next two decades in all aspects of public policy, with great debate about how to define it and worries that promotion of a traditional model may stigmatise those whose lives are different. It is a theme that will dominate thinking about reform of the welfare state.

Then there's the Pill factor. Society has yet to come to terms with oral contraceptives. Less than half a century has passed since sex became separated from pregnancy. It will take another two decades at least for global culture to adjust. The M generation are products of the 1960s and 1970s because that was the era their parents were brought up in. But very few parents of the 'free love'/'sixties' generation want those same values for their children today. They have lived through it all, done it all, felt the pain, and are hoping for something better for their own children. It's the same whether they are in Russia, Ukraine, Belarus, Spain, Italy or Canada. I see this every day in the work of the international AIDS agency ACET that I started in 1988.

M generation will keep the romantic ideal

Most young people are still very romantic. If you ask them what they want out of a relationship the great majority will tell you that their ideal relationship would be with a wonderful person, best friend, companion, great lover. Their ideal relationship carries on for more than a week or a month. Length becomes the test of a great relationship, in an age when people don't expect to stay together unless they are happy. The best relationship in the world goes on and on. It never breaks up. And there's increasing curiosity about what makes a great relationship work – just read the agony columns. Expect new specialities to emerge: relationship clinics and training centres, backed with government money.

Expect a new parent training industry as the state starts to panic. But these are expensive, partial solutions. A social shift in attitudes will do more, and will begin to deliver by 2020. With it will come some negatives, for example a growing intolerance in some countries of single parenting as a positive choice by young mothers. Expect an increasingly vitriolic rearguard action against such things as nineteenth century stigmatisation returns.

Many decades to reverse trends fully

Despite the beginnings of a pendulum shift, it will take many decades to reverse the trend for people to live alone. The Department of the Environment in the UK calculates that 4.4 million new homes will be needed by 2016, 80 per cent for single people. But that makes no allowance for the 1 million people who arrived in the UK between 2003 and 2006 and the further 2 million new EU citizens who may also arrive by then.

ADDICTION

Another feature of urbanisation is addiction. Drug dependency is a growing threat to civilised life and the greatest drug threat is heavy use of alcohol, which is now a global scourge and largely responsible for the fall in male life expectancy to just 57 years in Russia. Illegal drugs traffic is now 8 per cent of the value of all international trade, according to the UN. We tend to think of this as only a problem for wealthy nations but this is far from true. Heroin production is a key factor in destabilising Afghanistan, which produces around 600,000 tons of heroin a year, 92 per cent of the global opium crop. I recently visited people dying of AIDS in Manipur, north east India, on the Myanmar border, where 8,000 out of 40,000 people are daily injecting heroin. Every city in Asia now has a significant drugs problem. Each year $350 billion is spent on illegal drugs worldwide after allowing for drug seizures, most of it laundered through legitimate channels. Deregulation has made it far more difficult to stop vast flows of dirty money. The Net will make it almost impossible to track money flows in future. Criminals hate shipping cash, but why bother when electronic pulses can do it all? Laundering is carried out through all the world's main financial centres. The cost of laundering is less that 20 per cent of the total amount to be cleaned up even in the US or the UK, where controls are as strong as anywhere in the world.

Mexican economy high on drugs

Mexico is so hooked on drugs money that the profits from illegal trade would make the difference for the Mexican economy between boom and bust – 90 per cent of cocaine for the US market comes through Mexico. The forces of law and order are being subverted, with border guards carrying large quantities in their own vehicles. Mexico's narco-profits are conservatively estimated at $10 billion a year, 1–2 per cent of GDP. Up to 2,000 lorries a day pass through checkpoints to the US manned by a single customs officer, so inspections are rare.

Drugs in America

Some 900,000 US citizens are addicted to heroin and more than 2.5 million to cocaine. Americans spend $70 billion buying illegal drugs.

Drugs in Britain

In 2006 there were more than 250,000 heroin addicts and 250,000 others dependent on crack or cocaine in the UK. If each user spends an average £10,000 a year, the market in hard drugs is worth $5 billion to British dealers.

In Britain 20 per cent of all criminals use heroin and these heroin users are stealing £1.5 billion a year in property to pay for their habit. The average addict commits around 300 separate crimes a year. Expect tough new measures to deal with the problem. Expect more widespread random testing in prisons, with rewards for those who stay drug free. Expect whole prison wings to become drug-free zones, with extra privileges for those who live in them. Expect new partnerships between prisons and rehabilitation agencies.

Expect more money for residential treatment as surveys show significant numbers of those treated are able to stay off hard drugs. Many of these new treatment centres will be faith-based, particularly in the former Soviet bloc nations, where churches have played a dominant role in rescuing drug users, with impressive results. One Californian study found that every $1 spent on treatment yielded $7 in savings – crime losses and prisoner treatment costs, for example. UK treatment programmes have been shown to reduce shoplifting by heroin users by between 40 and 85 per cent.

A new prohibition movement starts with smoking

Expect a new prohibition movement by 2010, starting with tobacco and then giving increasing attention to alcohol. It will be a countertrend to the growing clamour for legislation of some or all psychoactive drugs. We can expect many other countries to follow the American outlawing of smoking. Smoking kills 419,000

Americans a year and drains $100 billion in healthcare costs and lost productivity.

This is no repeat of the temperance movement of the nineteenth century, backed by formal laws, but a mass movement controlling millions of people through minor inconveniences and regulations.

This creeping prohibition is affecting drug use in the workplace. The majority of large US companies already have drug-testing policies. Insurance companies are insisting on anti-drug measures following the discovery that drug and alcohol abuse costs industry billions a year in accidents and productivity losses. Recruits testing positive at interviews are five times as likely to injure themselves as others. Expect random drug testing at work to be a major issue in other countries such as Britain by 2010. Such programmes can reduce accident rates by more than 90 per cent, linking detection with counselling and treatment. Expect drinks companies to respond to the alcohol problem with innovations such as a form of alcohol that does not cause a hangover, alcoholic drinks with an anti-abuse ingredient, health warnings and so on.

Smoking will increase in some countries
The countertrend with smoking has been an increase in the number of British smokers for the first time in two decades. There is a notable increase among high earners, those in their late 30s and early 40s. However, smoking in teenage girls is also higher, partly encouraged by chic images of models on catwalks holding cigarettes. Expect smoking to fall worldwide in developed countries, with exceptions in particular social groups. In the poorest nations, however, billions of dollars of 'new' wealth will be spent on tobacco.

Increasing lifespans mean people may be careless
One reason that some groups may reject anti-smoking health messages is because of a third millennial fear of living too long. What happens to a generation that watch their parents grow older and frailer without any signs of dying? For many it may even be

good news to be able to die fit and bright at 85, having enjoyed life, instead of at 105 with no mind and very little body.

Therefore expect a boomerang effect when it comes to health messages, a kind of double-think – on the one hand an obsession with ageing and with staying healthy forever, and on the other an increasing apathy about personal health. Both will coexist and can already be seen in the same people at different times. Personal health has always been a fairly irrational issue and will continue to be so.

Smoking lawsuits

The pattern is not so much one of new, draconian laws but of a groundswell of public actions. Hence the avalanche of civil litigation which swamped the American legal system, forcing tobacco manufacturers to set aside $300 billion or more to pay for smoking illnesses over the next 25 years. Seriously large payouts have forced a rethink on cigarette promotion far more effectively than bills in Congress to ban adverts. In a world lighting up 15 billion cigarettes a day the compensation packages could be unthinkably large if America becomes a trendsetter for other countries.

It's not just people who want a cut in this mega-deal. State governments want manufacturers to pay their medical costs for looking after people with smoking-related conditions. Florida won $11.3 billion from five companies over 25 years. Such compensation suits are expensive. Expect the global fight for compensation to continue for at least three decades.

China cracks down on tobacco

China has banned cigarette advertising and smoking in public places in 71 cities. It has also banned smoking on trains. However, fines are small and the measures are widely ignored. Expect that to change. China burns 1.6 trillion cigarettes a year (25 per cent of the population smoke), making it the world's largest producer and consumer. Most smokers are male and smoking kills 500,000 a year, a figure expected to rise to 2 million a year by 2025. However, the industry is one of the largest sources of state revenue.

Bitter fight coming over dope (cannabis/marijuana)

Expect a bitter fight over dope, which proponents will claim (correctly) is less addictive and dangerous than nicotine, while opponents claim (equally correctly) that the use of other drugs is usually associated with previous use of cannabis, and that there is growing evidence that heavy use of cannabis has a long-term effect on brain function and can trigger mental illness. The fact is that one of the greatest predictors of smoking dope as a teenager is previously smoking tobacco. The battle will be fought one step at a time, with medicinal use of cannabis top of the list.

A number of experiments with the legalisation of cannabis will continue to be watched with interest (and some dismay) by other nations, with a counterswing against a dope-dominated culture. There is little doubt that wherever it happens, legalisation will result in a generation growing up for which cannabis use is as acceptable as smoking tobacco, if not more so.

Road accidents and drug use

Expect roadside skin-surface testing for illegal drugs to become common in many countries by 2010. Twenty per cent of all people killed in British road accidents carry traces of illegal drugs.

Designer drugs take off

We will see hundreds of new designer drugs in the next decade, acting not only on the brain but also on other parts of the body, for example to prolong sexual prowess and pleasure, to block the symptoms of a hangover or to enhance memory and intelligence. Expect great controversy over memory-enhancing substances and their widespread use in preparing students for exams. Some reports suggest that up to 20 per cent of American college students on some campuses are using drugs to try to improve their mental performance. Expect a huge black market in prescription-only sex enhancers, for women and men, until overtaken by over-the-counter versions, which will themselves be threatened by generic copies sold illegally online at far lower cost.

THREATENED NEW FOOD AND DIETS

Larger and fatter – epidemic of obesity

An example of how health conflicts with pleasure is the issue of food and obesity. Expect to see a battle of the bulge as whole nations get heavier – and heavier. Fat intake is falling in many countries, but not as fast as the taking of exercise. People eating less and less are getting more obese. Expect to see airlines redesign seat widths, even in economy class, as more people fail to squeeze in without risking injury. Car seats will follow.

Food – the new tobacco?

The percentage of overweight Americans has risen from 25 per cent in 1981 to over 35 per cent in 2006. Britons, on average, are 1 kilogram heavier than ten years ago while across western Europe as a whole, 15 to 20 per cent of middle-aged people are obese. For eastern Europe the figure is 40–50 per cent among women in some countries. Obesity-related disorders in the US kill 300,000 a year, and cost $100 billion in care. On current trends, one in three children born today in the US will develop weight-related diabetes – many as children. At the same time the US slimming industry has a turnover of $35 billion. Expect this to grow to an international obsession with laws preventing marketing of junk food to children and hundreds of other regulations – and debate about the definition of 'junk'.

Expect a new generation of 'safe' slimming drugs which kill appetite or prevent food absorption, for a market that could be worth at least $10 billion a year in the US alone. An example is likely to be molecules similar to the hormone thyroxine which can cause monkeys to lose 7 per cent of their weight in a week on a normal diet, with few side effects. Meanwhile the Fatlash movement will grow, promoting the erroneous belief that to be fat is healthy. Expect lawsuits against food companies alleging irresponsible promotion of unhealthy food, and a direct connection to sickness or death.

Anti-food for fat people

Expect to see a new food industry selling anti-food, or food with absolutely no nutritional value. The first anti-food was a new fat made from molecules which the body cannot digest. This can be used in cakes, ice creams or any other food. It cooks well, but once eaten comes straight out the other end unchanged. Bowel movements become greasy. There are dangers: fat dissolves vitamins, so a diet rich in this anti-food can produce deficiencies, as well as creating a generation of bingeing anorexics who are able to consume huge plates of food yet waste away to the point of death.

It will be a third millennial irony: 1 billion people starving or undernourished through poverty and millions of others using scarce resources to make food that they will waste 100 per cent through excretion. This is the ultimate in gluttony when taken to extremes, yet may be life-saving if it helps arrest obesity in a generation of food addicts who are increasingly immobile, unused to walking more than 100 yards without exhaustion. Exercise will be an optional extra in tomorrow's world. Why bother to walk when the world can come to your home, or when your home (your car) can travel?

Neurotic eaters

Expect to see growing neurosis, claims and counter-claims over the safety of food and drink, together with growing mistrust of government, manufacturers and labels. BSE was the consequence of turning vegetarian cows into cannibals in the name of farming productivity. The memory is still alive of rows over food irradiation, despite the fact that there is no evidence of any risk to human health. On the contrary: if 50 per cent of US food were irradiated, it would save 350 lives a year and prevent 900,000 people from becoming sick. Once again, we see that the future will be shaped not by science or technology, but by emotion, and food is a particularly emotional issue. Don't expect a change in consumer attitudes to food irradiation for a long time. Expect growth of 'natural' foods and 'natural' packaging as people begin to worry about oestrogen-like chemicals leaching out of plastic, some preferring old-fashioned, recyclable glass containers for milk and other products. Expect anti-additive food companies to create entire kitchen environments where nothing 'artificial' ever contaminates what people eat or drink. Expect new ranges of meat substitutes with the right texture and taste for some who insist on it. Expect a rash of new health scares related to vegetarian diets, such as nutritional deficiencies and worries about additives.

Expect more stampedes by consumers from one food to another, following the latest food scare, as happened with BSE and Foot and Mouth. Expect an end to the worst poultry factory farms, as worries over salmonella poisoning add another chorus to animal welfare campaigns. Expect food retailers and producers who break the rules to be 'punished' by increasingly militant groups, threatening boycotts and intimidation as well as shareholder action. Expect most changes in the food industry to come from consumer behaviour rather than regulations.

Expect confusion over what is safe and unsafe. Millions fled from drinking 'disgusting' tap water only to find that the bottled water they bought at high cost had higher levels of bacteria, was impossible to differentiate from the tap in blind testing studies and, what's more, was sometimes contaminated by pollutants from storage in plastic bottles. Expect global sales of vitamins to continue their spectacular growth upwards, although controversy will rage over what doses should be taken by whom and when – or even if they should be taken at all. Research suggests vitamins are best absorbed as part of normal food.

Vegetarians look for new products

Expect the vegetarian market to grow from 5 per cent to 10 per cent of the US population by 2015, with vegetarians eating some meat products occasionally, and millions of others eating far less meat than today. Red, fatty meat will be less popular, because of worries about bowel cancer and heart disease. In Britain 40 per cent of people often eat vegetarian foods, ten times the number of strict vegetarians, and the industry is worth £500 million a year.

Expect fast growth for certain 'veggie' products. For example, sales of vegetarian grills and burgers have increased by 139 per cent in five years in the UK, as technology and taste have improved. Expect new meat substitutes such as Arum to seize market share – a meat-like substance made from wheat gluten and pea protein with the bite, character, flavour and look of meat. It provides a good balance of amino acids from cereal and pulse proteins.

The latest studies imply that anyone eating as much red meat a day as in a quarter pounder has an increased risk of cancer of the colon and breast. Gene testing will be a rich person's way of sorting out whether an individual needs to reduce meat intake or not (see Chapter 5 for more about the implications of biotechnology). Only a minority of the population need to be careful about animal fat, because only they carry the disease genes. It is the same for many other diet-related conditions.

Expect organic food sales to increase by around 7 per cent per year in the wealthier parts of the EU and at a higher rate in the US. The EU and US are likely to continue to account for more than 90 per cent of the total organic market until at least 2015 – a market already worth $25 billion by 2003. Expect continued resistance in many nations other than the US to genetically modified food: 76 per cent of Polish consumers reject it, and 95 per cent of Russians who are aware of GM ingredients are seriously concerned and refuse to buy them.

Poor people eat more meat

While Western societies increasingly turn up their noses at meat, expect the emerging middle classes in many other parts of the world to celebrate their new wealth with increasing meat consumption. The result will be significant net growth in global production, at a rate far greater than the annual population growth. Expect a rise in the proportion of global grain production used to feed animals to more than 40 per cent beyond 2010. Expect countries like India to embark on another 'green revolution'. India's grain production has hardly increased over the last few years. Expect protests in wealthy nations as huge rural areas in places like India are taken over by industrialised large-scale farming, often of genetically modified crops. Concerns will be displacement of very poor labourers and environmental damage. Expect huge areas of food cultivation to be given over to biofuel production and a rise in the prices of some food such as maize as a result.

Future of the fishing industry

Expect growing demand for fish, placing further pressure on the ocean ecosystem. By 2006 40 per cent of all fish sold were already farmed, but farmed fish also require a diet of other ocean creatures. Expect intense efforts to solve this biological problem, allowing fish to be grown on a diet of land-grown food. Expect the proportion of farmed fish to increase to 60 per cent of sales by 2020, with far tighter regulation of marine fishing, in an attempt to allow wild fish stocks to recover. Expect major violations of international fishing treaties and failure by many governments to act in enforcement. The result is likely to be collapse of wild fish stocks in many parts of the world by 2025, further increases in fish prices and a further boost to the fish farming industry.

REPRODUCTION

Children having babies

Every year puberty comes earlier in both boys and girls. This dramatic change is seen most in larger girls, many of whom in some countries show pubertal changes as young as nine years old, in some cases at eight. By the age of seven, 27 per cent of African-American girls and 7 per cent of white girls in America have obvious pre-puberty body changes, for example breast enlargement. Expect to see pre-pubertal changes in even more seven-year-old girls by the second decade in the third millennium. Expect to see personal agonies, such as the one recently over an ll-year-old boy who is father to a child being carried by a 13-year-old girl. Expect to see nine-year-old fathers and nine-year-old pregnant girls, together with boys of nine charged with rape.

Doctors are having to rewrite the medical textbooks. What is normal, and who needs treatment? Children are being robbed of half a decade of childhood and are having to cope with huge hormonal and body changes before they are emotionally ready.

At present the age of puberty is considered to be a natural and highly personal event, a sacrosanct area that should not be interfered with. But in the third millennium many parents will want to manage puberty in their children rather than risk a full hormonal switch in a child. Society will be forced to take a collective decision about what the 'natural' age of puberty should be, and doctors, together with pharmaceutical companies, will do the rest.

Why is puberty getting earlier?

There are probably two reasons for the lowering of the age of puberty. Firstly it's a simple question of bulk. Female cells produce oestrogen and the larger the female body, the more oestrogen is in the bloodstream, to add to oestrogen from the ovaries. A child who is tall and well built will tend to reach puberty earlier and as we become, with better nutrition, a population of near-giants, so we become a population of child-adults.

Growth patterns are stabilising in developed countries so the effect there should level out. However, the second possible factor is environmental. There are a vast number of pollutants in the urban environment with oestrogen-like properties. An example is the string of chemicals which leach out of plastic containers into bottled water or foodstuffs.

One of the biggest sources of environmental oestrogen is food. Soya flour is a well-known source, so much so that a loaf of bread is being marketed which is claimed to reduce or eliminate hot flushes in women around the menopause. But what happens to male consumers or to unborn boys?

A sterile generation?

Environmental oestrogens in an increasingly urbanised society may also be the explanation for a catastrophic loss of sperm in men in industrialised nations, where counts have fallen by half in 50 years. We have also seen a significant fall in the healthiness of sperm. On current trends millions of men will be unable to father children because of this effect by the year 2050. If this decline continues at the same rate, healthy sperm counts will be seriously low in most men within the next 80 years.

However, these changes mainly affect the wealthiest nations and will not have a noticeable effect on population growth in the next 100 years at current rates. Other factors are more relevant, such as the age at which people start to have children and how many they choose to rear. In any case, men in developed nations will have all the resources of tomorrow's medical technology to help them father children, including cloning (see Chapter 5).

At the same time as sperm counts fall, testicular cancer and prostate cancer are rising. This feminising of the male population is subtle but progressive. Unfortunately the causes are so diffuse, so complex, that it could take several decades to be certain what they are. There are 100,000 widely used industrial chemicals in the environment and 1,000 are added every year.

Age of consent and child-bearing

As the age of puberty falls, the age of consent will also be reviewed. In Spain the legal age is 12 compared with 18 in Turkey, 17 in Ireland and 16 in Germany (all these countries have the same age of consent for both heterosexual and homosexual relationships). Expect a great debate over this, also where ages for same-sex relationships are different, as in Finland, Greece, Austria and Malta. Expect harmonisation downwards in many countries as law-makers shrink at the thought of putting teenagers in prison for having relationships with each other – assuming they object to paying fines.

Child puberty is a double hazard in millennial culture because adulthood – settling into a regular job and taking responsibility for others, including children – is being further and further delayed. Apprenticeships and training periods are longer, lasting until the mid-30s in some cases.

Child-bearing is being put off in almost half of all women in many industrialised countries until after the age of 30. That means a woman may have been ovulating for 20 years before she first attempts to become pregnant. But at that age her fertility is already in rapid decline. Expect an epidemic of infertility caused by a disastrous combination of older women trying to conceive, and the rapid spread of chlamydia infections.

A strange paradox in the next millennium will be millions of older women trying hard to become pregnant while millions of pregnancies in younger women are ended by abortion. It will be the era of the precious child, where anything that threatens the health or emotional happiness of a child will be severely frowned on. We see this already in growing public alarm over paedophilia, safety of children on the roads, exposure of children to undesirable influences at school and in the media. The new era will be one that worships the little child as a symbol of innocence and perfection in an increasingly tarnished, polluted and self-centred world.

'For the sake of the children' will be used as a motto to justify more or less anything, from marital fidelity to getting married in the first place or getting divorced, cleaning up the environment, banning cigarette advertising or imposing regulations on the volume levels of music in nightclubs (for the sake of adolescent children).

Expect parents to become even more preoccupied with child safety, creating cocoons for children in which (they hope) they are totally protected from risk. Fewer children will ride bikes on their own in the park or walk on their own to school. A countertrend will be a new generation of parents who believe children need to be allowed to grow up in the real world, less tied to adults for their every waking moment – parents who welcome risk-taking.

Problems of older mothers

In obstetrics any mother having her first child over the age of 30 is referred to as an 'elderly primip' because the human body is less able to carry a first child at such an old age. The risks are greater in delivery as well as conception, and there are added genetic hazards.

Expect a growing but controversial fashion for women in their 50s and 60s to have babies, using donated eggs or their own, held for years in freezers before use. The next two decades will see extraordinary advances in child-making technologies, each of which will push the boundaries of social acceptability. However, expect to see a reaction against 'playing God' (see Chapter 5), and a growing desire for 'naturalness' in conception as well as in delivery of babies.

All these biological time-bombs will have major effects in the first three decades of the third millennium. And others will emerge. They will fuel a general feeling in growing numbers of people that we are drifting off course and losing control, as a species, of our own destiny.

These issues will feed into much soul-searching over the environment. What kind of world have we made for ourselves? What are these unseen and unknown enemies around us that are making our children grow up too early, grow sick or even die? What is life for and what is our personal destiny?

THE CULTURE OF THE CITY

Nightclub culture, drugs and deafness

Nightclubs are booming and will continue to be a central part of urban life for millions of wealthier teenagers and young adults who only feel fully alive after midnight. The music played can be completely different from that played at home, highly repetitive and radically different from traditional pop – part of a culture dominated by the use of ecstasy and next-generation drugs. Expect to see a flood of research papers on deafness. Significant hearing damage can occur in some people following a single exposure of several hours at high volume. Ipods and other similar devices are capable of destroying the ability to hear certain frequencies, and this can be particularly risky since someone's exposure may be several hours a day without them realising. Expect thousands of lawsuits, much like those over tobacco, with people claiming that companies were aware of the potential for hearing damage in the 1980s and 1990s but failed to provide clear enough warnings or regulate sound output.

Many portable systems can power headphone or earpiece levels far above those from which ear protection is mandatory in factories. It will not be till 2030 that the problem really begins to bite, as the natural ageing process of hearing loss exposes the fact many people began adulthood with subtle but very significant hearing deficits. Expect an effect on music styles and dance culture, with the routine use of wax earplugs that enable music to be felt rather than heard.

Expect the common use of earpieces and earplugs by band members when performing, replacing old, loud onstage monitor speakers as a generation of older musicians find they can hardly hear. Everyone over the age of 70 experiences some hearing loss. Expect huge investment into ways to repair or regenerate hair cells in the inner ear using adult stem cells, viruses or other advances. The basic science to do this has already been explored.

So what will third millennial music be like?

Like previous musical eras, each built on the new technology of the time, third millennial music will harness new tools. We already have the capability to create any waveform we want – but the future will be in reproduction. Whole new ways of creating ambient sound in rooms, so they sound like concert halls or the open air, for example. Three-dimensional sound imaging creates instrumentation that flies through the air and then under your feet, voices that create a sense of total immersion, quite unlike anything ever experienced before – even in real life. These sound constructions will make all existing CDs redundant and every early 2000s album will sound dull, except when played through old equipment used to capture the 'genuine' historic sound, or when remastered in a studio. There will also be a music of extremes – with many rejecting the results as music at all. The ultimate test for every musical style will be whether it communicates. Does it connect emotionally? Does it change how people feel as they listen?

And third millennial films?

Expect to see major changes in the film industry. Expect a flood of remakes with better and more expensive special effects. The films of tomorrow will be dominated by computer-generated virtual sequences where stunt men are replaced by virtuality, and actors become virtual entities. But some film-makers will reject digital effects altogether.

Expect the creation of hundreds of 'see what it is like' films, creating entirely unique worlds in stunning detail, which will eventually be in trouble-free high-resolution 3D. Large wall-screens in homes will mean films that create audience atmosphere or offer vast, even 360-degree, imaging. But celluloid is dead, together with all traditional photography, except as an eccentric art form or as a leisure activity for those who enjoy echoes from the past.

And third millennial fashion?

You will see the same trends in fashion, on the catwalks. New designs will be influenced by new materials as revolutionary as stretch lycra became in the 1990s. Fashion parades will also continue to push towards every extreme, with models parading semi-nude, completely veiled, clean, muddy, soaked, icy, body-painted – anything and everything to get attention. But none of this will create popular third millennial fashion. The dominant styles will be different, but by definition mainstream. Expect to see wide use of intelligent clothes that change with temperature in colour or texture, and accessories that contain microchips and are 'wired' with functionality, such as belts, hats, glasses, watches, gloves or trainers – for example, providing readouts of distance run.

CRIME

Crime and personal security are the number one concerns for people in the US, Russia, South Africa and many other parts of the world. The fact is that urbanisation creates an environment where crime can flourish. In remote rural villages people still rarely bother to lock their doors, because crime is rare.

Crime tends to be a juvenile activity, fed by urban decay and social disintegration, that the vast majority grow out of. Expect draconian new laws in many countries, with new sanctions against youngsters and their parents as a desperate attempt to knock some responsibility into this age group. Prison populations continue to soar. In Britain the prison service had to try to convert holiday camps and ships into emergency prisons to hold them all. At current rates a large new prison will have to be built every six weeks.

Curfews after 9 pm for under ten year olds

Expect widespread use of curfews in badly affected cities or estates, to cut down on delinquency. More than 100 US cities already require everyone under the age of 17 to be at home by 8 pm every night of the week, except on Friday and Saturday when there is an extension to 11 pm.

Scientific evidence shows overwhelmingly that in industrialised nations, the collapse of the family is one of the most important risk factors in a teenager becoming involved in crime, along with academic failure and personal unhappiness. In the UK most child crime is committed by those from the underclass, those who drop out of school and are often illiterate. Expect social powers to focus on these issues.

Death of the police force

The first police force was set up by British Home Secretary Sir Robert Peel in 1829, but a revolution is under way. In 1970 the ratio of police to privately employed guards in the US was 1.4 to 1, but by 2006 there were three times as many private as public police. Private security in America costs almost three times as much as public police. Expect private security spending to increase globally, especially in areas with the greatest contrasts between rich and poor.

Countries like Russia and South Africa boast ten times as many private as public police. In cities like Johannesburg the wealthiest live in walled compounds surrounded by barbed wire and electric fences, with armed guards linked to instant response teams.

Russian law and order is chaotic. The interior ministry bill of $2 billion a year exceeds by far state spending on health. The new Russian revolution is still young and vulnerable. Expect Russia to take two decades to stabilise, and achieve some 'memory' of stable democracy, sound tax and legal frameworks and an enviable crime record.

SHADOW ECONOMY AND TAX AVOIDANCE

Millions of relatively anonymous people are hard to locate and hard to tax. No one sees what they do. While the Net provides new ways for the wealthy and educated to evade tax, at the bottom end of the scale the cash economy continues to thrive.

No tax, no regulation. Research at Linz University suggests that more than 20 per cent of GDP in Belgium, Italy and Spain is created in the shadow economy and 10 per cent in Britain, France and Germany. Compare this, for example, with the Belgian government's own estimate of 3.25 per cent of GDP and Britain's own official figure of only 1.5 per cent. If these figures for Europe are correct, the shadow economy is growing at three times the rate of the official one. Across Europe as a whole the shadow economy probably equals the entire legitimate output of Germany and Spain combined and is one reason why in a digital credit card age the amount of cash circulating is rising so fast in the EU.

Expect far more discussion of shadow economy figures, now that the EU requires them to be included in calculating true GDP and national contributions to EU budgets. In Russia the underground economy is probably greater than the official one. Russian tax inspectors carry stun grenades, tear gas and an assault rifle. In a year 26 people were killed, 74 were wounded and one was kidnapped at work.

In countries like the UK or France a figure of 10 per cent is highly significant. Since most of these cash deals are likely to be at the lower end of the wage scale – say a gardener or painter and decorator – it probably means that two out of five people are involved in the shadow economy in some way as earners, and the vast majority of the population are purchasers.

In Italy and France it costs a company three times the worker's net pay to take someone into an official job, so there is a huge incentive to employ casual labour on an unofficial basis. In Germany the ratio has been as high as 2.3 to 1. The service sector is growing fast in most industrialised countries and so are self-employment and part-time work. As incomes rise, more people are paying others cash to clean, shop, cook and do maintenance work around the house, while the Net and globalisation are also making income flows harder than ever to monitor. The greater the add-on costs of labour and the greater the regulations, the larger the shadow economy. Thus some measures to increase revenue or protect workers become largely self-defeating. That is one reason why countries like Russia, Slovakia and Ukraine have recently adopted flat-rate tax set at a lower level for income and purchases.

FEMINISATION OF SOCIETY

Many countries are becoming radically feminised. Men are in retreat, labelled as testosterone addicts: dangerous, ill-behaved variants of the human species prone to violence, predatory sexual acts and general loutishness and irresponsibility, the victims of a growing chorus of negative comments and abuse. Patriarchal society is rapidly becoming matriarchal. Female instincts and reactions are set to become the future norms.

If a man is strong he is macho, dangerous, stupid and a typical testosterone product. If he is soft and intuitive, sensitive and caring he is an effeminate, 'boring' wimp. And some women have begun to decide that romance has died.

A backlash against feminisation has already started. For example, Promise Keepers in the US is a men's movement, associated with the religious right, aiming to encourage responsible male citizenship and to restore men to their traditional role as head of the family. Some 1.2 million people gathered together at a series of rallies across the US and half a million in a single rally in Washington DC. It has tens of thousands of volunteers.

More jobs for women

Most new jobs in Britain are going to women – an estimated 70 per cent. Most of the jobs lost are those traditionally done by men. Since the 1970s, female employment has risen by 20 per cent while male jobs have fallen significantly. Tomorrow's jobs require flexibility, teamwork, efficiency – favouring women, according to some feminists. The greatest growth of jobs is in part-time service and leisure industries, while traditional full-time manufacturing workers are a dying breed.

The feminisation of society is probably most clearly seen in Japan, a strongly male-dominated culture. From 1975 to 2005 the percentage of women attending a four-year university course rose from one in eight to more than one in four. The female workforce has increased from 32 per cent to over 40 per cent in the same period. However, women still have only two in 40 managerial positions (double the number in 1984 but far to go to reach parity). Sex discrimination in promotion has been outlawed by the courts and 12 female staff of a bank recently won $890,000 in compensation for sexual harassment.

Women dominate online spending

Seventy per cent of all online purchases of many kinds of products are by women in Europe and the US. Seventy per cent of all online bank accounts in the EU are opened by men but 70 per cent of transactions are by women. They buy most household goods, most books, most food and most holidays. Women also dominate spending in traditional retail stores, yet despite this most marketing executives and customer relationship managers are men. Expect this to change as companies look to rebrand in a more feminine way.

Feminist movements are going to have to think where to go next

Expect men's liberation movements to parallel women's activist groups. Expect gender-role confusion to continue, with a backlash from many women over the negative stereotyping of men. Expect major shifts in corporate culture, especially as populations age, creating skills scarcity. Expect many more women to occupy senior positions. Expect continued agonies over the welfare of children brought up in two-career homes as more studies show a strong link between behavioural problems in children and households where both parents have demanding full-time jobs. Expect men to sue for sexual harassment, intimidation and prejudice in recruitment. Expect men to demand male quotas for jobs and continued debate over whether, for example, male nursery nurses should be allowed to escort toddlers to rest rooms.

Expect the M generation to question some of their parents' ambition when they feel it resulted in damage to them as they grew up. Expect them to organise their own child-rearing years differently, with increasing numbers deciding to sacrifice one or both careers for the sake of longer-term family happiness, although with less income. Men will more often be at home looking after children, and will combine this with part-time teleworking.

Feminisation slow to deliver at home and at work

Despite all the above, feminisation still has a long way to go. Men clean the house, but not much more than they did. There is still a glass ceiling blocking promotion for women in many areas and women still have far less leisure time than men. Most large corporations still have very few women at the most senior levels, despite half their best people being women further down the organisation. Expect corporations to pay far more attention to retaining talented women, with many changes in culture and working practices, with more part-time jobs and flexible hours.

AGEING POPULATION

Two-thirds of all those in human history who have ever reached their 65th birthday are alive today. Yet at the same time the number of children in schools in some countries is falling fast – halving in some German towns, for example, over the past decade. The impact of these kinds of demographic changes will be felt in every 'old' EU nation and every business trading in the EU over the next 30 years. Ageing will be even more dramatic in developing countries with a 15-fold increase in men over 60 and 20-fold increase in women over 60 in the next 30 to 40 years.

The most important health budget factor will be ageing

Age-related illnesses are responsible for almost all medical needs in those over the age of 40. Those over 65 cost 65 per cent of the health budget in the US – $470 billion a year. Since all this illness is a result of several common ageing mechanisms, at the cellular level, expect pharmaceutical companies to try to solve several problems at once with single therapies.

Expect a significant jump in life expectancy with medical advances in therapeutics and biotech (see pages 111–13, 229–38). There are already more than 75,000 people who are 100 years old in the US, and the number is expected to double in a decade.

So are we just adding years to life, instead of life to years?

Babies born in Europe and the US in the next ten years will live at least twice as long as those born 100 years previously. Killers like pneumonia or childbirth are being replaced by rheumatoid arthritis, cancers, dementia, crumbling spines, blindness and deafness. Gone are threats in wealthier nations of polio, tuberculosis and whooping cough. Instead there are fears about dependency, and pressures on the retired to become carers for parents who are also retired. Grandchildren will find that illness in a parent can leave them caring for two or even three generations above them.

Balance-sheet crisis for multinationals

General Motors already spends more on healthcare alone for those who used to work for the company than it does on steel. If life-expectancy forecasts are increased by just 3–4 years, the impact on the balance sheets of many corporations in the UK and US becomes very significant. Every year of added life means an additional 3 per cent pension fund liabilities for corporations, individuals and for government. Companies have to show sufficient funds in pensions to meet future obligations but their life-expectancy forecasts are almost certainly inaccurate, as we will see later in this chapter. Expect significant increases in official figures, but these will be announced in many small steps to try to avoid market shocks.

Europe is dying.

However, the real cause of the ageing problem is lack of babies rather than longer living. If the average European couple were still having three or more children there would be no ageing problem and no pension crisis.

In most EU countries the average couple is having 1.3–1.7 babies – well below the level needed of 2.3 to achieve a stable population. That means four couples will be needed to create a single great grandchild. The solution is simple: make more babies, import more people or retire later. We can expect all three strategies to be popular with governments. France has already offered large incentives to couples to make babies and birth rates have risen slightly.

Thus making babies will become a major policy issue, one affecting future national well-being. Expect countries like Germany, Italy and France to relax immigration controls following the UK example, which led to 1 million people entering the country in under four years.

Baby famine in Europe
- ◆ 2.3 births per couple needed to sustain population
- ◆ 1.5 live births per couple average
- ◆ 1.2 Spain and Italy
- ◆ 1.4 Germany
- ◆ 1.5 Sweden
- ◆ 1.7 Netherlands, Britain, France

44 million immigrants will be needed by 2050 to keep the population stable on current trends within the old EU nations, but many are likely to come from new EU entrants such as Poland, creating severe shortages of young adults and their own needs for immigration from further afield e.g. Ukraine, Belarus, Russia.

In Japan the number of children aged 14 and under has dropped to 15.5 per cent of the population from 35 per cent in 1955. By 2010 Japan could have the smallest workforce in the world in percentage terms and the largest proportion of elderly people.

German and Italian pensions bill will threaten the EU

By 2007, 80 million people were alive in Germany. Of the adults, three were of working age for every one retired. Current predictions are that by 2035, 71 million people will be alive in Germany. However, the ratio of adults will be only five of working age to three who are retired. The reality will be even tougher. Some of those five will not be working. They will be retired, in training, or chronically sick. Of course it is possible, but unlikely, that the few younger adults left over the next couple of decades will abandon restraint and have very large families. But even if they do, it will not be in time to ameliorate the problem significantly before 2025 without huge immigration.

By 2035 there will be 4.5 million pensioners in Germany over the age of 80 – up from just 3 million in 1997 and more than enough to swing any election. Germany's pension problem could be the undoing of the European superstate. Expect radical measures to deal with it. Britain has vast savings in pension funds for the future. But Italy has a similar challenge to Germany. There will be 1 million Italians over 90 years old by 2026, 85 per cent of whom will be women. As a result expect further falls in the percentage of over 15-year-old Italians in work – below today's 50 per cent compared with 70 per cent in some Nordic countries.

Who is going to pay the bill?

So who is going to pay? Will there be higher corporate taxes? Sales taxes? Income taxes? Will other European states foot the bill? Who is going to want to live and work in Germany or Italy if taxes are far higher than elsewhere? Expect relaxation on immigration to provide more workers and drive ageing economies. Other EU nations will be forced to follow the UK, but with an ever-present risk of an economic downturn, and rising unemployment blamed on recent influx of immigrants.

France will wake up from sleep with riots and demonstrations

France's public sector workers are still under the delusion that they can all retire on good pensions many years earlier than their colleagues in industry. France has a strong tradition of government or policy change through large scale protests. Expect this pattern to continue. There will be more rioting on French streets when a government finally has the guts to grasp that nettle – as well as continued restlessness among ethnic minorities who resent negative public attitudes, low-level discrimination and the lack of jobs, partly a result of restrictive practices.

A generation ago, five French workers were paying for one retired person's pension. Today there are around 2.2 pension contributors for every recipient, a figure expected to become 1.75 by 2015 and only 1.1 by 2040. By then, if nothing changes, every worker will have to finance 100 per cent of another person's monthly pension payout, as in Germany. France is in a serious situation, having virtually no privately funded pensions. Already 10 per cent of its GDP is spent on pensions and there is no fund of investments for the future. In contrast, the UK government spends 6 per cent of GDP in total today. The increase in French public worker pensions alone by the year 2015 will be equivalent to an extra drain of 1.25 per cent of GDP. By 2015, 25 per cent of France's population will be over 60. Most will be entitled, as things stand, to between 66 per cent and 75 per cent of their finishing gross wages, index-linked, all paid from the wages of working people. Meanwhile Italy's state pension system is supporting 18 million pensioners with the contributions of only 21 million in the workforce, and is currently running an annual deficit of around $50 billion.

EU pension fund assets are one-third of US assets, paying for 100 million more people. And what is more, the UK and the Netherlands account for 75 per cent of that. A staggering 85 per cent of European pensions are 'pay as you go'.

Double taxes for future generations

To sort it out future generations may have to be doubly taxed in countries like Italy, Germany, Spain and Sweden where private pension fund investments are less than 7 per cent of GDP. First, they will have to fork out for the vast numbers of people without a pension who need one today. Second, they will also be forced to start saving hard so that they don't need a state pension when they get old. In effect that's a double tax. You pay into a private pension for yourself, and into a state pension for those older than you. Unfunded liabilities in pay-as-you-go EU countries are over $14 trillion. Where will it come from?

One way the money will be found will be by cutting 'safety net' benefits for the sick and the unemployed – a recipe for widespread labour unrest. A French government was recently elected promising to create 700,000 jobs, half in the public sector, cut the working week from 39 to 35 hours with no pay reduction, cut VAT, raise wages and pensions, boost state spending on culture and research – without increasing borrowing, spending more or increasing taxes. Expect a passionate debate between generations on solving the pensions crisis – made more difficult by the growing number of active older voters and their power to decide the outcomes of elections. So what will individuals do? First, some will move out of countries where they are heavily taxed to pay other people's pensions and go to live in low-tax countries where they just save for their own. Second, expect far greater attention to the performance of pension funds and to the levels of contribution.

Over 65s own most of US wealth

People over 65 account for 50 per cent of US income and 75 per cent of all financial assets. Expect a wide range of new products for the 'grey market', such as super-cruise ships and luxury air trips. Well-off older people tend to be careful spenders who enjoy new experiences and travel. Older consumers expect more: personal advice, easy parking, seats in shops, supplier choices and larger print size.

Expect a rethink about packaging, restaurant menus, instructions and marketing materials, which are often printed too small for anyone under 55 to read without glasses – and even then with difficulty. This is a generation that think young, with a mental age of 40, physical age of 50 (compared with their parents) and actual age of 65. Expect many of the role models used in advertising to age 30 years from the up-and-coming 20 to 30 year olds to those whose children have long left home. Grey power will be far more visible on the high street, in clothes shops, sports shops, car showrooms, garden centres, travel agents, theatres, cinemas and restaurants.

Personal pension plans and investment funds will be growth markets for those nearing retirement, and high-value personal services such as face-to-face banking will be especially aimed at those who are retired. There will be a boom industry in converting life insurance policies into cash pre-death, aimed at people in a disintegrated society who have no wish to pass on capital to their descendants.

How people will survive their pension crisis
- ◆ Delay complete retirement beyond 70
- ◆ Save more before retirement
- ◆ Move to smaller house – live off capital
- ◆ Release equity from house and stay there
- ◆ Inheritance from parents
- ◆ Move to lower-cost country – rent out original house
- ◆ Live with children in extended family
- ◆ Cut down on luxuries e.g. travel/clothes

Other consequences of the 'grey factor'
Countries short of labour will need to import it from other nations. The increase in immigration from poor to wealthy nations will have a profound effect on the ethnic mix of younger populations in towns and cities, especially when combined with higher birth rates in some existing minority communities. It will also result in rapid depopulation of cities in countries such as Poland, Ukraine and Slovakia.

As I say, we can expect many older people to carry on working until 75, some enjoying a partial pension at any stage from 45 to 75 so as to take on less well remunerated roles for worthy causes. Most people find it hard to imagine a world where they are as fit

and agile at 75 as their parents were at 65. Expect state benefits
to start at higher ages by 2010, 70 years by 2020 in most countries
with a severe pensions deficit. However, those with their own
personal pensions will continue to choose to retire, or semi-retire,
whenever they like. A key strategy for recruitment will be tempting
out of retirement such people, many of whom may have intended
originally to stop work at 55 or 60 at the latest.

Compulsory retirement will become illegal – a form of ageism.
Many will work beyond 70 and still have a long, wonderful retirement. Many will inherit wealth in their 70s from over 90-year-
old parents – $4 trillion dollars will pass from one generation to
another in the next decade in the US alone. Expect an army of
fit and active 75 year olds to become volunteers for hundreds of
charities, especially geared to the social and emotional needs of
older people whose lives are helped by helping others. Expect
these organisations to provide a sense of family, destiny, belonging
and personal well-being.

At the other end of the social scale, expect a growing underclass,
and a layer just above who work part-time until they drop in their
70s, 80s or beyond, unable to survive on miserable state pensions
and out of touch with their children, eking out a pitiful existence
doing menial service-industry jobs for almost no pay. They will
appear on few statistics, since their earnings will often be informal,
in cash and undeclared. No rights, no representation, no benefits,
no security. A huge problem will be the growing numbers of people
in 20 years' time who failed to invest adequately in pension funds.
A separate, traumatic problem will be experienced by those whose
funds fail to produce what was promised or expected.

In summary, governments and individuals will use many strategies to help fund retirement, and combinations of all these efforts
are likely to soften the impact of the crisis for the majority. But of
course all these strategies will be affected by wider issues affecting
the future growth of economies.

Expect older people with long-term, successful and happy
marriages to become a respected source of wisdom on content-
ment, following a growing recognition that happy, stable marriage
is a major predictor of general emotional and physical well-
being throughout life. Expect the spread of informal fostering

or adoption in wealthier nations of retired people as substitute grandparents by those with children at home, where generations are separated by distance or family tensions. Some of these arrangements will attract state funding because reconstructed family groups save money in care bills.

Can we stop ageing?

The first 150-year-old human being could be sitting next to you today as a five year old. We know that a common gene is often found in people who live for more than 100 years, identical to the one in long-lived yeasts and worms. Expect huge advances in our understanding of the relatively few common mechanisms of ageing that affect living cells and ways to interfere with them. Expect intense efforts to unravel the mystery of how some animals don't show any measurable evidence of getting older – such as some rock-fish and some hump-back whales. Rock-fish life expectancy ranges from 12 for the Calio to 205 for the Roughi. By 2010 some of the genetic differences between these rock-fish will be clear, which will give us new clues about ways in which we could try to interfere in the ageing process in humans. It is likely that similar mechanisms have evolved in the sturgeon and turtle, pointing to new approaches that could be taken in humans. Expect research to show why mice can be kept alive for the equivalent of 150 years old in humans by restricting their caloric intake or by treating them with the anti-diabetic drug metformin. This reduces cancer deaths by 80 per cent and prolongs life by 20 per cent. If you knock out the insulin receptors in rats, they lose 70 per cent of body fat despite eating 55 per cent more – and they live 18 per cent longer.

Expect growing numbers of people to treat themselves with drugs like metformin hoping to extend their own lives. They will not be willing to wait for formal trials in humans, since evidence in rodents is that the earlier these drugs are taken the greater the effect.

Adult stem cell research offers intriguing glimpses into our medical future. We have already seen improvement of heart function by up to 85 per cent using adult stem cells from the person's own bone marrow following bypass surgery. Severe spinal injuries have been successfully repaired in animals and steps are being made to repair brain tissue after a stroke. We now know that brain regeneration is a normal part of daily life, and that bone marrow stem cells released into the blood play a role in this process. Therefore it is no surprise to discover a woman's brain containing a large number of male cells following a bone transplant that she received from a man before she died.

Adult stem cell breakthroughs will leave embryonic stem cell researchers seriously short of cash as investors flee from controversial approaches that will remain illegal or unpopular in many countries.

Adult stem cells have proven far more adaptable and useful than researchers thought back in 2000. New pig's teeth have been grown inside the bodies of rats, while mice have grown new teeth from nerve cells or gum tissue. Adult stem cells are found in our own bone marrow, blood, corneas, retinas, intestines, liver, muscles, nerves, spinal cord, brain, pancreas and skin. Expect stem cell research to treat blood disorders, cystic fibrosis, diabetes, heart disease, kidney failure, stress incontinence, liver damage, lupus, osteoporosis, spinal cord injury and disk damage.

Expect the first successful repair of blindness caused by macular degeneration by 2016, offering hope to 10 million in the US alone. Expect the first successful attempts by various means to restore hearing by 2020.

Expect intensive research into replacement of joints with new prosthetics and joint repair using your own cells. Expect progress in treatment for deterioration of the brain, including adult stem cells from your own body to renew brain tissue. Expect new ways to diagnose brain deterioration before symptoms develop and effective drug treatment to slow progression. Expect stem cells to be used in motor neurone disease, multiple sclerosis, Alzheimer's disease, Parkinson's disease and stroke. Expect new creams and drugs that arrest cell ageing and death. Expect many new health management companies to fight for the lion's share of hospital and nursing home management for a new generation of older people.

7 Ways that cells get old
1. Atrophy – cell loss
2. Nuclear DNA mutations
3. Mitochondrial DNA mutations
4. Death-resistant cells
5. Extra-cellular junk accumulation
6. Intra-cellular junk accumulation
7. Formation of extra-cellular cross-links

Total body life and cure for blood pressure?

Imagine a drug that is taken for just a month and causes a permanent lowering of blood pressure, as well as permanently restoring the elasticity of the skin in your face and the whole of the rest of your body. It is already in clinical trials after dramatic results in rodents. So far, there has been slight evidence of benefit to those with severe heart disease but no effect on human skin (Alteon research). Expect many new discoveries of this kind by innovative biotech companies, with curious combinations of effects that result from targeting single mechanisms.

Is it right to live forever?

Around 40 per cent in the US say anti-ageing therapies should not be developed as public policy – yet the same people spend huge amounts on anti-ageing remedies for their own use. In other words, people very much want to live longer (assuming the extra years are active and symptom-free) but they worry that everyone else may find out how to live longer too. The aim of most anti-ageing research is compression of morbidity or the 'Duracell effect', allowing people to stay on full power for almost their entire lives before a short final illness. Length of final illness has remained six weeks in many developed countries despite longer life expectancy.

How much will life expectancy increase?

Death rates in each decade of life will need to fall on average by 80 per cent from levels in 1985 to produce an average life expectancy of 100. Life expectancy jumped in the last century from 49 to 80, but mainly for one reason: a huge reduction in deaths of babies and those under the age of two. One child life saved adds 80 years of life. However, saving the life of a 70 year old from illness may add only 10 years before she dies of something else. That is why even if we eliminate all cancer, heart attack, strokes and diabetes, it would only raise the average life expectancy in the UK from 82 to 94.

Euthanasia calls will grow stronger

Euthanasia will be a number one hot medical issue for the next three decades as populations age. This issue will not go away. The 'right to die' will be packaged with other issues, including the right of doctors to take a decision to end the life of someone who is unfit to take the decision. Doctors or a court of law will always have to decide, because someone has to decide whether the person is 'of sound mind', has all the facts and is not under undue pressure from others.

Expect to see doctors taking the law into their own hands, high-profile court cases and the legalisation of 'mercy death' in some countries. Expect more organisations like the Voluntary Euthanasia Society, Hemlock Society, Compassion in Dying and Death with Dignity to be set up. Also expect a backlash in countries where euthanasia is allowed. Expect to see a compromise where active medical curative treatment is abandoned far more frequently at a far earlier stage, allowing 'nature to take its course' with symptom control measures.

Countries allowing the freedom to kill those who want to die will find the elderly and dependent take this way out as the 'responsible' thing to do. The length of stay in nursing homes will fall, and doctors will become lazy regarding pain relief. People who suffer will be terminated. In the Netherlands, hospice medicine is badly developed as a direct consequence of some of the most liberal euthanasia laws in the world. One per cent of all deaths are the deliberate killing of a patient by a doctor without the patient requesting it. The criteria for euthanasia now include chronic illness and emotional distress. So now we seem to be in the business of killing people just because they are miserable.

Expect a new emphasis in medical training, not just to cure but to manage death and the dying process. Expect palliative medicine to be a key growth area in emerging nations. Expect new break-throughs in the relief of pain and sales of pain-relieving drugs to rocket globally in the next decade.

HEALTHCARE PROVISION

Rationing will produce many moral dilemmas

Health rationing is nothing new but will become far more obvious, with high-profile public debates about whether, say, a 70-year-old man or woman should be given a death sentence because of kidney failure, in order to allow a young child to receive twice-weekly dialysis treatment for the same condition. The number one health issue will be to work out guidelines for 'affordable treatment', having the interests of the whole community in mind. The idea of free or low-cost health for all will come under severe pressure. Doctors will be accused of playing God and will blame politicians, who in turn will tell the people (accurately) that health spending has never been so high, and is increasing far more rapidly than inflation.

Changes in healthcare

Expect healthcare in the US to be mainly state-funded by 2010, with major implications for price controls and profitability of all healthcare industries. Expect further rapid shifts to home-based care with extra emphasis on wellness, prevention and performance rather than on treatments. Expect new therapies like Melanocortin-4 stimulators – which could help you tan, lose weight and get ready for sex.

Expect radical steps to solve the global shortage of trained doctors and nurses, with wealthy nations having to plug labour shortages by tempting care professionals trained by poorer nations to emigrate. This 'theft' of care teams from the countries needing them most is already causing huge hardship in parts of Africa and Asia. Expect new agreements between wealthy and poor nations to compensate for losses of trained doctors and nurses. These payments will fund further training of healthcare workers. Meanwhile, trained professionals in wealthy nations will continue to leave their posts for other careers, blaming poor pay, overwork and low morale.

Health will therefore be a dominant industry in wealthy nations, and increasingly so in aspiring nations, with significant global growth throughout the next century. Doctors, nurses and other healthcare professionals will continue to be needed in increasing numbers, despite robotics and other technologies. People power will continue to be the main source of care delivery, whether it's helping someone turn in bed, or listening to someone in distress who is feeling unwell and afraid.

Emotional ill-health will be a growing issue from now to 2020, with depression and anxiety increasingly dominating many people's lives to the point where normal coping mechanisms fail. The history of Western civilisation has been that as people grow more affluent, and as their lives become healthier and easier physically, their stress levels rise and they become more and more emotionally fragile. Hence the US boom in therapy and a host of other services designed to care for the emotions. Expect 20 per cent of all men and women to need formal psychiatric help at some time in their lives, up from one in six women and one in nine men in the UK today.

Expect a new medical specialism to appear, linked to human happiness. Happiness will become a focused theme of the early third millennium. Since improvements in material wealth seem to produce no discernible increase in national or personal content-ment or fulfilment (among the non-destitute in developed countries), where is happiness to be found? New designer drugs will be increasingly used by doctors to elevate mood or control anxiety, as a partial solution to a growing crisis. Widespread prescribing of these mind-altering substances will be a back door to legalised drug intoxication.

NEW EPIDEMICS

One consequence of the increasing population is a growing risk of global epidemics. We are already seeing rapidly changing viruses emerge in different parts of the world. Every time a new person is infected there is a small risk of a significant mutation. As the world population increases, so the risk of mutation increases. High mobility also encourages spread. We have no medical protection against viral plague, no equivalent of penicillin for viruses.

New bacterial threats are also being seen, for example the Buruli outbreak in the Ivory Coast, and new drug-resistant strains of other bacteria, infecting 1.7 million people in the US each year, with 100,000 deaths, and many more in Europe.

A new global threat

AIDS is just one example of these new viral threats, and is now out of control in many of the poorest nations. The number infected with HIV every year is equivalent to 20 times the number killed in the 2005 Tsunami disaster. We are seeing one new infection every 15 seconds, with around one in 100 adults alive at the end of 2006 carrying the virus. Ninety-five per cent of all new infection is among heterosexuals and 60 per cent of new cases are among women. In a single year more US citizens died of AIDS than in the entire ten-year Vietnam war.

If the interval between infection and death were only six weeks, the US alone would have seen more than a million AIDS fatalities and would have declared a national state of emergency long ago. Instead most infections are hidden as America learns to live with a 'secret' illness, which complex treatment has turned into more of a chronic condition.

Some African countries are reporting that more than one in five of all adults carry the virus. In some communities, infection rates are as high as 70 per cent. But the greatest impact may turn out to be in Asia. India now has more cases than any other nation, with 1,000 new infections in Mumbai a night. By 2020 India could have more HIV cases than the entire world today. Neighbouring countries are likely to follow, including China. Meanwhile the fastest rate of increase of HIV is in Russia and Ukraine. Expect wealthy nations to invest more in prevention as part of developmental aid. Prevention works and is the only answer – as we have seen in countries like Uganda where infection rates have fallen dramatically, from 22 per cent to 7 per cent among teenage girls since 1990. It costs very little to save a life: what is needed is political will and community mobilisation on a massive scale. When people are motivated to talk about AIDS, and equipped with a clear health message, infection slows right down.

HIV treatments for rich not poor

Antiviral drugs prolong life, but the most effective can still cost more than $10,000 per person per year – science fiction for a country like Burundi with $3 a year per person to spend on health. Expect a 'morning after' pill for HIV in less than five years, with worries about partial efficacy and side effects. Expect no effective vaccine for at least another decade. We remain no closer than in 1990. Once such a vaccine has been developed, expect huge pressure on the patent owner to make it available globally at low cost. For this reason, drug companies will continue to pour more money into HIV drugs for wealthy nations than into vaccines.

Expect huge consequences following the decision in 2001 by drug companies to accept legal defeat in the fight to stop poor nations making copies of AIDS medicines. It will be part of a relentless global attack on intellectual property rights, where those rights seem to enable rich companies to exploit poor nations. Expect HIV testing to become a major weapon in containing spread by helping identify those infected and encourage behaviour change. Testing will be more acceptable as low-cost treatment becomes more widely available. Expect wide use of short courses of antivirals for infected pregnant women, reducing risk of transmission to their babies to less than 5 per cent at a cost of $15.

SARS: bird flu and threat of other new viral plagues

In 1918–19 Spanish flu swept the world infecting 300 million people and killing 30 million people. More died from this mutant form of flu than in the entire First World War. It spread globally in three great waves of death over just 18 months, in an age of horse-drawn carts, steam trains and slow passenger ships. Today such a virus could spread globally in a fraction of the time.

For years scientists have warned that another virulent strain could mutate into being at any time. In March 2003 a strange new virus swept across parts of China and Hong Kong. With no treatment or vaccine, SARS was rapidly carried around the world, causing alarm and huge efforts to contain spread. Such mutants emerge at the rate of one a year. By the time you read this it is possible that another mutated form of bird flu may have success-fully adapted to spread rapidly among humans. The World Health Organisation regards such an event as a 100 per cent risk – the only questions are when and how dangerous it will be, and how prepared nations will be with infection control, quarantine and mobilisation of healthcare. Just 8,600 SARS cases and 861 deaths were enough to wipe billions off the Asian economy. But govern-ment estimates for mutant bird flu or similar new pandemics are for up to 90 million cases in the US alone and a similar number in the EU – with death rates that could be as high as 1–2 per cent.

Expect governments to invest huge efforts in reducing the risk of bird–human virus adaptation, and in plans to slow down the spread of an epidemic, to gain time to make enough specific vaccine.

Even a small international outbreak is likely to cause widespread anxiety and rapid changes in behaviour. Expect up to half your workforce to want to stay at home in the early stages of what looks like a significant epidemic, especially those with young children who may worry about taking them to school (if schools stay open).

Past experience suggests that the greatest risk will be in the first wave, which will probably last only a few weeks, but with no vaccine cover and little medical experience. By the second wave some vaccine will be available and more by the third – but by that time many nations will have acquired some immunity in those who have recovered. If the virus turns out to be virulent, it is likely that healthcare services will be overwhelmed. If a global pandemic causes significant deaths, it is inevitable that priorities will change, with radical steps towards more effective global control of disease, new models for funding and conducting medical research, and a profound impact on how people feel about life, priorities and their future. If it mainly kills older people, it may turn out to affect the ageing crisis.

THE FUTURE OF THE PHARMACEUTICALS INDUSTRY

It costs almost $1 billion to bring a new drug to market – rising every year. Expect consumers and pharmaceutical companies to campaign for faster approval processes. But sales can be more than $8 billion a year so the stakes are high. Expect most new drugs to be just variants of previous molecules. Few will tackle root problems. Pharmaceutical spending is larger than the combined GDP of 135 nations, yet the great majority of new drug approvals come from small companies with tiny budgets. The traditional pharma companies are expensive and relatively inefficient. As a result few new drugs are in the pipeline. It takes 15 years to get a drug right through the system. Expect a radical rethink about how best to carry out pharma research and encourage innovation.

Expect consolidation of big pharma companies with hundreds of new partnerships with biotech companies, by just five or six large multinationals. Expect a narrow focus on the elusive search for more 'blockbusters' with potential sales of at least $1 billion a year. This will knock out research on many hundreds of other treatments where the numbers affected are small or where most people who have the illness are in the poorest nations.

Pressure on drug pricing

Expect huge pressure on earnings from pharmaceuticals in wealthy nations where many governments will insist on setting their own prices, or will control a restricted list of approved therapies, and where insurance companies increasingly interfere in treatment decisions.

At the same time, we are likely to see growing challenges from generic manufacturers, which will continue to flood the market with identical copies of expensive drugs, made perfectly but without permission or royalty payments.

Enforcing intellectual property rights will be almost impossible for a wide range of urgently needed medicine in emerging nations – not because of lack of legal systems, but because of unwillingness of big pharma companies to engage in potentially brand-damaging prolonged legal battles.

Even where the moral will exists to take aggressive action, it may be difficult to get adequate protection of intellectual property in countries like China until well beyond 2012. These pressures will combine to form a toxic mix for the future of the traditional pharmaceuticals industry. Expect alternatives to grow, for example partnerships between pharmaceutical companies and organisations like the Bill Gates Foundation.

Tomorrow's drugs are about performance and desire

Yesterday's drugs were all about need, while tomorrow's medicines will be about performance and desire. The definition of ill-health will shift significantly by 2020. Today's life-enhancer will be tomorrow's health need. Examples of problems that many governments today say are outside their responsibilities are male baldness, infertility treatment and cosmetic surgery. Others include appetite suppressants, skin anti-wrinkle creams, teeth whitening, gum disease, eye-sight correction, hearing repair, menopause and general processes of ageing. We can expect that many of these conditions will be seen in future as significant personal needs for which free treatment should be given. Expect also a reaction, with accusations that pharma companies are creating 'cures' for diseases people didn't know they had (see smart drugs, page 232).

Expect major consolidation of over-the-counter drugs companies in a market worth $170 billion a year, which will grow by more than 10 per cent a year in the next decade. Expect huge growth in pharmacogenomics: using gene-screening to decide individual treatment. This will help identify the 35 per cent who typically don't respond or have serious side effects, saving up to 100,000 deaths and 2.2 million serious drug reactions every year in the US alone. Medicines are the sixth biggest killer in the US. Expect more high-cost drugs like Herceptin, which is given to only 30 per cent of women with breast cancer who have the right gene.

. . . .
CHALLENGES TO MANAGEMENT
. . . .

Megacities
◆ Do you need a strategy for seizing market share or developing new markets in megacities?
◆ Who understands megacity culture in your organisation?
◆ Who is advising you on big questions, such as to what route to use or what speed to go at in regard to emerging countries such as China or India?

Maintaining appropriate differentials
◆ Expect pay scales to come under increasing scrutiny, with growing questions over vast differentials, not just in the same country and the same company, but between nations in the same company. Do you have a global pay policy which can be justified?

Relocation policy
◆ A key challenge for many corporations in the next decade will be whether to relocate – and if so, where? Expect a flow in and out of the central areas of big cities of companies with household names.
◆ Are your offices the right size and in the right place for rapidly changing circumstances – including the need for easy access to a global travel hub?

Water restriction
◆ What effect will water restrictions have on your business?
◆ Do you have added value here – e.g. making distilled water while smelting aluminium?

Family and relationship issues

◆ Have you considered how your company can help those who are married to stay happily married?

◆ Have you reviewed areas of policy for their 'family value'?

◆ Have you factored in the loss of productivity and increased staff turnover from family break-up?

◆ Have you thought of creating family-friendly policies as a means of attracting and retaining staff?

◆ Is your company providing an appropriate level of child care or flexible enough options to retain key female staff?

◆ Is your company providing fast career paths for high-flying women?

◆ Do your female staff agree or is there a glass ceiling?

◆ Have you defined and dealt with sexual harassment?

◆ Is there a written and understood policy?

Unemployment and insecurity

◆ What kind of staff training programme do you have?

◆ Do staff feel that even though their jobs may be insecure, they are becoming steadily more employable elsewhere as a result of working for you?

◆ What retraining and consultancy/advice packages do you offer those who become redundant?

Addiction

◆ What is your company policy on addiction and how is it defined?

◆ What is the policy on intoxication at work and how is it measured?

◆ Are employees screened for mind-altering substances, including alcohol, if they are in sensitive situations where the health and safety of others may be at risk?

◆ What sanctions are applied to those who test positive or are intoxicated, and do all employees understand what the sanctions are?

◆ What is the company smoking policy and is it being applied consistently?

Diet and weight
◆ What is the company policy on nutrition – e.g. canteen/ restaurant – and has it been reviewed recently?

Crime
◆ How would your company survive the theft of every piece of computer equipment at a key site, including all tape streamers and other backup storage devices and related media?
◆ What protection do you have against corporate spying, electronic bugging and other information losses?
◆ How secure is your business from attack?

Ageing population
◆ Have you reviewed retirement policy in line with demographic change?
◆ Have you considered abolishing a compulsory retirement age?
◆ Is your recruitment ageist?
◆ Have you considered changes in job design and hours to attract older people who may stay longer and be more loyal, as well as being more mature and experienced?
◆ Is your pension provision adequate, and if not, are your employees aware they may need to top up with voluntary contributions?
◆ Are you ready to move out of countries where social costs are going to soar, or to enter growing 'grey' markets?

Health provision
◆ Is your company's healthcare provision in line with what others are about to provide, in the light of the reducing role of free state healthcare?
◆ Does your company offer support for staff with emotional problems, as a means of enhancing productivity and loyalty?
◆ Has your company taken health promotion seriously, particularly regarding AIDS in high-risk countries?
◆ Do you have contingency plans in place for up to 50 per cent of staff not turning up to work because of worries about a new, rapidly spreading virus?

. . . .
PERSONAL CHALLENGES
. . . .

Transport hub – how close are you?

◆ How important will air travel be to you in the future, and are you near enough to a major international airport? Life's too short for frequent fliers to spend several hours driving to catch a flight, when it takes less time to travel across an entire continent.

Happy home life – competitive edge

◆ If you are married or in a long-term relationship, how important is its success to you and are you investing enough in it? A happy home life gives you a strong competitive edge. Domestic disaster will wipe you out emotionally and physically.

◆ When did you last programme in some quality time for your most important personal relationships?

◆ What about your oldest and most faithful friends?

Family issues

◆ In view of the rising infertility problems in many countries, how long dare you leave it before beginning to try to start a family?

◆ Where does all that fit into the rest of your plans for the future?

◆ Are you talking to your own children enough about the pressures they feel to take drugs or to experiment with early sexual relationships?

◆ Are they getting enough quality time with you?

◆ How are they coping with the fast, urbanised life you lead?

Tobacco, alcohol and other drugs

◆ Is your use of tobacco, alcohol or other drugs holding you back?

◆ Are you happy about that?

◆ If so, what are you doing about it? There are many other ways of winding down and relaxing.

◆ What would happen if you were randomly tested for drugs or alcohol at work?

◆ Is there a risk it could affect your future?

◆ Are you able to smoke freely when and where you want to at work?

◆ If not, how does it affect your performance when you want a cigarette or when you have to keep leaving the office to go and have a smoke?

Feminisation of society

◆ How comfortable are you with the feminisation of society?

◆ Do you feel secure in your own role as a man or a woman in the workplace?

◆ How would you like attitudes to change?

◆ What steps can you take now in your own situation to encourage this?

Planning to say goodbye to work

◆ When would you like to retire?

◆ How will you use the time?

◆ Is your own pension plan adequate for the future?

◆ Is there enough of a contingency there to cover periods of unemployment, when contributions will be hard to make, or unexpected early retirement?

Elderly relatives – what's the plan?

◆ How would serious illness in an elderly parent affect your plans?

◆ What do you hope will happen when you become old and frail yourself?

◆ Is that what you are modelling to your children with the generation above?

And finally…

◆ Do you feel comfortable with the gross inequality of wealth between the richest and poorest – and if not, what are you doing about it?

◆ Have you installed any water-saving or energy-saving devices in your own home?

CHAPTER 3

Tribal

Identity crisis: conflict of culture and conscience

Tribalism is the most powerful force in the world: more powerful than the combined military might of America, Russia and China. Tribalism creates belonging, identity, family, community, teams and nations, but can lead to separatism, violence, wars and genocide. All terrorism is extreme tribalism, fuelled usually by perceived injustice. Unless governments sort out the growing gap between the wealthiest and poorest nations, they are likely to see new protest movements become terrorist groups.

We tend to associate tribalism with African tribal wars in places like Malawi, Rwanda or Sudan, but tribalism is seen in any group of people who agree to belong together. The greater the globalisation, the greater the tribalism, particularly when one tribe of tribes is so dominant – America.

That is not to say that the end of the sovereign state is at hand. Tribalism simply means more sovereign states, smaller units of jurisdiction, while universalism dictates that larger issues such as defence will tend to be handled regionally.

The Economist wrote recently: 'The virus of tribalism risks becoming the AIDS of international politics – lying dormant for years and then flowing up to destroy countries.' We see tribal conflicts everywhere, whether in the Middle East, Bosnia, Kosovo, Northern Ireland, in Spain with Basque separatists, in Canada with Quebec separatists, in Chechnya, Rwanda, Kashmir, Indonesia or between black and white in America.

Wars today are mainly between family and family, and set street against street, town against town. These are not wars between nations but wars inside nations, or wars fought in new ways by an informal enemy whose greatest weapon is fear.

Tribalism will continue to dominate the Middle East, with the constant risk of major regional conflicts spilling over from Israeli–Palestinian grievances, anarchy in Iraq, Syrian and Iranian ambitions, and the battle for influence in Saudi Arabia. US foreign policy has historically been sympathetic to Israel's need for security. This perception of favouritism risks fuelling intense hostility to the US over the next few years, not only in Iraq, Iran, Syria, Lebanon, Saudi Arabia and other Arab nations, but in some communities in many other parts of the world. This is likely to have an adverse impact on US business and national security.

Tribalism will wear down the US in unwinnable, long-distance, asymmetric conflicts, where relatively small numbers of people manage to provoke the government into disproportionately costly responses over long periods. Extremes of tribalism will continue to cost the US billions of dollars a year in increased home security – against a small number of potential terrorists, who may be US citizens or residents. Of course, a small number could create havoc with a dirty bomb or a weapon of mass destruction, and that fear will haunt intelligence agencies.

TRIBALISM WILL THREATEN EUROPE AGAIN

Tribalism will be the downfall of Europe. A United States of Europe has no chance of being a reality for the next 100 years without some kind of imposed authority. In Europe we have nations who can't even hold their own people together. How can they all merge as one? We don't even have an elected president.

Another major problem is in defining what Europe actually is. It was all very clear before the Iron Curtain collapsed, but now? The old cluster of established industrialised nations has been changed forever by many new additions of very different economies. How can all these be welded together? The old-style European Union is dead.

Language identity

We see tribalism in the resurgence of language identity. For example, Gaelic in Scotland was more or less a dead language 20 years ago. Now it is spoken in shops and on the radio, it is taught in schools and road signs are in both Gaelic and English.

Then there is French radio. There is a strict limit on the amount of English-language music that can be transmitted on air. The medieval French Langue d'oc is experiencing a revival. The first Langue d'oc school opened in 1979; now over 1,400 pupils receive tuition in the language, backed by state funding. In Russia there is a ruling in some cities that business signs over shops must be in Russian as well as English. Belgium is a country split between Flemish and French. Switzerland runs on four languages: French, German, Italian and Romansh.

There are 329 languages spoken in the US. Out of the total population of over 260 million, 198 million speak English at home, 17 million speak Spanish and the rest speak one or more of the other 300-plus. Despite all this, the overwhelming evidence is that ethnic groups have children who adopt the dominant language of the country they live in. Diversity will depend on parents encouraging languages at home and school.

Language is very important: it helps express our national and cultural identity. Language preserves ancient literature and poetry as well as songs. Language communicates who we are – even the accent in which we speak our mother tongue reveals our tribe. This new love of old languages is a direct reaction to the almost overwhelming threat of English, which is used in 60 per cent of world broadcasts, 70 per cent of world mail, 85 per cent of international calls and 80 per cent of all computer data. Mexican Nobel Prize winner Octavio Paz once wrote: 'With every language that dies, an image of mankind is wiped out.' At present between 6,000 and 7,000 languages are spoken. A third of all languages will disappear within the next 100 years. Only 600 languages are considered secure. Expect more vigorous efforts to preserve those that remain.

TRIBALISM FEEDS TERRORISM

Terrorism thrives on tribalism. Expect to see terrorist groups multiply in the third millennium, the products of tribalism and single-issue activism. Most terrorist groups will continue to be small, fragmented, mobile and short-lived. They will tend mainly to be local rather than globalised with informal networks, using new technologies to frighten, sabotage and attack for the sake of a cause, seeing themselves as moral freedom fighters.

Expect to see a shift from suicide bombs, random shootings and remote control explosions using the tools of the mid to late twentieth century. Tomorrow's terrorists will be interested in things like germ warfare agents that can threaten city or countryside yet be carried in a briefcase. Sarin nerve agent attacks on the Japanese underground railways are the style of things to come as will be media-grabbing outrages. Terrorists will seek greater psychological power and media attention for less effort, using more automatic weapons and heat-seeking and other kinds of stolen missiles, readily available since the end of communism.

The collapse of the World Trade Center in 2001 set a benchmark against which terror groups will measure success. Never have five men with box-cutters demonstrated such power. Angry groups of many kinds will devote great efforts to similar acts – perhaps flying into a nuclear power station, or contaminating a city with a 'dirty' bomb, explosives mixed with radioactive waste. Suicide attacks will be seen by supporters as noble and courageous.

Yet despite this, and despite the impression from watching news channels, the actual numbers injured or killed in terror attacks will remain almost insignificant compared with other causes of deaths. The lifetime risk of witnessing an act of terrorism will remain effectively zero. Deaths from all acts of terrorism over the past 30 years have been almost immeasurably small (and will continue to be so) compared with deaths from conventional armed conflicts and civil wars. Even if a dirty bomb were to be detonated in London or New York, or a nuclear power station were to be attacked, that would still be the case as deaths in combat in every decade are comparatively huge.

Terrorism becomes a way of life

Expect to see economic and anti-corporate terrorism: the spiking of more food products in shops, the cutting of optic cables, damage to huge satellite dishes, the creation of computer viruses and spread of animal viruses like foot and mouth. Expect more tribe- and state-funded terrorism as conventional wars become more difficult to fight against an army with ultra-high-tech weaponry. The greater the perceived imbalance in military power, the greater the temptation will be for militant groups or nations to resort to low-level 'terror' attacks designed to cause maximum disruption and fear.

Expect most governments to spend more on anti-subversive activity. Security forces will use ever more sophisticated spying technology to track down and destroy terrorist groups, and in so doing will violate the privacy of many innocent citizens. The same forces will also target drugs activity and globalised crime syndicates. Eventually, the public hysteria over terrorists will subside to a more rational and pragmatic response, recognising that the greater the reaction, the greater is the win for the terrorist. Terrorism will become an accepted part of third millennial life, as an irritant rather than a major feature.

Expect new research efforts to try to understand why young people become convinced that acts of terrorism are their only option, and to try to identify root causes of community anger and bitterness that create conditions for easy recruitment, so that positive action can be taken. Expect significant changes in foreign policy as a result.

TV makes big wars harder to fight

Live TV pictures and videophones will make wars harder to sustain because their horror will be seen so close to home. The Iraq war, Afghanistan, Bosnia, Kosovo – conflicts have become more difficult to manage from the public relations point of view. The media brings home to us the absurd and obscene contrasts in our world. It focuses on violence and discord, rewarding protest groups and tribal factions with huge coverage, hijacking national agendas, and disturbing the sense of well-being of millions. Expect growing unease about the way in which unrestricted media reporting tends to focus on sensationalist and distorted coverage of our comparatively mundane daily global existence.

THE DEATH OF NUCLEAR WEAPONS

Conventional weapons such as land mines have been in great demand while nuclear weapons have been dying. The changing military and political realities will result in further rapid reductions in nuclear warheads – with continued worries about safe disposal. By 2012 expect the US and Russia to deploy only 1,700–2,200 strategic warheads each, two-thirds lower than the 2002 figure. Expect further reductions by 2020.

However, surplus missiles are a great temptation to the crime syndicates which control much of Russia's economy. Russia will be a major official source of surplus arms sales for the next 20 years, selling to virtually anyone with money (with the exception of nuclear sales or attempted sales which will be controlled by crime syndicates). Expect to see major nuclear scares over the next 20 years as countries or groups claim to have got hold of nuclear weapons or material, or to have developed their own, and threaten to use them. Bluff and counter-bluff will threaten regional security. There could be some risky stand-offs.

Expect an accelerating nuclear arms race involving India, Pakistan, China, Iran, North Korea and others, in a bid to protect national security and as a bargaining tool. America's failure to ratify the Comprehensive Nuclear Test Ban Treaty (together with China) will make it far harder to persuade India, Israel, Pakistan, North Korea and Iran to do the same.

No nuclear warhead has been used in war for 60 years. Expect someone to threaten it somewhere and massive international confusion about how to respond. Do other countries threaten to go to war against a nuclear weapon-using nation, if a warhead is used by such a country in self-defence, after repeated warnings to an aggressor? How would such a war be waged? How do you counterstrike against an invisible terrorist group? What happens if a nation or group threatens again, and explodes another warhead?

Do the collective opposition then decide to let off a warhead themselves and if so, where? Countries may have only days or hours to debate these issues when the situation emerges.

There'll be lots of news about ultra-smart weapons and near-empty battlefields fought over by unmanned drones, cruise missiles and other technology. But the fact is that most wars tomorrow will be guerrilla wars fought wall by wall and house by house, ethnic conflicts or terrorist attacks; mucky wars where tanks park themselves inside the compound of a large children's hospital, where civilians are caught up in bombing attacks.

There is no such thing as a designer battlefield, apart from the areas where test exercises are done over and over again. Battles will be fought in shopping precincts, around public libraries, by ancient stone bridges and in fields of corn. Digital positioning systems can pinpoint every vehicle in fog or darkness in a 200 square kilometre area. But 'smart' wars will continue to get bogged down in urban chaos with the ever present risk of killing unarmed men, women and children.

National arms factories will continue to overproduce

As I predicted, there has been significant consolidation in the arms industry. Expect further mergers and partnerships between European defence companies. The five big leaders still compete to win military contracts worth less than half the $150 billion the US spends a year, just part of the total $500 million defence budget, itself 50 per cent of all global military spending. Expect US defence spending to grow, influenced by 80 per cent of Americans who see military force as an appropriate option to deal with threats, compared with only 20 per cent of those in the Netherlands or Spain.

Expect more joint ventures to satisfy national governments which seek to protect jobs at home. However, new mergers or joint projects will not solve an underlying problem, which is that defence research spending makes sense only when there are larger economies of scale and that means selling to other nations whose policies and behaviour may make many uneasy.

The British and French economies will suffer as the non-US

arms trade shrinks. This is an industry which produces offensive weapons, designed to shoot down, destroy or otherwise incapacitate an enemy. If an enemy is seen as the aggressor, action is seen as defence. But many of the weapons sold to other countries are used aggressively.

Expect increasing unease in developed countries about the building of national economies on the sale of 'death machines', and growing ethical concerns among the workforce as well as shareholders. The argument until now has been that if we don't sell, someone else will. This argument will not be so persuasive in the future.

Expect China's military spending to grow faster than its economy, reaching more than $320 billion a year by 2020. Expect Russia to increase military budgets using oil and gas revenues.

Landmines and other messy weapons

So what happens to all this production? Either the world fills up with more and more weapons, millions of rifles, tens of thousands of missiles, or for every weapon made another has to be decommissioned. In practice two things happen. First, weapons move down the arms chain towards the bottom of the pile, into the hands of the poorest (and often most unstable) nations where they are often used for internal repression rather than national security. Then arms fall into the hands of gangs and criminal groups, the lowest layer of all.

Second, weapons are lost or unaccounted for. Landmines are a prime example. Tens of thousands of square miles are uninhabitable because of the indiscriminate use of anti-personnel devices, which will remain dangerous for at least two decades. Over 110 million mines have been scattered and lost, affecting at least 70 countries. Cambodia, Angola and Mozambique are among a number of countries which have been severely affected, with large numbers of civilians killed or injured every year, including children. A third of all the land that could be farmed in Afghanistan and Cambodia has been rendered unusable. Worldwide, 1 million people have been injured or killed in 25 years. There are a further 100 million land mines in military stores.

Expect to see today's high-tech weaponry used by 2015 in many developing countries against neighbours and internal threats.

TRIBALISM BROKE UP THE SOVIET UNION

Tribalism, expressed as nationalism, broke up the Soviet Union and will threaten Russia as it is known today. Tribalism will affect the future of countries like Ukraine. Anti-Russian feeling will continue to find expression far beyond the era of President Putin.

The 12 countries of the old Soviet Union are drifting further and further apart and the new Commonwealth of Independent States (CIS) has failed, whether as a military union, a currency union or an economic union. So long as Russia continues to try to dominate, the CIS members will continue to be forced either into further economic dependence on the old mother state or, as many of them are, into looking west, possibly as far as trying to join NATO – an act the Kremlin once described to be as dangerous as 'playing Russian roulette'.

The Soviet economic order has gone for good. Privately owned business now accounts for more than half of the region's GDP. All this has been achieved with remarkably little unrest.

Foreign investment is picking up, especially in countries like Poland and Hungary, and the region's stock markets are becoming popular. Expect westernisation to accelerate, and an increasingly wealthy middle class to begin to travel across Europe frequently.

The future of Russia
Russia will remain a high-growth and high-risk market, with business threats from organised crime syndicates, local corruption and erratic government decisions. Russia will benefit from oil and gas wealth, but will also find these assets hard to manage in a global economy, where economic realities and political ambitions are often in tension. It will take Russia at least 25 years on current trends to begin to satisfy the expectations of its citizens for a more comfortable, prosperous and secure life.

Expect Russian leaders to continue to fear peaceful revolutions like those in Georgia in 2002 and Ukraine in 2004, with sharp crackdowns on anything that looks like foreign funded political activity disguised as humanitarian work. Expect President Putin to make great efforts to install a rubber-stamped successor in 2008. He will demonstrate complete mastery of the media and intolerance of any business interests that try to challenge him. Putin's strong will will be welcomed by the majority of Russians, who take comfort in powerful leadership in preference to the painful chaos they experienced in the early years after the collapse of communism.

Expect significant political changes in Kazakhstan, Uzbekistan, Kyrgystan and Tajikistan as they seek more to free themselves from Russian influence, with pressures from both Russia and Islamic groups.

The future of the former Eastern bloc

Much of the region will remain in deep recession for some time, but people living in larger cities will experience growth. In half of the economies in central and eastern Europe output fell by 50 per cent after 1990 – this was a catastrophe, since the original levels were already low compared to the rest of Europe. The entrepreneurial spirit in many communities had been crushed.

It will take another decade for these Eastern bloc countries to settle down economically, and even then there will be a huge gap with the rest of Europe. It will take two decades for democratic traditions to take root. In many of these countries there is a political immaturity which could lead to unrest. Some democracies are only skin-deep, brittle and fragile. Unless there is a great leap forward in economic growth, growing dissatisfaction could lead to riots, civil disobedience, internal military action or worse. Expect wealthy nations to take positive action to reduce the risk of this, including further extensions of a broader, redefined European Community. New tax systems, regulatory authorities, laws and other components of civic life need to be introduced and adapted, and they will be.

If most or all of these central and eastern European countries become part of the EU, it will add to the disruption of the original simple concept of a western European Economic Community. Enlarging the EU from 15 to 27 countries has changed it forever. For example, unanimous decisions are much more difficult. The combined GDP of 12 new entrants is barely 4 per cent of the current EU total, yet they account for a big chunk of the votes.

Ninety million new EU citizens have created a community of over 500 million people, a $9.5 trillion economy. But 45 per cent of the EU budget will be subsidies for new entrants. Poland will take 40 years on current trends to reach the UK's level of wealth, and huge numbers in the ten new nations earn less than $450 a month.

The future of central and eastern Europe

Shaking off entirely the legacy of communism will take another generation and will be costly. Just look at the huge investment made by West Germany after reunification. Despite this, unemployment and social problems remain huge in East Germany. Regeneration has been slow and a major drain on Germany's finances.

Until recently, take-home pay in countries like Hungary and Slovakia has been a mere 20 per cent of total employment costs – compared with 50 60 per cent in the EU. In 2006, many millions of pensioners in countries like Russia, Slovakia and Poland continued to face great economic hardship with rapidly rising prices and static or erratic pension support.

Expect radical land reforms in central and eastern Europe by 2020 – 4 million jobs will need to be sacrificed to reach even 50 per cent of EU productivity. The average CEE farm size is still only 20 hectares. Expect this to treble by 2015 with increased mechanisation. Tens of thousands of smaller farmers will be forced either to ignore EU directive or go out of business, while larger farmers will benefit from generous EU subsidies.

In Poland, 19 per cent of workers are semi-subsistence farmers, compared with 5 per cent in the Czech Republic, Slovakia and Hungary. Therefore, Poland will see the greatest rural to urban migration, and the greatest number of displaced rural workers travelling to other countries (mainly the UK) in search of work.

Over 1 million had already left by 2006, of which a significant number returned wealthier to start their lives again.

Expect major CEE government reforms to create a more flexible labour market with lower taxation, attractive investment incentives and stronger, more transparent legal processes. Expect fierce legal disputes with Brussels over the relevance and appropriateness of tens of thousands of minor regulations, which will threaten the viability of the majority of smaller businesses, ranging from pavement hot dog stalls, to small-town slaughter houses or local garages.

THE EU – SUM TOTAL OF EVERY COUNTRY'S NEUROSES

The idea of a united Europe is not new. It was the foundation of the Holy Roman Empire which lasted from 800 to 1806, extending over large areas of central Europe including what is now France, parts of Italy, Germany and Belgium. The trouble is that when standards are combined on such things as health and safety there is a tendency to push for the highest rather than the lowest.

The result is a sum total of every country's neuroses – on how cattle should be slaughtered, or how clean water should be for drinking, or whether double-decker buses are safe. Every country has its own petty neuroses. These things become part of national culture, dominating chat shows and parliamentary discussions. The British are deeply shocked by animal cruelty, so they want to ban the transport of live animals and fox-hunting – as well, presumably, as bull-fighting in Spain. The Spanish have been neurotic about the safety of British beef and lamb, as are the Germans and French, who, incidentally, are also indignant at the thought of Cadbury's chocolate being labelled as chocolate. Add it all together and you have a multi-neurotic community, obsessed with small regulations.

Rules about insecticide residues or the shape of cucumbers. Rules about the cooking of food in restaurants, the killing of animals in slaughterhouses or the sale of national cheese. Rules about the bumpers of cars. Rules about the sale of beer. But these rules are often rooted in national culture. Standardising rules on

10,000 matters of life is impossible without standardising culture – or destroying it.

Hamburgers in the US are now subject to 41,000 regulations and involve 200 laws and 110,000 precedent-setting court cases. They range from the thiamine content of a bun to the thickness of ketchup and the level of pesticide in meat. Europe is going the same way.

But laws make life more difficult and expensive for manufacturers, distributors and retailers. The cost of living rises, salaries rise the cost of production rises, while jobs fall as there is a move to countries where the bite of the law is less fierce.

Strains in Europe from monetary union

The strains in Europe will be immense. Monetary union means that the foundations of economic policy are now dictated in most countries by a majority of others who do not even speak the same language, and perhaps have never lived in that country. But monetary vision without progressive alignment on all major issues will be impossible. Common immigration, asylum and visa rules, common defence (or attack) policies, common foreign policy – all these things to agree on or be steamrollered over. Then there are the legal strains.

So what will happen to Europe?

The core nations of the old EU will continue to move together to align their economies and many other areas of life, in a process which will continue until the day the whole thing starts to fall apart. No nation will want to risk being left out, even if it means economic gridlock. Yet those same nations may in the future be just as relieved to get out of the all-embracing European mega-politics.

Pressures will remain to protect national economies from currency instabilities through regional economic alliances, and these pressures will increase as further globalisation produces ever larger surges on the foreign exchange markets. The way ahead will therefore be very difficult and messy.

In the meantime, expect continued pressure to enlarge the EU further from countries like Ukraine and Turkey – whose entry will pose major challenges. Turkey has a young population, with 18 million under 15, and a strong national culture which is very different in some ways from the 'old' EU. Integration will not be easy. Although negative EU attention may focus on such things as human rights and freedom of the press, the fact is that Turkey alone is as large as the entire group of ten countries that joined recently. Until the enlarged community has stabilised with an agreed constitution it is hard to see Turkey's admission to the EU being approved. So do not expect Turkey to join before 2012–15.

European Monetary Union

And what of the single currency – the euro? One thing is clear: it won't be sustainable without pain. The individual countries are in too much of a mess for that. It will continue as a fudge, with France, Germany and other countries squeezed into a straitjacket from which there is no escape. The harder the squeeze to get in, the greater the agony of staying in. Countries with different economic problems and in a different stage of their business cycles will often experience great pressures. Imposed squeezes on budget deficits will continue to create agonies for public spending on health, education and social security – all three sensitive areas for the electorate.

Never again will a member country be able to allow its currency to devalue to offset inflationary pressures, or to set interest rates at a higher level than its neighbours to control inflation. All Eurozone members will swim or drown together. But conditions that enable some to swim will drown others.

Many businesses are keen. They cannot understand how nations in Europe could have hung on to their own currencies in a globalised world which demands currency stability.

So there will be a conflict between 'corporate' tribes who want a simple trading area across the region, and 'people' tribes who will sometimes be very hostile to the emerging mega-state.

One of the destructive pressures on the 'United States of Europe' will be unemployment caused by changing conditions and labour force immobility inside 'old' Europe, combined with a progress-ive, long-term shift of manufacturing and service provision to the lower-cost Pacific Rim economies and to other countries such as India and, later, African nations. Germany has recently seen more people out of work than at any time since Hitler came to power, with 4 million on the dole. This problem will partly be offset by labour shortages in some areas caused by an ageing population.

For individuals, this all adds up to a difficult, rapidly changing labour market where those with rare leadership and communi-cation skills command vast salaries, while growing numbers of manual labourers may be semi-permanently unemployed. Senior executives will dominate a global stage, but the next layer down will often be under pressure to relocate east, to manage subsidiar-ies in Asia.

Unless there is a radical rethink on policy, all 'old' Europe will have left to offer by 2035 will be a massive cultural museum (history for tourism) and the intellectual capital of its relatively immobile, ageing workforce (for example, software development skills and management consultancy). However, Europe will benefit in the short to medium term from relative instability elsewhere, becoming a haven for investors. Dictatorship-led economies are inherently unstable because of the lack of openness, account-ability and transparency in their governments. This has been a factor among many in the currency crises in Asia and elsewhere. Dictatorships also have a habit of being overthrown, followed by further internal conflicts and uncertainty.

Europe will also benefit hugely (if attitudes change) from some of more than 500 million people in emerging economies who would like to live and work in the EU. Many of them are highly educated, while others are willing to do much needed but unpopular jobs for low wages, helping reduce labour costs and boost the economy.

Productivity challenges in the EU

Productivity growth in the EU is likely to fall further behind that of the US and Asia for several reasons which EU governments will try to tackle. There is a lack of techno-innovation. The EU venture capital industry will remain small compared with that of the US with lower levels of investment at each stage. EU culture is likely to continue to be less entrepreneurial and less tolerant of risk-taking, while also making cross-border mergers and new market entry difficult. Expect old EU governments to relax many labour laws to encourage business investment, while many new EU nations gradually tighten their own. A major issue within the large EU will be to find a middle way that is appropriate for countries as diverse as France and Poland.

THE EMERGENCE OF THE ENGLISH TRIBE

Anti-imperialism (a reaction against control by one country of another) is tribalism. Anti-imperialism is so strong as a global force that any kind of new world order will be extremely difficult to establish without force, unless as a creeping bureaucracy of international regulations or response to common threat (see Chapter 6). Any hint of imposed rule by one tribal group over another will continue to be fiercely resisted. That is why there is such an (often violent) reaction against American cultural and military power. That is also why the Scottish nation has been so obsessed with the thought of being free from Westminster rule 'by the English'. It is the reason why for generations the British Parliament has over-compensated, by allowing the Scottish electorate far more MPs than by rights they would otherwise have been allocated given the small size of Scotland's population.

The English have suffered an identity crisis of their own. Historically they were strongly globalised and strongly tribal. The Empire was the centre of power on earth and the Union Jack a potent symbol of global supremacy. 'Britannia rules the waves.' Yet England itself has very little native culture left – apart from the pomp and ceremony associated with royalty.

Royal reforms and a national flag flying
There is, of course, the Royal Family, with a dearly loved Queen, but with a set of children and their partners (or ex-partners)

whose antics sell newspapers but who have lost the moral capacity to lead by example. The British people may not stomach a Grand Monarchy in the third millennium headed by King Charles III after all the troubled events involving his former wife and mistress although acceptance is likely to grow with time. The trend to a 'welfare monarchy' will continue. There will be less pomp and more social work, royals fund-raising for good causes and encouraging business to help create a more caring society.

The tragic death of Princess Diana will continue to overshadow the monarchy throughout the young adult years of Prince Harry and Prince William. The Royal Family will never be the same again, experiencing huge pressures to complete a reform process, become less formal, less distant and less expensive. Nevertheless, tribalism will save the monarchy, precisely because there would be so little left otherwise to make us British. The fundamental problem is that by definition royalty is based on genetic discrimination: unless you have the right combination of royal genes, you cannot fill certain roles. This genetic elitism will seem increasingly bizarre and morally suspect to a people who have fought for equality of opportunity, fairness and lack of discrimination.

There is a class system in Britain which is as destructive in some ways as the caste system in India. There is a ruling class, which by virtue of its family line has enjoyed genetic rights to sit in the House of Lords forever. Royalty is part of this system. I am a monarchist, not a republican. I think the British people will be the poorer without a constitutional monarchy – but expect radical reforms by 2015 following major cultural changes that are already obvious.

Then there is the national flag – but of what nation? Scotland can fly a national flag but those in England will probably fly the Union Jack. A few might fly the English flag of St George, but confusion and guilt over the Empire meant that from almost the last day of the Second World War until the anniversary of VE day some 50 years later, there was hardly a Union Jack or a flag of St George to be seen fluttering from a public or private building in the whole of England. Most Union Jacks in Britain were printed on cheap T-shirts and plastic hats for tourists.

As the UK continues to disintegrate in the final death pangs of the English imperialistic dream, you will see a rebirth of the

English people: a fresh energy in a new generation who want to express that they are as English as the Scots are Scottish or the French are French. National state funerals, international football matches and other events will help focus national identity among a people increasingly feeling the need to be proud to be English, and worried about multiculturalism.

The M generation are tribalists: 88 per cent of teenagers in England would choose their own country to live in, 66 per cent think of themselves as English not British, 72 per cent say nationality is important to them, and most teenagers expect the UK to divide into separate states with their own border controls and passports in 20 years' time. While the Scots may look to Europe as a way of staying together in a broader alliance, preferring to accept some rule from Brussels rather than close rule from London, the English are likely to become increasingly resentful of the new non-elected emperor, sitting somewhere in Europe, presiding over a strengthened but distant and distrusted European Parliament.

TRIBALISM IN ASIA

Tribalism could one day undermine the cohesive might of China. This ancient superstate has 1.2 billion people, more than 48 languages and many ethnic minorities. While over 90 per cent of the population are Han Chinese 'sons of the Yellow Emperor', large areas are inhabited mainly by other groups.

An example of recent pressures is in Xinjiang. Since a major uprising in the border area in 1962 there has hardly been a year without trouble there. The local population of Turkish ethnic minorities outnumber Han Chinese by two to one. Kazakhs, Tajiks, Kyrgyz and Uighurs are seeking to rebuild ethnic and nationalist ties with the new central Asian republics. There have recently been pro-independence Muslim riots (there are 20 million Muslims in China).

Such separatist tendencies are strongest in Tibet. The Chinese government has used its usual technique of control by flooding Han Chinese settlers into Tibet's towns, but with little effect. Even in Inner Mongolia, where Han Chinese outnumber Mongols by six to one, Mongolian nationalism threatens to flare up at any time (see pages 61–4 for more on China).

Japan facing problems

Japan will face severe problems from an ageing population and cultural isolation, as well as from a mentality that does not encourage creativity or allow immigration. Japan produces 10 per cent of the world's economic output. But less than 15 years ago it produced more cars than any other nation and 15 per cent of the world's steel, launched more ships than anyone else, produced more televisions and radios than Europe and more watches than Switzerland, and was a dominant player in the computer, aircraft and space industries.

Expect Japan to have difficulty maintaining its economic might, surrounded by emerging but vulnerable economies with cheaper labour and high technology. Expect trade restrictions to ease, allowing Japan's high trade surplus to settle. Expect Japan to own big 'foreign' industries and parts of cities abroad, and to make far less at home. China will affect Japan's future.

Expect Japan's economy to gradually improve, held back by consumers' lack of confidence and recent memories of deflation.

Tribalism in India

India is the greatest democracy in the world, yet with its deeply rooted caste system few countries are so tribally based. Tribalism will threaten India, for it is more a continent than a country. With over 1.3 billion people, a single state has more than three times as many inhabitants as the whole of the European Community. A flight from one end of India to the other is equivalent to flying from London to Moscow in terms of millions of people flown over and language groups passed by. India already shows signs of fragmenting.

To the far east, beyond Bangladesh, close to the Myanmar border, are the north eastern states such as Manipur. These have been run almost in a state of emergency due to tribal fighting and strong independence movements. More soldiers died in the north east in 1997 than in Kashmir. Ethnic groups here are very different in every way from those in the rest of India. In facial appearance they are almost Chinese. But India will survive despite recent religious tensions and the growing militancy of the Hindu majority.

So this is a paradox. People want to be part of a globalised planet and to function in free-trade areas with freedom of goods, services and people. Yet most groups of people are still fiercely territorial, and are becoming more so.

ETHNIC CLEANSING

In the meantime, tribalism expressed through the horrors of ethnic cleansing will continue to haunt Europe, its memories still raw from the Second World War and more recently from Bosnia and Kosovo.

There is nothing new about ethnic cleansing. The deportation of unruly minority groups has been a common practice of victorious armies since ancient times. After the end of the Second World War the allies allowed the Czechoslovakian and Polish authorities to expel 7 million ethnic Germans. But the results are often horrific: 1 million dead in 1947 during the partition of British India; over half a million dead in Rwanda in the mid-1990s; tens of thousands butchered in Bosnia. The complete exodus of the Asian community from Idi Amin's Uganda in the 1970s was less bloody but no less sudden or dramatic. Expect ethnic cleansing to become an entrenched pattern in Iraq, leading to attempts to zone different communities in different parts of the country.

Expect to see more ethnic disputes as mobility and immigration muddle up the original racial mix of nations, transforming cities and rural areas. Tribalism will produce troubles which have no simple solution, with terror and bloodshed followed by yet more refugee movements.

And yet, as we have seen in many countries, such ethnic conflict tends to settle and be followed eventually by stable and peaceful coexistence.

Tribal minorities demand compensation

In Australia, a court judgement has raised the spectre that almost 80 per cent of the country could be subject to legal claims by Aborigines. The High Court ruled that the Wik people had a valid claim to land leased from them in 1915 by white farmers. Already 40 per cent of the country has been subject to native claims, including the bulk of western and southern Australia. Relationships with the Aborigine population have not been helped by the discovery that thousands of children were removed compulsorily and sent abroad or relocated with the country in previous decades. This scandal has yet to be sorted out. Expect similar disputes to continue in many other indigenous groups.

Population pressures will be used to justify ethnic massacres

As we have seen, 98 per cent of the growth in world population is in developing countries.

'There are too many people on the earth'

Since the late 1980s I have heard many comments that the AIDS disaster in Africa hardly matters because it is a way of 'controlling the population'. These shocking comments have come from the well educated and less well educated, from influential 'movers and shakers' and the poorest in other continents. More recently I have heard the same comments in a chilling response to the rapidly worsening AIDS situation in Mumbai and Kolkata: an indifference to plague because those people think it is nature's way of thinning out the unwanted and unneeded. This is particularly the case in India, where at present many of those dying with AIDS are in the lowest ranks of society.

Expect the same arguments to be used by undisciplined armed mobs as they target unpopular ethnic minorities. Expect to see the 'culling' of human populations by horrific acts of slaughter, justified by the claim that 'there are too many people on the earth'. The same idea will be directed at the old, infirm, sad and marginalised and all those who at the least pressure drop off the edge of mainstream society. Expect more mass graves, and mixed feelings in some at the news of massive loss of life in densely populated poor countries from flood, avalanche, disaster or plague.

The larger the world population, the more spectacular the scale of human disasters as more and more people are packed into more and more hazardous areas. The low-lying landscape of Bangladesh is a prime example: it is permanently at risk of catastrophic flood as a result of annual monsoon rains, a risk that will be made worse by changes in the use of land. There are 116 million people, a figure increasing by 2.6 per cent a year, who live at the convergence of three great rivers: the Ganges, the Brahmaputra and the Meghna. Much of the land is less than 15 metres above sea level. Rising population densities and rising sea levels caused by global warming are dual risk factors pointing to a vast human disaster in the region by 2025. But tribalism will ensure that few of these millions are welcomed into other nations.

Territory is at the root of tribalism and national identity

When increasing numbers of visitors become residents, then nationals, then voters, then rulers, resentment is likely to occur at a certain point, unless the newcomers integrate in a way that makes them invisible as members of a 'foreign' group. Immigration laws and laws against racial harassment are almost impotent against minority extremist groups who take the law into their own hands. You cannot guard the front door of a vulnerable family on a tough estate every hour of every day. You cannot prevent all the cruel taunts at school, all the petty bullying, the catcalls from those in the street, the mindless verbal abuse, graffiti and stones thrown at windows. These are the realities, and they are one reason why ghettos form.

Here are trend and countertrend: racial mixing and ghettoisation. Or are they both part of the same thing? Who do I belong to? Do I belong to a nation that I was not born in, or to an ethnic or cultural group within it? Ghettos will continue to flourish in big cities as relatively safe, geographical culture centres for different groups, whether identified by ethnicity or by lifestyle.

TRIBALISM AND GLOBAL BUSINESS

Global citizens

Expect to see a new breed of hyper-mobile globalised people with no national loyalty or identity and no commitment to any geographical area, yet with friends in every city. These industrialised techno-gypsies consider themselves global citizens. They will be hard to tax and hard to count in census surveys, as well as hard to police. Countries with strong human rights legislation will feel particularly vulnerable in future to legal challenges which undermine their accepted way of life by small numbers of immigrant activists with radical agendas. An irony will be that such activists may also be people whose agendas would include abolition of such rights in future if their own favoured form of government were ever to come to power.

We see global citizens already: for example, the executive who spends more than half the year away from home, equally divided between two other continents, and who decides to take a flat in another city, which he visits frequently. Where is home?

Many people are looking for new tribes, having lost their own through permanent migration, family breakdown or weakened communities. While this can disrupt society, it also creates opportunities for business.

Tribal conflicts can brew up fast

The start and end of major tribal conflicts can be hard to predict and may affect corporate investment. For example, a huge mining company may be faced with multiple ethnic challenges. In the light of recent tribal warfare, should it risk a new six-year commitment in central Africa to develop a new mine from scratch, including infrastructure investment such as building a road to the mine? What will the current instability be like then? Is it sensible to think in such a long time frame? Many corporations are turning to short-term, in-out projects in emerging countries where they fear loss of longer-term assets. They want to be able to make their profits fast, cut their losses and run.

Pacific Rim pushes west

After the huge growth of the Pacific Rim economies, what next? Wages will rise as these economies heat up again with local shortages of skilled labour and increased expectations for living standards. It will take several decades for the process to have its greatest impact on China. India and neighbouring countries. After this there will be only one part of the world left with the best part of 1 billion people available for ultra-cheap labour – Sub-Saharan Africa. However, the automation of most production worldwide will marginalise them – too far away to be employed in service industries. Aggravated by AIDS, malaria, TB and water-borne disease, poverty in Africa will remain one of the world's greatest challenges, despite rapid economic growth in many of the larger towns and cities.

Southern Africa growth engine

South Africa and Zimbabwe should have had the wealth, expertise, networks and infrastructure to help drive the rest of Africa into the third millennium. There are many entrepreneurs in South Africa (including white Zimbabweans) who have grown their bases and are looking north, capitalising on rising costs of labour in East Asia. Many of their companies will experience spectacular growth. Import/export, manufacturing and a host of other new industries will flourish, working against severe effects of AIDS and local instabilities. However, the southern region will remain risky in the eyes of many investors until the end of President Mugabe's disastrous rule of Zimbabwe.

Does the lift factor actually work?

What will happen to the poorest of the poor? Will they be lifted as these national economies grow, or will they be trampled? Some have argued from experience in Indian cities such as Mumbai, which have experienced a boom, that the rich get richer while the poor starve and die. That may be true in the short term but not in the medium to longer term, so long as developing countries develop a social conscience alongside their increasing national income. This is likely to happen as part of the process of westernisation, which continues to export Americanised Judaeo-Christian values about human rights and worth. The larger the economy, the greater the state revenue and the greater the choices about redistribution of some of that wealth to protect the most vulnerable.

Logic dictates that the trickle-down effect will help relieve absolute poverty while not dealing with increasing inequality. How else can the extremely wealthy spend their income except by paying others for their time or their property? Either way, money begins to circulate in higher volumes than before. Productivity rises as the unemployed or only partly employed have the chance to work hard, increasing the standard of living of the community. And those who are already employed become steadily more efficient with new tools, technology and education.

The greater the contrasts between rich and poor in a society, the greater the risk of instability as antagonism, aggression and organised opposition grow. Therefore healthy societies will always tend to redistribute wealth to some degree, even if in the interests of self-preservation rather than because of a troubled conscience.

Despite this, expect gaps in gross pay to widen, with even higher remuneration packages at the very top for outstanding leaders and advocates, people who make things happen. One reason why such large packages will be needed is to entice such people into helping companies perform, since all the most successful will by definition have no real economic need to work any more. Many senior executives will be driven mainly by the challenge of the task, rather than by financial rewards.

Another reason for big payouts will be the severe scarcity of world-class leadership, communication skills and creative genius. If a multibillion turnover company plunges into the red following two disastrous CEO appointments, it is in the interests of the company to pay a huge price to guarantee that the problem is sorted out fast. Payment by results is the easiest way to get the biggest deals approved, and this will continue to be common. But how do you measure results? Pay packages based on balance sheets often encourage the wrong decisions in the longer term. Expect to see more sophisticated measures.

At the other end of the scale, expect micro-banking income

generation projects to grow spectacularly in many deprived mega-cities, each lifting tens of thousands out of absolute poverty in less than 20 years, creating a new generation of middle-class business owners. The results in Indian slums are spectacular.

Tribalism means respecting culture

All the globalisation in the world will not produce identical nations. Indeed, national identity will become even more important. There are too many differences, for example, for global TV to be run by robots, offering the same channels every-where all the time – as a French technician found out recently to his cost. His pulling of the wrong switch resulted in children's TV being replaced in Saudi Arabia by hard-core pornography from Club Privé de Portugal. To add to the insult, the programmes were beamed via a Saudi-controlled satellite operator, ArabSat, which was in partnership until that moment with Canal France International, a state-financed French television company. That was the end of a sweet relationship. The companies that succeed in a globalised world will be those that understand local culture, for example in management styles.

TRIBALISM IN RETAILING

Successful brands create tribes and all successful companies nurture tribes – of customers and staff. Tribalism is a dominant force in retailing: people have intense brand and retailer loyalty. Designer clothes thrive on tribalism. Brands like Nike will continue to charge big premiums for the privilege of wearing a label, particularly among teenagers and young adults where labels will continue to attract cult followings. Brand name forgery will continue to grow. Buying the label is buying a place in the family. The more upmarket the customers the more tribal they tend to be. Customer loyalty means that 'I buy all my food at Marks and Spencers and all my clothes from Harrods'.

Fashion itself is built on tribalism. A style is by definition a means of identifying with a group. There is no such thing as individual style. The style of a single person is not a style, just an expression of eccentricity. Style is a common theme adopted by many.

Expect rapid growth of tribalism in every area of retailing as a reaction against a uniform globalised world. Expect global retail chains to make great efforts to adapt to local language and culture. Expect some global brands to be particularly vulnerable to association with one particular country (e.g. the US) in some territories.

Expect rebranding of global products as we have seen in the beer industry, with local packaging changed to look like a country-made item – especially in large and important national markets such as India, China and Russia.

Niche marketing is usually tribal

People who occupy a particular niche are likely to have a host of things in common and successful marketing will use every one of those factors to hit home. Marketing not only forms the image of the tribe; it also plays on and exploits the tribe.

Expect niches of one person only with customised cosmetics, unique cocktail mixes, personalised clothes (within a common design range) and many other innovations. Expect rejection of package holidays and more personal trips arranged in a unique way with friends or family. Experiences will matter most.

Product tribalism

In a world where people crave secure relationships it is strange that relationship marketing should be such a relatively new science. Interviews with hundreds of consumers have created a picture of 15 different relationships that consumers have, in which they 'belong' to their products or the other way round. These range from the long-term, committed partnership an athlete has with a make of trainers he believes helps him win, to a childhood friendship when someone buys food that they used to eat as a kid, to a secret affair when someone sneaks down at night to raid the freezer for a hidden tub of luxury ice cream. Expect to hear much more about this. Relationship marketing will mean 'fostering a special alliance with customers by gathering and employing massive information about individual behaviours and buying habits'.

Hundreds of corporations have already jumped on the relationship bandwagon. Their heads of relationship marketing and relationship marketing departments are advised by relationship marketing consultants. A key target is direct marketing.

But relationship marketing can backfire. A major supermarket chain sends a mailing about disposable nappies to a man, addressed as: 'Dear shopper, being a mum can be such fun!' There can be no more effective way to advertise that you have no relationship than to make such an error. After all the hype, relationship marketing will come to be seen in future as little more than what companies always did: care for existing customers and target marketing to specific groups – but using better information systems.

Tribalism and network marketing

Expect rapid growth of informal marketing networks imitating those successfully powered by Tupperware and Avon – especially in emerging markets. Most of these networks will be domestic sales by women to female friends.

Expect targeting of online communities such as MySpace with viral marketing campaigns, using amusing or shocking video clips and other tools.

Tribalism in sport

Tribalism will continue to drive sport as much as the love of sport itself. Take tribalism away and sport falls to pieces as a spectator industry, becoming just a collection of individuals trying to excel. Even single-person competitions such as golf create tribal followings. Successful football or baseball clubs are only as successful as their tribalism. Tribalism brings in crowds, sells merchandise, attracts sponsorship.

Advertisers love tribes

Consumers are already exposed to €1 billion a month of advertising and 30,000 brand names. Expect marketing directors to pay closer attention to their customer groups in an effort to overcome marketing saturation. Direct marketing will become more focused, partly as the general public look for protection from junk. Over 30 million people in the US opted out of telemarketing in just five weeks in 2003, and the rate of name-removal is growing by 600 per cent per year in some countries. In comparison, response rates remain very high for e-mail campaigns where individuals have given their permission to be informed of new offers which are specially tailored to their own situation. Click-through rates can be as high as 70 per cent per mailing.

Tribal gatherings are an advertiser's dream. Create a tribe and money follows. So the organisers of a conference of doctors know that they can bank on massive subsidies from drug companies, who pay for stands and other promotions. Create the World Economic Forum for global leaders in industry and large-scale company sponsorship begins to arrive. Start a new radio station with a very narrow (high-income) target group and you can set the budget high. Forming, manipulating and exploiting tribes will all be key functions of many successful organisations beyond 2010.

By 2012, more than 10 per cent of advertising spend will be online in some countries, leaving newspapers and TV stations with less income. The online world allows far more precise tribal marketing – without any human intelligence needed – see page 13 on Google Adsense.

The future of marketing

Expect large multinationals to spend up to $500 million each on global rebranding over the next 15 years, to refresh their image, and the value of the largest advertising accounts to soar. Despite this boom in big marketing projects, traditional agencies will come under threat. In the past their creative genius was free, and clients were charged for implementation with commissions on print, advertising bills and so on. But in an online age, the roll-out of new campaigns can be free – as, for example, in the case of a clever e-mail video clip, which 200 million people copy to their friends.

Expect, therefore, a rethink about how advertising agencies earn their money, with a move to charge for ideas instead. However, agencies will find it challenging when they have to prove an idea was original. Who had the idea first? Agencies often develop ideas in discussions with clients, and clients in future may argue that some or all of the idea came from their own people in a brainstorming session with the agency.

The real 'added value' may therefore be stretching a previous idea that the client had already generated – but how do you charge for that? Some agencies will attempt to move to a consulting model, but in all this, the end result will be major consolidation among advertising agencies and rapid growth of freelance consultants in this area.

TRIBALISM AND THE MEDIA

Tribalism will have a huge effect on news reporting in the media over the next decade, especially on TV. Tribalism means that you identify with your own kind and are less interested in news from elsewhere. Expect ratings to continue to fall for pre-millennial style news bulletins on TV. Slayings, beatings, spectacular suicides and disasters, together with pictures of starving millions and other tragedies, will be turn-offs unless they are relatively local. There is not enough real local news to keep ratings high. Most days are fairly boring and repetitive. CNN's daily audience in the US in 2005 was a mere 448,000 viewers. If each watched a whole hour of news a day, then the average US CNN audience for any given bulletin was little more than 18,000. Wars boost ratings – but the underlying trend remains.

Expect CNN and other stations to try to lose their US 'feel' so as to compete better in the global arena.

When you have a population of 6.3 billion people, every day the law of averages dictates that somewhere in the world there will be an aircraft crash, a terrible industrial accident or an appallingly violent crime. But TV news is driven by images. Sensational footage of a train plunging down a ravine will guarantee that the story has a high profile, regardless of location or how many killed.

But news driven by the sensational will always tend to be news of the dreadful, and an unlimited diet of the dreadful is depressing – the opposite of entertainment. Expect much soul-searching over news in tomorrow's world. News as entertainment and as tribal gossip – the ratings war will do it all.

Newspapers and online sites work better than TV for news because they contain more stories (a news bulletin will cover only four or five), and that allows selection. Expect TV news to hit back aggressively with online offerings and interactive news.

Expect news gatherers of the future to be members of the public equipped with nothing other than a video phone, able to be eyes and ears, transmitting live pictures and excited commentary around the world, seconds after phoning CNN or the BBC, from their location in the thick of major events.

POSITIVE TRIBALISM

Many of the earlier examples of tribalism have been negative, to do with nationalism, racism, elitism and sectarianism, yet tribalism is an immensely positive force. Tribalism is the basis of families, teams and belonging. Tribalism provides a sense of identity. Tribalism helps us understand who we are, where we've come from and where we're headed. Teams are to do with tasks, tribes are about whole groups moving together.

Tribes hold the whole of society in a common community. Neighbourhoods are tribes, members of sports clubs are tribes, football supporters are tribes. If there were no tribes, human beings would create them in a day. We need tribes to exist, to make sense of our world.

Tribes are like countries on a map. Without tribes there is no geography in our relationships because there are no groups, just atomised collections of isolated individuals relating equally to everyone. Therefore if you want to understand the forces in someone's life, their motivation, the basis of their values and decisions, you need first to understand the person's own tribal culture.

Of course these cultural factors are particularly obvious when working in a multinational corporation, with executives from very different countries, but they are often no less significant in other, more localised working situations.

Corporate tribalism

Tribalism is a very powerful concept for large organisations. Every organisation is a tribe and there can be many tribes inside corporations: front and back office, HQ and regions, sales and credit control, research and marketing. Tribalism in a company makes us proud to belong. Tribalism can weld teams together in a very healthy and competitive way. Corporate tribalism raises key issues: can we have one culture for an international company? What about cultural adaptation? What about corporate discipline?

Tribalism is one of the most powerful tools managers have for increasing productivity, competitiveness and company loyalty. Every manager needs to understand how to create and keep a tribe, and how to belong to a larger one.

Building a tribe is more than team building. Teams are groups with common goals and functions. By definition there are severe practical limits to the size of an effective team. But tribes are different: proactive, competitive, proud-to-belong groups which can form and re-form with their own culture, identity, loyalties and driving force. Tribes embrace everyone in the workforce. Developing a successful tribe depends on inspirational, dynamic, visionary leadership. The greater the leader, and the stronger the corporate sense of identity and mission, the larger the tribe can be. Tribal leadership is able to move an organisation of tens of thousands in the same direction. Watch out for tribal leaders: figureheads who change large companies with single-minded purpose.

To some extent tribes form naturally across whole departments or entire organisations. But strong tribe formation in companies requires a shift in management style. It means active promotion of culture and feel-good identity, vision building and communication.

Changing a tribal structure is often far more than mere team building. Take a multinational: if Frankfurt HQ wants the New York office to change, it needs to target the tribal chiefs in New York. Who really commands respect? Replacing a New York chief with someone from the head office in Germany may backfire. Team logic might suggest it's a good idea to bring HQ priorities and culture right into the operation, especially if the remaining senior team work well with the new chief. But the rest of the tribe further down may be far from happy. We could be talking about powerful negative perceptions throughout the entire US operation. And those negative perceptions may directly hinder change as well as damaging morale, productivity and bottom-line profit. Smart managers take care of their tribes, understand them, work with them and harness their strength.

Tribes don't form in companies overnight. You can create a team in a week but a tribe gradually comes into being. Tribes can be the basis of pressure groups within an organisation. You can work with tribes or you can find they work against you. You can accelerate their development but it is hard to cause their destruction – without mass redundancies and relocations.

At a time of constant change, a real challenge will be to preserve the vitality of an effective tribe. Take two large companies in a merger. Are both to lose their unique identity? Is one culture going to be dominant? Mergers often involve large-scale redundancies. If tribal identity is also lost for those who remain, the result is a double demotivation. The process requires strong leadership, pulling two tribes together.

Tribes in companies make money

Research shows that creating a sense of family at work increases productivity. Friendship between employees helps significantly. A recent study found that groups of friends produced three times more manufacturing output than did groups of acquaintances and 50 per cent better decision making. They benefited from increased trust, honesty, open communication and respect.

Family business

Most economic growth will come from small tribes. Expect 80 per cent of new wealth to be created (as at present) by small companies with fewer than 20 employees – 75 per cent or more of these companies are family owned or controlled, and have been started with family money (or with loans against equity such as the home). Expect these family-based firms to resist employment legislation such as equal opportunities, quotas and other restrictions. They will continue, despite legal challenges, to discriminate widely in favour of relatives, friends and friends of friends as future employees.

Expect new government initiatives to help provide longer-term venture capital for smaller businesses, driven increasingly by pressures from commercial lenders for near-instant results.

. . . .
CHALLENGES TO MANAGEMENT
. . . .

Tribalism as an issue
- ◆ Has your company ever looked at tribalism as an issue – national culture, target groups, markets and corporate tribalism?

Language identity
- ◆ What is company policy regarding national languages and company language?
- ◆ Does this need reviewing in the light of current trends?

Culture sensitivity
- ◆ What kind of preparation do you give staff when posted cross-nationally?
- ◆ How sensitive is head office policy to local cultural issues?
- ◆ Is it sensitive enough?
- ◆ Is your company able to capitalise on new tribal forces – for example, emphasising the American-ness or Frenchness of a product?

European instability
◆ Is your company prepared to exploit economic union but with the possibility of inter-country tensions, protests, marches and other popular disruptive action?

Ethnic cleansing
◆ How effective are your anti-discriminatory policies?
◆ How possible is it for someone with very negative views of another people group to pursue departmental actions which discriminate, e.g. in employment?
◆ How vulnerable is your company to charges of racist actions?

Tribal marketing
◆ Has your company invested enough in relationship management, building a tribe of loyal happy customers?
◆ What about relationship marketing?

Tribal team building
◆ How strong is the corporate 'pride factor' among your workforce?
◆ What steps can you take to increase positive tribalism inside the company, including competition between strong teams?

. . . .
PERSONAL CHALLENGES
. . . .

What tribes do you belong to?
◆ Where do you belong?
◆ What groups do you identify with?
◆ Where do you get your inspiration from?
◆ Are you happy about the tribes you are identified with?
◆ How do people label you?
◆ Is there an exclusive tribe you want to belong to?
◆ How could you join?

Changes in Europe
◆ Are you prepared for major changes in Europe?
◆ Do you have contingencies in place both for the success of

further integration, and for problems and conflicts?
- How would these things affect you personally?
- How European in thinking are you?

Racial discrimination
- Are you aware of racial discrimination in your workplace, and what are you doing about it?

Tribalism as a management tool
- After all the management emphasis on teams, have you considered working in tribes, harnessing these human forces to create larger dynamic, competitive groups with a common sense, identity and purpose?

Cross-cultural understanding
- How good are you at relating to people of very different cultural backgrounds?
- What are you doing to increase your understanding of different cultures and ways of doing things?

CHAPTER 4

Universal

Global management

The fourth face of the future is the exact opposite of tribalism, and is universalism: McDonald's everywhere. The greater the globalisation, the greater the tribalism. One accentuates the other. Tribalism and universalism feed each other, each the reaction to its opposite. The greater the global uniformity, the greater the drive to maintain tribal identity. The more secure people are in their own identity, the less they are threatened by globalised sameness.

Globalisation has been a long-standing feature of the media. American culture has been exported on a large scale since before the Second World War, mainly through films, TV and popular music. Nations have cultural power, or soft power, that is greater today than the hard power of military strength, through the influence of culture, values and the perception of a technologically superior society. As China has recently recognised, in world power stakes nuclear weapons matter less in influencing international affairs than the promotion of global values in the mass media.

Globalisation is an unstoppable force: the result of the digital revolution and lower transport costs, combined with freedom to move capital, goods and services across national boundaries. It will continue to increase competition and lower profit margins in many countries while also centralising wealth and power in a diminishing number of super-national corporate giants. Globalisation has been accelerated by decisions by most nations' governments to operate more and more as part of one global unit. Where does it lead us? No currency flow restrictions. No import or export tariffs. No national protection against sudden fluctuations in external market forces. Greater freedom for capital movements which may result in severe, destabilising currency volatility. At the opposite extreme are Myanmar (Burma) and North Korea, which have been impoverished by their extreme isolationism.

A WHOLE WORLD TRADING TOGETHER

For the first time in history almost the entire population lives in a global capitalist system. The driving force towards globalisation has been the promise of economic growth and prosperity, especially for poorer nations whose economies have often been the most restrictive in the past. They have been propelled by statements such as these from the World Bank: 'There is a positive link between freeing markets and trade and the eradication of poverty in the long term.' and 'There is no evidence to justify fears that free trade pushes down wages for unskilled workers in developing countries.'

But the UN has a different view. 'Increased global competition does not automatically bring faster growth and development... In almost all developing countries that have undertaken rapid trade liberalisation, unemployment has increased and wages have fallen for the unskilled.'

There is a fundamental problem with globalisation which will cause international tension and trade disputes without arresting the process. The problem is the irrational nature of the global market, coupled with the extreme vulnerability of the poorest and most marginalised in emerging economies to sudden changes in exchange rates, interest rates, or big investment decisions.

Consider the following scenario: Country A has a rapidly growing economy. Many companies are booming. Foreign investment is pouring in. Property prices are soaring. Businesses are borrowing ever larger sums, with little or no security except their expectation of future large profits. Every month these companies have to borrow more to buy more stock to make more goods for ever larger orders, which will be paid for in the future (they hope there will be no bad debts). They are also exposed through large assets held in property. There is little inertia in the economy. Currency reserves are tiny compared with hourly currency flows in global institutions.

Then comes one piece of unsettling news and currency selling begins. Traders may be confident that the currency is now undervalued, but they will go on selling as long as they believe other traders think the currency is still overvalued. In other words, buying and selling becomes driven not by objective data, but by what they think others will do, which in turn will be influenced by their emotional reactions to events as they unfold. But this is a recipe for overshooting, seen over and over again in currency, commodity and stock markets.

A bizarre situation can exist in which everyone privately thinks that the currency is already too low, but continues to sell hard only because they are certain that everyone else thinks the currency still has further to fall. Rates fall through the floor in a wave of panic selling, as dealers dump currency in the near-certain knowledge that they can buy it back at a profit in a few minutes, hours or days. The big issue is not what the real value of the currency should be in the light of the economy, but how the rest of the market is likely to behave in the very short term.

Free market dogma is that these peaks and flows will always sort themselves out. 'Don't try to buck the market.' True as this may be, it ignores the monumental impact of these arbitrary swings on families, communities and nations.

The big difference between Britain and the US and, for example, Thailand, is that in the first two countries the ex-workers of a bankrupt company can often still eat, drink and have homes. In Thailand there are very few safety nets. If you have no job and are already poor, you don't eat. A massive fall in currency may last only a few weeks before partially correcting itself, but that is plenty long enough for multiple bankruptcies. Some companies can't afford to buy the foreign components they need for manufacture. Others are crippled by sudden increases in interest rates to support the currency. Yet others collapse because a large creditor is suddenly unable to pay a bill. Banks fold as companies default on repayments and property prices fall below the value of huge speculative loans. Thailand is just one of many recent examples of a nation brought to its knees by a currency run. More will follow.

Many talk glibly of the benefits of complete, rapid globalisation without any idea of the very real, human, tangible tragedies that are being created. The most vulnerable nations are making huge steps at the insistence of multinationals which refuse to invest unless they do. I have sat in meetings where the most senior members of the governments of emerging nations have been systematically bullied into scrapping regulations, in order to become more globalised. But they are being rewarded with what appears to them to be callous contempt for their own people and the flouting of the fundamental principles of free trade by some of the wealthiest nations, which subsidise agricultural and other products, and dump them on the world market. Of course, many of these governments of emerging economies have a track record of callousness themselves, despite their recent adoption of a more compassionate rhetoric. But the poorest countries cannot change as fast as the markets swing. And they have no cushion.

Borrowing to break the bank

The foreign exchange market is now a major investment tool in its own right, rivalling stocks and shares. And there is plenty of surplus cash around to invest with – often very short term. Once currency speculators spot a vulnerable target they borrow huge amounts of that currency and sell it for another. If the currency falls sharply, they buy back at a profit to repay the loan. Once a campaign gets under way, other investors start to panic, dumping currency and adding to the chaos. However, as George Soros himself told the Banking Committee of the House of Representatives, if everyone rushes to sell, there are no buyers, and those still with positions in the market are unable to bail out and may suffer 'catastrophic losses'.

Some would argue that his foreign exchange interventions, and those of others, actually stabilise in the longer term by selling when currencies are too high and buying when they are too low. It could be argued that central banks tend to destabilise when defending a currency, because they operate in reverse – they buy when the market feels a currency is already too high and sell when it already feels too low. In the longer term it is true that free market forces operating on floating exchange rates will tend to produce greater stability – protecting a currency is usually destabilising because it risks a sudden fall or rise.

As the American economist Paul Davidson puts it: 'In today's global economy, any news event that fund managers even suspect that others will interpret as a whiff of currency weakness can quickly become a conflagration spread along the information highway.'

Governments are quickly defeated by huge flows. Very few nations have currency reserves deeper than the pockets of speculators and the combined panic capacity of the global market. Few can afford to raise interest rates high enough to stop large-scale speculative borrowing before they have wrecked their economies. The only other way out is to stop trying and let the currency float.

If globalisation is to proceed rapidly and harmoniously in the short to medium term, it can only do so if nations adopt a more holistic approach. Lifting all exchange controls and just hoping for the best is not enough. Wealthy and poor nations need to agree that the opening of economic boundaries will also be accompanied by support packages, to help stabilise currency fluctuations and interest rates in these countries. To some extent this is already happening. But this route is risky and fraught with danger. Expect to see major steps taken in the interests of short- to medium-term global stability, with the International Monetary Fund taking the lead. Expect huge retraining initiatives, especially in African nations, partly funded by wealthy governments, partly by the corporate sector, to assist the bottom-end losers from globalisation to become winners, gaining new jobs.

Expect growing calls for global taxes on all foreign exchange transactions so as to 'throw sand in the wheels'. Such attempts are likely to fail. The forces of globalisation are already too strong. Foreign exchange transactions are now impossible to prevent since anyone, anywhere in the world, can now trade whatever they like instantly, using the Internet and secure encryption. The black market would be vast, cheap and efficient.

Expect economic decisions to be taken increasingly out of fear of market reactions rather than out of true conviction. National economies will be increasingly controlled by the fickle and often irrational reactions and counter-reactions of the currency and

stock markets. In the longer term, expect governments to take
refuge in ever larger and 'safer' alliances or trading blocks, with
many grouped, linked or fused economies by 2020. The aim will
be to provide economic stability against speculative attack, but it
will be won at high cost and will not be entirely effective, as global
speculators also grow with extraordinary power.

China currency reserves

Expect large nations such as India and China to continue to
observe all this activity from a bemused distance, since they already
have two emerging economic areas between them serving almost
2.5 billion people, and China has reserves of more than $1 trillion.
They will be hoping not to have the same market vulnerability as
Malaysia or Thailand or the Philippines over the next decade, but
will find themselves facing their own pressures.

Expect to see aggressive vocal minorities in some emerging countries, angry at what they see as fat, imperialistic money-makers who
over-sell and over-buy, manipulating stocks and currency up and
down for their own mega-profits. Expect these reactions to grow
ever stronger as global players increase in power and weight. By
2012 there will be several institutions whose decisions are controlled by very few people, able to shake a national economy to pieces
in the short term and make huge profits doing so. Expect false
rumours and reports to be part of the process.

For ordinary workers in emerging countries, the globalisation
of finance seems good news at first, with huge inward investment,
new factories, jobs and infrastructure. Family income rises, homes
are built, cars bought, university education paid for. It seems that
good times will last forever and little is saved. And then comes the
crash – the job goes, the loan is called in on the house leaving
huge debts because of the property fall, the car is almost worthless
and the children are suddenly pulled out of education. Whatever
savings there were are wiped out as the value of the market falls
through the floor and banks become insolvent.

And then confidence begins to return. The grossly under-
priced currency once again encourages inward investment. This
time foreign speculators get even better mega-deals, buying up

whole factories and neighbourhoods at a fraction of their former cost. Gradually the economy recovers, jobs are created again. Life goes on. But at a terrible cost. In the big shakeouts many smaller investors, small business owners and workers lose everything, while some large (foreign) institutions make vast profits.

Overshooting will continue in currency markets

In the past a disincentive for smaller speculators was the cost of commissions, but technology has reduced these to such low levels that multiple short-term switches are now a common pattern. Expect therefore that markets will also be increasingly destabilised by millions of individual decisions to buy and sell, made by people who have only a partial understanding of the underlying factors in price movements. This effect will further encourage overshooting.

For example, in Uganda many local offices of non-government organisations place overseas grants into currency accounts, and switch the money repeatedly according to their own view of what exchange rates will do. They are not finance houses and have no specialist expertise but are playing the market like everyone else as amateurs. And large institutions in London, Tokyo and New York are playing the same game against them. After all, the only way a London house will consistently make money is from foolish decisions by others.

Every big winner means a big loser – or many small losers

For every big winner on the currency markets there are big losers. If, for example, New York teams are more skilled than those in most poorer nations and also have more clout, we can expect poorer nations to be systematically weakened by New York or London market activity. Of course, globalisation is here to stay and in the longer term is the most effective way to generate wealth for every nation, rich or poor, but these are some of the undercurrents which by 2015 will be causing international tension and concern.

Expect emerging nations to try – and fail – to tame the process.

Expect ASEAN currencies to move together in East Asia, giving life and strength into SADC in southern Africa.

The ERM debacle in the UK proved once and for all that the fixing of currencies cannot work unless it is a part of financial union. But even complete financial union will not prevent global industry pressures from controlling governments. When governments no longer control their own exchange rates, interest rates are held in common across nations, and import and export restrictions and capital movement controls have been abolished, they are vulnerable indeed. Foreign capital is notoriously fickle, but the only alternative is raising domestic capital, which is a major challenge in a developing nation.

Who is now running the country?

Expect growing frustration as many countries recognise the reality, which is that they have almost completely lost control of their own economies. Expect many nations to slow down the relaxation of controls on the finance sector between now and 2015 as a direct result of market instability.

Globalisation means that large interest rate differences between nations become less sustainable, capital flows unstoppable. As the process of globalisation continues, all they will be left with is national laws and the raising and spending of taxes – but even here governments will be forced to harmonise laws, taxes and benefits. Countries out of line with what the global investment community thinks is reasonable will rapidly lose investment. Expect to see many government policy reversals as political conviction gives way to practical issues, such as whether Nissan will build a giant car factory in your country or place the project next door.

So who is now governing the country? The answer, of course, is the market, or collective decisions by some of the largest multinationals, which themselves are controlled by a few very powerful players. It's the death of democratic power.

WORKERS OF THE WORLD UNITE

Trade unionism was founded in developed countries to provide protection for workers against oppression. Nation after nation was forced to legislate to provide basic rights such as holidays, sick pay, redundancy pay, maternity benefit, a maximum working week, health and safety at work, the right to challenge unfair dismissal and so on. These agreements were fixed nationally, to prevent one company undercutting another by employing workers at lower cost with no such benefits.

But that was the old world, which has been destroyed utterly by globalisation, unless we develop global protection of workers' rights.

'Ethical' employers (maybe forced to be ethical by law) who treat their employees well are losing out to 'unethical' employers in the poorest nations, or will do so in the future. Globalisation means that there is a level playing field for trade, and it's getting even flatter. The threat that jobs could go abroad lies behind job insecurity, the erosion of non-wage benefits and the catastrophic weakening of trade unions. These will all continue.

Factory workers in rich countries who enjoy a good health service, unemployment benefit, pensions and education will do so in future only if they produce more or faster, or better quality, or at lower cost than those in poorer countries. But how will they do this, since those in the poorer countries may have the same technology in their own factories and cheaper labour? Workers there may be paid almost nothing, have no job security, may be exposed to health and safety risks, and have no sick pay or other rights. Unless this hole is plugged, efforts by workers to secure rights in one country will end up destroying their own jobs. It will always be cheaper in the short term not to ventilate factories properly than to ventilate to a high standard, or to give no sick pay rather than to be generous to workers who do not turn up for work.

Ironically it is often the same multinationals that employ both groups in both parts of the world, making 'ethically employed' workers redundant and replacing them with 'unethically employed' workers. Some hoped that workers in rich nations would earn more because their factories would be more automated with higher productivity, but new factories can employ the latest technology wherever they are built, whether in America or China. Many management, consultancy, service and support jobs will command high salaries, but that will not protect Western nations entirely from the globalisation shakeout.

Third millennial trade unions must be global or die

Third millennial trade unionism can go down only one of two routes. If it stays in a national rut, fighting for national rights and for protectionism, the end will be massive job losses, and job gains in poorer nations by non-unionised, unprotected labour forces. This will be the final death of trade unionism. Every day we see the further weakening of old labour movements because they have failed to grasp the nettle of globalisation and have remained stuck in last century irrelevance. In Germany, for example, membership of the DGB trade union federation fell from an all-time high of 11.8 million in 1990 to below 6 million in 2006.

The only other option is for them to form a global labour movement seeking to negotiate 'fair' labour rights for the entire global village. Such a formal movement would need to be capable of organising, say, global pickets of ports or global protests against particular companies. Expect some attempts at this, with little success because of the diffuse nature and great strength of globalised companies. However, the online world, linking 1 billion people, will soon be used to mobilise instant protests of tens of thousands of people on a range of issues at more or less any point on the surface of the earth. In the meantime, informal protest movements of activists will continue to win publicity, influence and (indirectly) power.

This third millennial labour movement will be driven from the wealthiest nations, by people concerned mostly to protect their own jobs, trying to make sure that workers in emerging nations become almost as difficult and expensive to employ as they are and therefore less a threat, and also by those with wider agendas.

Of course, globalised companies hit back at the label 'unethical' when it comes to working conditions. They will argue correctly that they are providing otherwise destitute peasant farmers or street dwellers with a living wage, training and a future, building national prosperity, contributing to the balance of trade. In a competitive world, paying their workers more or giving them extra benefits could mean they all lose their jobs.

Global agreement on minimum labour conditions

Expect the beginnings of global agreements on labour conditions, health and safety and other issues by 2010, as a condition of global trade. It is already starting as a result of consumer pressure. Take, for example, child labour. Few household name companies today would risk 'knowingly' employing six-year-old children ten hours a day to make clothes. Yet in Bangladesh alone it is estimated that 80,000 children under 14, mostly girls, work at least 60 hours a week in garment factories.

Sadly, knee-jerk reactions and simplistic campaigns can wreck the lives of the very people they were meant to protect. In the child labour example, an international campaign led to millions of children being dumped as workers. But they and their families needed money to eat. Many children went straight onto the street where they were rapidly forced to become child prostitutes, repeatedly raped, often to die later from AIDS. The lesson is that while all these labour issues are important, and must be addressed, they need to be tackled in the context of overall community development.

I have seen these child tragedies at first hand in India. Child labour is a very complex issue. Children with no parents, living on the street, either work or beg or starve or get exploited as sex slaves. It is as simple as that.

Free trade mandate driven by America

Europe and the US are the two engines behind free trade negotiations worldwide, but Europe has its own distractions and these will continue. Therefore expect America to be in the driving seat of far-reaching trade initiatives but increasingly nervous about the 'overwhelming' threat of low-cost imports from China and the rest of Asia.

Expect organised labour movements worldwide to campaign increasingly against free trade and in favour of hostile trade blocs. Expect such voices to grow powerful in the US. If the US becomes strongly protectionist (possible but unlikely), expect a severe defensive reaction from more than 100 other nations. Big trade agreements will continue without America if necessary, but with the serious risk of becoming derailed by some other anti-globalisation backlash.

Old economics is dead

Old economic theory was built for a world which no longer exists. It stated that, for example, 'high unemployment causes wages to fall', and 'low unemployment causes wages to rise'. But in recent years unemployment has been low in some industrialised countries without inflationary pressures. Why?

The old boom and bust economics is nation-based and semi-redundant in a third millennial world, where forces are infinitely more complex. We will see big booms and big busts and disruptive business cycles, but their causes and time-scales will not be as easy to manage or predict as before.

Two factors have combined in the new world order. First, globalisation means global competition, which is now restricting the ability of workers in any one country to demand higher wages. In the global village they know that another, less greedy country will win the contracts. Second, the digital age and other technologies are triggering a massive increase in productivity along with rapid downsizing in manufacturing, and deflation of costs.

The future of outsourcing and offshoring

Outsourcing and offshoring will continue to generate heated debate, especaially offshoring where jobs move out of the country. Expect 200,000 jobs a year to be lost in the US and a similar number in the old EU nations until 2015, by which time this process will have slowed considerably due to salary inflation in many emerging economies. Expect similar gains by India, China and other Pacific Rim countries and former Soviet bloc nations. Growing reactions against offshoring are likely to lead to several more US states passing legislation in an attempt to limit the process. However, expect the tide to turn. In 2006, 82 per cent of large US, EU and Asian companies were offshoring a significant amount of their operations, but only half were happy with the results. Some of the jobs created are already being brought back to the US and EU.

The future impact of offshoring is likely to be less than many fear. Job losses are likely to be relatively modest in the longer term for several reasons. First, the purpose is to reduce cost, which means that prices fall. That in turn means that people spend less on things like DVDs or computers, and more on local services, which create new jobs. In any case, when a product is manufactured in China instead of the US, the Chinese producer is likely to see a maximum of 15 per cent of the total retail price. The rest remains as before in the host country, being spent on research, design, marketing, wholesale, retail and distribution costs.

On the other hand, every time a dollar is spent on employing an outsourced worker in a country like India, it stimulates the local economy. A full-time call-centre job, for example, is likely to contribute significant wealth to at least 50 other people. In developed nations, a monthly salary flows relatively slowly around the economy. In contrast, money flows rapidly in the poorest nations among people who have no bank accounts and live from day to day. $10 spent on buying a SIM card is used almost immediately by the street vendor to buy food. The food seller in turn uses the money almost immediately to pay rent and so on. Thus, $10 can be spent ten or 20 times over in as many days – and each time it changes hands it creates additional turnover in the economy.

It is no surprise that these nations are growing fast – and as they do, we see the emergence of a larger middle class and fresh demand for Western goods and services, which also creates jobs in industrialised countries to replace those outsourced in the first place. When you add these two effects together, of lowered prices and increased demand, the result is likely to be less dramatic than many suppose.

Expect huge growth in personal financial services in Asia – of at least $300 billion from 2011 to 2020 – equivalent to four times the growth of US personal financial services from 1994 to 2001.

Expect huge growth in India's insurance industry, where total premiums in 2006 were only 2 per cent of GDP compared with a world average of 7.8 per cent. Expect a shift from insurance as a tax saving investment vehicle to risk cover, including health insurance.

Finally, large-scale offshoring will also accelerate wage inflation in China and India which will inhibit the process. If the US and EU are really hit hard, the result will be falls in the dollar and euro, which will also make offshoring more expensive, and help protect domestic markets.

FACTORS AFFECTING REGIONAL GROWTH

Geography matters – or does it?

In the past, different policies in different regions produced huge differences in economic growth. In the future, while policies will tend to converge, some developing countries will be left behind, partly because of geography. It will always be true that sea trade is cheaper than long-distance land (or air) trade. It is no accident that 300 million people in China are on the move to more rapidly growing and dynamic coastal provinces.

A container can be shipped from London to Shanghai for the same cost as driving it in the EU on a lorry for just 150 miles, even when allowing for loading and unloading at the two ports. It costs less to ship water melons to Naples from Istanbul than to drive them down the road from Palermo. Thus in economic terms, Singapore is closer to Rotterdam than Rotterdam is to Brussels. This simple fact will continue to be a major driver of globalisation.

Throughout history coastal states have tended to develop freer market policies than inland landlocked neighbours. Mountainous states have neglected market trade due to isolation. Despite the transport and communications revolutions, landlocked countries will tend to grow more slowly, as will those in disease-hit tropical areas, those with corrupt or inefficient governments and those with the highest population growth. All these factors consume resources that could be spent on production.

Population grows as medical care improves. Then birth rates fall as households adjust to longer life expectancy and lower infant mortality. East Asia is into the second phase while Africa is still in the first. Thus Africa has a huge bulge of dependent children (up to half the population in some areas is under 15 years old) with no bulge in workers, a problem made far worse by the selective destruction of young adults by AIDS.

Two of the most effective ways to help Africa will be to tackle AIDS with far better aid programmes, including treatment of other sexually transmitted diseases, and to tackle malaria which kills 1 million a year and affects between 200 and 400 million others. Ninety per cent of the deaths are in Sub-Saharan Africa. A simple, low-cost malaria vaccine could revolutionise large parts of Africa. Expect an effective vaccine to be developed by 2012.

Companies switch many times from country to country

Many US toy manufacturers have moved their factories from Japan to Taiwan to Singapore to Thailand, chasing lower labour costs, finally ending up in China. In contrast, some engineering jobs will stay in countries close to where final production is needed – especially in high-tech areas where specifications change rapidly.

Sunlight is the greatest barrier to the global village

Globalisation means long-distance travel for executives, because technology has not yet caught up with the movement of capital and other components of international trade – or rather the technology is there but social skills are not. Most pre-millennialists just can't cope with loads of electronic meetings, but their jobs will depend on them.

The greatest barrier to the global village is sunlight. In an ideal globalised world every inhabitant would be on the same time clock. And that is the crux of a growing problem. The third millennium will see a whole new pattern of working. Days of 9 am to 5 pm, 8 am to 6 pm or even 7 am to 9 pm will be replaced by a different rhythm, dictated by business efficiency and what globalised customers and corporations want.

Consider the example of a private banking client who in an ideal world would like to call her banker from wherever she has just flown today, without having to look at her watch and do a mental calculation across a time zone. Ideally she wants to be able to talk anytime. She can. Technology allows her banker to be constantly available by phone, e-mail, text, video link. But what happens to the banker's own life?

The answer is that work patterns change. Instead of having, say, five very important clients that he services during traditional hours, he now is available at all hours, but less intensely. As compensation for offering such a premium service, he can afford to have only four clients and still have the same income. Most of the work is still done during normal hours, but out-of-hours unscheduled work and pre-booked meetings are compensated for by shorter hours overall, and time off during the day.

So he might be playing golf all day Monday. His clients are educated to know that this service means that when they phone he could be anywhere, doing anything.

Many people already live like this, myself included. For a start, anyone involved seriously in the media as a commentator on global events has to. News stories can break at any time, day or night, 365 days a year, and when they do, media researchers need instant access to expert comment and advice. Television and radio are particularly demanding, and can be on the doorstep within 40 minutes of an event happening.

Living 'on call' is nothing new. Doctors and many people in other professions have been used to it for decades, as have all those who organise themselves so that (after the proper screening of calls) they are very rarely if ever uncontactable.

For holidays and special family times phones can be carried by others, calls diverted and contingency plans laid. Cover can be arranged – and should be. We are not talking about communications slavery, but about using technology to liberate us from the pre-millennialist expectation that we should all enjoy full-time leisure interspersed with very intensive full-time work.

Some say that this new pattern of global time-keeping is unhealthy or unnatural. The reality is that it is far more in tune with the old hunter-gatherer pattern of life, and of course identical to normal patterns of life for mothers or fathers at home alone with several small children.

Life in those circumstances is not a set of neat on-off buttons. But it does involve a different mindset from conventional office workers. It also has implications for where we work: when executives need to take or make calls very early or late in the day, or over weekends, the trend to home working is accelerated.

Without an attitude change the result will be burnout and the destruction of families. We already see workaholic techno-freaks with mobile phones and computers sitting on beaches on holiday. Office addicts who cannot relax. Techno-junkies driven by insecurity about what might be happening back at the office while they eat at a local taverna.

But without a massive rethink about hours and daylight, global village life is never going to work. It is far easier for a company based in South Africa to work in close partnership with Britain than with Hong Kong, from the point of view of working hours. The problem of daylight incompatibility is made even worse by cross-cultural differences. A company in San Francisco trading with Dubai finds not only a disruptive time difference, but also that Dubai works from only 7 am till 1 pm and does not work on Fridays – but works a normal day on Sundays.

Globalisation will be patchy at first

Expect big differences and inconsistencies over the next two decades in the degree of globalisation in industry, as in the last decade. This will follow national and regional consolidation. Take banking, for example. The 10–15 largest US banks control more than half America's assets – up from 29 per cent ten years ago. In 1985 the US had more than 14,500 commercial banks, mostly operating by law in only one state. By 1995, limited interstate banking allowed this to drop to 10,000. This will probably fall to less than 2,000 as further deregulation allows national banking. The largest US banks in future could be several times the size of a Citibank or an HSBC today. However, as in most other sectors, at least half of all mergers will be likely to destroy shareholder value, mainly because of failure to understand tribalism. This pattern of consolidation will be paralleled in Europe, driven by a belief in economies of scale, and the ambitions of CEOs to grow further by acquisition.

Expect the number of conventional banks to be also reduced dramatically in the EU, especially in heavily 'over-banked' nations such as Germany and Switzerland. Banks will go on making deep cuts in their labour forces, at a time of great overall profitability, concentrating on premium or relationship banking for higher net worth individuals and corporates.

'Future branding' – universal and tribal

'Future branding' is the reshaping of a brand not only for today's needs but also for tomorrow's globalisation. For a while British Airways abandoned its British-style logo for a new brand image as a global carrier. Tail emblems were based on designs from different nations. But many fly BA precisely because it is British (tribalism). British Airways has a strong, staid, conservative, ultra-safe character in many people's minds.

Expect a rebranding of national airlines throughout the world, together with continued consolidation. There is not room for every nation to have an unsubsidised privately owned 'national' carrier. Country images inspire loyalty, hostility and a range of other emotions and national images change. As airlines become multi-national they will need to think and act globally. Many national airlines will struggle to develop and embrace a new global culture in competition with low-cost budget airlines with higher efficiency and weaker national brand identity.

VIRTUAL COMPANIES

All successful global companies will work virtually in many areas of operation by 2015. During the early 2000s, many executives were doubling their air travel every two years (with a temporary dip immediately after 9/11). A significant number were already spending six weeks a year cruising at 35,000 feet, not including time wasted in airports and so on. These corporations were still playing at globalisation. Expect a structural shift from 2010 to 2020, with a greater proportion of international meetings conducted by voice or video, enhanced with file sharing and multimedia displays.

Corporate leaders will be expected to be communication experts, able to win trust and confidence over very long distances. The aim will be to achieve a 30 per cent drop in international face-to-face meetings, with a 60 per cent increase in output. However, business travel is still likely to increase as international deals continue to grow faster than the development of virtual teams. Companies will increasingly come under pressure to justify air travel to meetings because of global warming activism and carbon-use reporting requirements. However, the real driver will be personal productivity. Of course, we need face-to-face meetings, and that is where the most important decisions will be made, but it will be a question of balance, and balance will be an issue of corporate survival.

Globalisation means subcontracts and partnerships at every level. Expect more virtual organisations with far fewer employees than you might expect from their global operation and high turnover:

◆ team members in many different locations
◆ rapidly changing and flexible structure
◆ many functions carried out by partners.

A rapidly growing number of organisations have no permanent staff. They hire freelance workers, typically home-based, on a project-by-project basis, in the same way that Hollywood puts teams together to make movies. Roles can be reversed when several groups of people have several companies between them. In slack times for one company, a director may find himself contracted to a new project run by a company belonging to one of his or her own freelancers.

Around 75 million Americans are now working from home, occasionally, part-time or full-time, using e-mail to work with others. The spread of virtual companies will accelerate this.

However, virtual working can affect many families and marriages, with people working long hours and a blurring of the gap between work and home. There is often no cover for sickness, training or other traditional employee benefits. The upside is that productivity can be sky-high with self-motivating employees. There is no hanging around the door for a chat. All you can do is work.

Virtual companies avoid high-risk start-up costs, such as were seen recently with biotech initiatives. When biotech started, companies built scientific teams, rented big laboratories – and then caught colds from big overheads when facing problems getting their products to market. In contrast, the biotech virtual CEO works in an office by himself with everything contracted out. The company is generally in a university and pays no rent; drug discovery is carried out at additional universities under contract.

Virtual corporations

A virtual multinational is a collection of companies, some perhaps virtual themselves, organised to behave as if it were a larger, multi-faceted organisation. Expect more of them. Headquarters will no longer indicate size or profitability, only how hierarchical the company structure is, and how much money the shareholders are willing to waste on a prestigious monument to past greatness.

Virtual corporations can be seen only on paper, video or the web. The nearest you will come to visiting one will be at a large corporate gathering, attended by key people from across the world, representing every aspect of the virtual structure. At first many people will refuse to take virtual organisations seriously, until they find their profits and jobs disappearing. If virtuality means almost the same output for less cost, and a faster response time to major changes, what is the point of not being as virtual as possible? Expect all kinds of high-tech experiments, for example CEO offices lined with a dozen screens so that at any time people, data and other images are on display, including perhaps the view in the virtual corridor outside.

Knowledge management is the key to virtual working

Knowledge management will make all the difference between survival and death in the virtual future. New specialist posts are springing up everywhere: Chief Learning Officer at General Motors, Group Director of Organisational Learning and Development at UBS, Chief Knowledge Officers at Skandia in Sweden and Chapparal Steel in the US. It is all part of the same trend towards marshalling information resources and making the right decisions quickly by using multiple channels and partners.

Many of the largest manufacturers will push towards decentralisation and subcontracting. As part of the process, niche globalisation will increase: there are now only three large suppliers of car seats in the whole world.

Customers count more

Expect a further huge shift to customer/client contact in all areas, whether health, law, retailing, financial services or any others. Everyone has customers, external or internal. Expect more selling of products and services by one department to another in the same corporation, and then further outsourcing as the real costs of internal provision are exposed.

Adding shareholder value – but what is real value?

As shareholding becomes more globalised, pressures from shareholders will change. Adding shareholder value will continue to be important, but this emphasis will encourage short-term return on capital rather than long-term corporate strength. Short-termism will be made worse by remuneration packages which continue to depend on last year's company figures, rather than on 360-degree assessments, where each worker is asked to assess the performance not only of juniors, but also of peers and superiors. Expect a shift from such year-on-year blindness as investors increasingly recognise longer-term assets, such as work in progress.

Expect growing numbers of corporations to seek delisting from stock exchanges, so that they can run their businesses in a more sustainable and stable way with longer-term horizons, under private ownership.

In future a company may be only as good as its shareholders, with more board decisions governed by what shareholder reaction is expected to be. Expect large institutional investors, such as pension funds, to become increasingly involved in major corporate decisions, effectively hiring and firing the most senior executives and exercising a veto on new policy. But these institutions will not be well placed to judge what is best for the longer-term future of the company.

Already institutional trades account for almost 90 per cent of the volume and value of trades on the New York Stock Exchange (pension funds, investment companies, foundations, mutual trusts and banks). Institutions will continue to own the vast majority of US stock beyond 2010.

Company valuations will continue to develop as a specialist blend of art and science, with an increasing number of 'soft' variables such as the intellectual capital of the current workforce, and its future likely worth in the light of expected staff turnover and possible 'brain poaching' by rivals. The extra value derived from such things as completed internal reorganisations and the re-skilling of staff will increasingly be recognised and debated.

SUPER-CORPORATIONS – RIVALS TO STATE POWER

Expect the opposite trend as big companies merge to become a colossus of global expertise and economic power unrivalled on the face of the earth, more powerful than most governments.

The process of globalisation has hardly begun. In the 20 years following free capital flows and global networking we will see new super-corporations, each larger in economic weight than many sovereign states. These complex institutions will have the power to dictate terms to governments and set the agenda for commerce, and will attempt to create global monopolies. They will be beyond state control, so globalised that their power base shifts geographically whenever it suits, and will provoke protests.

What happens when a single investor has the capacity to wreck an economy or resurrect it? Those days are already near. Calls for super-state control will grow stronger as global monopolies grip more tightly. This will become a key issue for governments, which will find themselves outmanoeuvred by rapidly changing corporate decisions, and also for voters, who will be disempowered.

A government might take a year to change or reverse a particular policy, while a corporation may take a major decision as a response within a day. Twenty large super-corporations with unimaginable combined economic power will make many of tomorrow's governments look like dinosaurs, struggling to comprehend the world around them, to react fast enough. This will be particularly the case in emerging nations.

And while remuneration packages for CEOs in industrialised nations remain so much higher than for prime ministers or presidents, many governments will also find themselves crippled not only by cumbersome decision-making machinery but also by a serious lack of brain-power. The brightest and most talented leaders of tomorrow will tend to go to where the real power is. They will choose to run corporations rather than pretend to run countries. As a result many national governments will be led by weak and incompetent teams, incapable of wise, incisive judgement at times of rapid change or crisis.

This will be an issue with huge consequences for geopolitical stability. These often relatively inexperienced and inept teams will be in constant danger of making ill-advised and disastrous decisions about such things as going to war, making peace, or finding urgently needed solutions to some of the world's greatest challenges.

While many super-corporations will dominate specific fields, such as satellite broadcasting or computer hardware/software production, they will also show a remarkable ability to jump into unrelated fields, and to dump old businesses.

Mergers and acquisitions – and liquidations
Expect a new wave of mergers, de-mergers and acquisitions, with the chaos increasing in a huge global realignment. Expect crazy pricing: further cycles of unsustainable price cuts in short-term bids to win market share. In many industries, mergers, acquisitions and aggressive expansion plans will contribute to lower margins.

Consolidation will be most radical in mass-market services where we will see almost zero margin, except in developing countries. This will be especially the case in the financial sector, for example online banking. Most profits in banking will be found in face-to-face premium relationships and other specialist areas. Expect many 'buy and dismantle' operations, where the break-up price is greater than the complete sale value. Many companies that might just have turned around will be ruthlessly liquidated, producing a fast return on capital.

Expect growth of super-giants in the retail sector. Wal-Mart will grow to more than 500 billion sales and 2 million 'associates' by 2012, while at the same time, expect the chain to stall or decline in some countries which reject the cultural package. Expect Carrefour to take risks to grow faster in new territories, but with mixed results. In most developed countries, the largest four retailers will take more than 60 per cent of actual retail spending by 2012.

Big shakeouts

Globalisation means big swallows small. It means huge retail chains gobbling up thousands of small independent outlets. It means huge discounts because of greater buying power, lower prices on some goods and inflated prices on others because of virtual monopolies in some areas.

Microsoft is a good example of a corporation with money to spare. At one point the Seattle-based software house was sitting on $9 billion in cash, growing by $18 million every day. A major challenge for them is what on earth to do with it all to ensure proper returns. Watch out for a string of new acquisitions and more anti-monopoly challenges as Microsoft battles for supremacy in the next-generation digital world, against Google and other third millennial players such as Skype. Google will drive many of the most exciting online innovations over the next decade, powered by one of the most talented and creative teams in the world, working in a highly creative culture. Expect Google to rival Microsoft's range of office and personal user products with new tools.

Globalisation and consolidation

Industry after industry is facing big shakeouts. Once-stable markets like banking are shedding weaker players and merging into new big groups. Software houses are seeing faster and more intense shakeouts while their sales grow.

Seismic shifts have been hitting mature industries. Examples include drug companies since governments began to insist on generic prescribing and global pressures forced them to concede patent rights to poor nations.

Keeping in business

Early warning signs of a big shakeout include:

◆ Belief in a company that it can't happen – it probably will
◆ Entry rates of new competitors
◆ Excess capacity in industry
◆ Pressure on margins as prices drop
◆ Scenario planning based on different forecasts
◆ Identifying which competitors are likely to survive best

The end of mass products?

Factory production has been based on economies of scale – big factories, high volume, low margin. But new technology allows smaller players to enter, make niche products at low cost and move on before old dinosaurs have had time to react. Thus small new players will continue to enter markets successfully, despite domination by super-corporations.

Mass customisation will be a key feature. In a sense it's nothing new. Back in the 1970s you could order a car with any one of hundreds of variations like quality of trim, paint colour, type of radio. Every vehicle on that conveyor belt was built to order. The final car rolled off the belts with a delivery name and address neatly packed in a polythene sleeve attached to the windscreen.

The most obvious new area for mass customisation will be interactive TV, where viewers will find themselves targeted with adverts specially selected for them. Digital TV will copy what is already happening online. With so many millions of pages to browse around, it is easy to place ads on just the right pages to fit with your products.

The future of air travel

The next decade will be dominated by huge expansion of budget airlines, forcing the consolidation of traditional operators, which for decades have been protected by government subsidies and restricted practices. All the world's largest carriers by 2015 will be operating with an adapted budget-airline model: online booking, minimal in-flight service, low baggage allowance, free seating and rapid turn-arounds. However, long-haul business travel will be an even more luxurious experience.

China and India will dominate the market for new planes by 2015. By 2020, expect 600 billion revenue passenger air miles in China alone each year.

Budget carriers will grow dramatically in India, with more than 30 million seats sold by 2015. Despite global warming and new carbon tariffs on air tickets, the growth of the Asia-Pacific economies will mean that at least a quarter of all 1.6 billion seats sold in 2020 are likely to be on long-haul flights. Airlines will be hammered by ecology groups, despite the fact that global carbon emissions from planes in 2006 were only 3 per cent compared with 22 per cent for surface transport.

Expect many parts of the leisure and travel industry to focus on the needs of totally networked business executives, at the same time looking to provide ever more unusual and exotic experiences for premium leisure travellers.

Air freight set to grow

Speed brings savings in storage and enables just-in-time solutions. High-value goods such as computers, software, medical equipment and other time-sensitive goods such as fashion accessories will increasingly be carried by air. Air cargo has doubled in a decade, and accounts for a third of global freight value. Expect a further doubling over the next five to ten years.

GLOBALISATION IS CHANGING COMPANY STRUCTURES

The old-style company began as a kind of a pyramid:

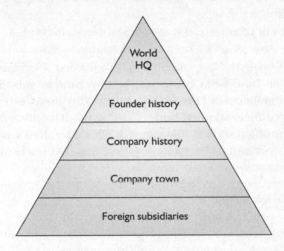

And the subsidiaries really were foreign, subservient, lacking in power, controlled from the top down. This kind of structure is increasingly irrelevant in a globalised world where location becomes less meaningful. The future is about partnerships and alliances.

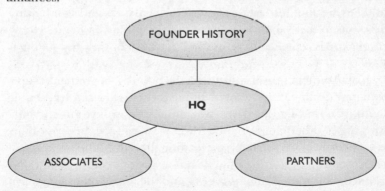

Globalisation forces corporations with strong tribal (national) identities to ask: 'Who is us?'

Many companies, wherever they have their HQs in the world, will have boards where the majority are from other nations. Indeed it will become almost impossible by 2015 to manage a globalised company effectively without globalised representation at the top, partly because of tribalism and a perception of staff and public image problems.

The majority of large national companies will have very diverse global operations, where turnover outside the 'home country' will be greater than that produced in the domestic market. Expect a spate of company name changes as large corporations refit their images to become global citizens rather than national entities.

Workforce left behind

Financial controls have crumbled so that the cost of capital is converging between countries. Factories can be located anywhere, and can be moved rapidly as conditions change.

The trouble is that rapid relocations leave people behind – except for a few specialists. People are less mobile than capital, technology, information and raw materials.

Home ownership makes moving more difficult and expensive. In France, Italy, Spain and Belgium the cost of selling one house and buying another (estate agent fees, legal costs and stamp duty) amounts to more than 15 per cent of the price of a home. Home ownership is less of an issue in the US, where buying and selling is easier.

Home ownership will continue to be popular, but owner occupation may decline. Expect many home owners to become absentee landlords, renting out their own homes as an investment while working in other cities or countries. As we will see, hypermobility is very costly in personal terms, leading directly to the break-up of marriages, the scattering of children in various countries because of fixed educational commitments, and the loss of other long-term relationships.

Executives need more than money to move

But if people get left behind as industries come and go with remark-able speed, shifting themselves around the globe, then retraining is going to be an even more important national priority. Companies may not be able to guarantee jobs in the future, but at least they can invest in their staff so that when the company moves on, it leaves behind employees with the right skills to find new work.

Many middle-ranking executives need more than money to persuade them to move. It is true that a starving man or woman will travel a long way to win daily bread for a family. But in many Western nations other factors become more important. Relation-ships and family keep many rooted. Parents with teenagers at a critical stage in their education are often extremely reluctant to move. As are those on their second or third marriages, having learned painful lessons from the past about neglecting home life, perhaps now with a 'new' set of very young children they are deter-mined not to neglect as they did the set who are now grown up. Increasing numbers of older executives in very senior positions are also bound to a locality by responsibility for elderly parents, at a time when their children have finally left home.

Lower down the social scale there are armies of mobile workers in countries like India and Poland who are used to spending 11 months a year away from home, earning money to support a wife and family. Many Indians, for example, work in Dubai as taxi drivers or construction workers, returning only once every two or three years to see loved ones. But this is globalisation.

VAST AND INVINCIBLE

Small may be beautiful but big means powerful. Who is going to regulate the new super-corporations? Monopolies and oligopo-lies have hardly formed yet on a global level – globalisation is too young – but they will. But where is the global control going to come from? Expect this to be a key issue by 2010, with attempts at regulation by 2015 – which will be only partly successful.

•
CHALLENGES TO MANAGEMENT
•

Globalisation as an issue

◆ Has your company recently addressed the new challenges posed by globalisation?
◆ Are all senior staff up to speed with the extraordinary changes in the global economy over the past three years, and the likely impact?
◆ How globalised is your head office in mentality?
◆ How would you know?

Currency instability

◆ How vulnerable are you to increasing political risk and currency instability, especially in emerging markets?
◆ Are you in a position to profit from it?
◆ What 'insurance' have you to cover this risk?
◆ Are you prepared for very hostile attitudes to foreign investors who rapidly remove capital?
◆ How ready are you for government policy changes at short notice, precipitated by fear of the markets?

Global pressure from labour force

◆ How prepared are you for labour movements in several countries to join forces against you?

Working hours in a global village

◆ What is your expectation of staff that are required to interact with colleagues very early in the morning and very late at night, because of time differences?
◆ How should your office hours culture adapt in the longer term and what are you doing to encourage this?
◆ What is your policy on home working and mobile working (e.g. dataphones) and how does it need to change?

Rebranding

◆ Do your products need rebranding for a global market?
◆ Do your 'global brands' need better management as a portfolio of niche brands?

Virtual companies

- How easy would it be for a virtual company to set up in competition with you and take some of your business?
- Are you as virtual as you should be, given the possibilities created by workforces and new technology?
- How could you be more virtual and more profitable or efficient?

Shareholder value

- Is your company being valued correctly, e.g. by the use of new measures such as intellectual capital?
- How well are you managing shareholder expectations regarding the need for longer-term views of success than last year's balance sheet?
- Where are the threats and opportunities in mergers, acquisition and disposals?
- How well can you survive in a huge global race on your own?

Disintermediation

- Is your company fully exploiting new technologies to cut out 'middle merchants', with direct buy and sell?
- Are you vulnerable to being 'cut out of the deal' in the future?

Switching countries

- Is your location policy due for review?
- How certain are you that company activities are all located in the right country?
- Do you have rapid exit strategies for countries which may become unstable?

Market research

- Are you using psychographics and other new technologies to predict what customers will really want tomorrow when surveys tell you only what they can see from today?
- Do you have good access to accurate global trend forecasting, taking into account discontinuities?

Company structure

- Is your company structure changing as fast as the world you operate in?

◆ What is the future of your HQ in a world where partners, associates and competitors are networking continuously?

◆ Does your current structure give you a competitive advantage
– or is it a fudge?

Company identity

◆ How important is the current image of the company, and is it
the right image for the third millennium?

◆ Is national identity an advantage or disadvantage?

• • • • • • • • • • • • • • • • • •
PERSONAL CHALLENGES
• • • • • • • • • • • • • • • • • •

Personal globalisation

◆ How globalised are you in your own thinking?

◆ For example, do you read a newspaper like *The Economist*? Do
you watch a global news channel such as CNN?

Multiskilling

◆ What would you do tomorrow if a big merger or acquisition
meant that your company and role was likely to disappear?

◆ What kind of insurance policy have you taken out against
unemployment – for example, do you have a second or third
skill which you could use to get a job?

◆ What can you do now to keep yourself in the mainstream job
market?

Multilanguage and multi-English

◆ How many languages do you speak, and do you need to improve
your language skills? If English is your mother tongue you may
not understand the need. English may be the dominant global
language but we are talking about building relationships,
communication and confidence raising.

◆ Is your English world-class standard or could it hold you back?

◆ Do you understand the difference between your own version
of English and international English? The words used, the
grammar and accent are entirely different from British or
American or Caribbean or Indian English.

◆ Are you speaking the right version of English at international forums?

◆ Do you speak clearly or do you mumble?

Moving to a virtual day

◆ What steps have you taken to move away from a traditional working day with a beginning the middle and end – towards working across several time zones? That means taking leisure time in the middle of a traditional day in the office, and being on call for up to 18 hours a day. It also means taking whole days off – apart from being on call – during a 'normal' working week.

◆ How prepared are you for virtual working?

◆ If your company had to choose the most virtualised team members for their next initiative, would they choose you?

Mobile home

◆ How mobile do you want to be in the next five years?

◆ Is that compatible with the personal commitments and preferences of other members of your household?

◆ Have you talked those issues through enough to have a joint plan?

◆ Have you considered developing alternative career paths so that you can have the option to stay where you are rather than relocate if your job changes, or to be able to relocate because your partner is relocating?

Greater knowledge means more power

◆ Do you know how to use your company intranet effectively?

◆ Do you have a thorough understanding of how knowledge is managed inside your company?

◆ How valuable is your own contribution to this growing knowledge base?

◆ If staff were rewarded according to how many times other people accessed their own unique pages of information, would you rank as a net provider or taker of data?

And finally…

◆ How vulnerable is your own portfolio of investments to a major currency crisis?

CHAPTER 5

Radical

Reacting against twentieth-century values

The future will have a strong radical element to it, as traditional political movements shrivel and die. The digital revolution created the global village and globalisation the rules for trading within it, but neither has taught us how several billion people should live inside such a tiny 'cultural space'.

GOVERNMENTS – LOSS OF POWER

All over the world the political scenery is changing and old forces are dying. What will replace them all? Governments are losing power. As we have seen, the global economy rules nations. Trading areas are regional. Currency is decided by markets. State services have been privatised and there is a trend towards local government.

In the case of Britain, most laws are now made by Brussels and national decisions are often overruled. Loss of power upwards is balanced by loss of power downwards, with the creation of a Scottish parliament and a Welsh assembly, and devolution of power to Northern Ireland. Westminster will be left as the mini-Parliament of Little England – minus London and other large cities, which increasingly want local powers of their own.

At the same time government runs less and less of the economy. Gone are ministerial responsibilities for water, electricity, coal, gas, British Airways, telephones and much of public transport. This trend to privatisation is now global and unstoppable. There will be major opportunities for corporations to run these privatised

industries. We will see growing concern as nations lose control of
their own utilities through international ownership, with, say, a gas
company in America buying a huge stake in an electricity provider
in France, yet the process will accelerate.

Non-profit organisations set to grow

The welfare state will be privatised extensively, to non-profit organisations (NPOs). In an age that will increasingly question the
profit motive, especially when meeting the needs of the sick or
vulnerable, expect NPOs to grow fast. Half their income in many
countries is from government contracts and grants. NPOs will be
increasingly popular, 'run by people for the benefit of people',
rather than with the prime motivation of securing return on
capital. NPOs will be characterised by greater rigour, professional-
ism, audit and evaluation. Fierce competition between agencies
will equal anything in the commercial sector today. Expect huge
voluntary sector growth in America, where already 60 per cent of
adults give on average 200 hours of time a year.

There will also be competition between commercial and non-
profit organisations, with accusations by commercial companies
that NPOs are artificially undercutting prices by using unpaid
voluntary labour, or by cross-subsidies using donations. The whole
concept of charitable work will be called into question as many
agencies find themselves more and more as simple subcontractors
to government, with severe restrictions on their activity. Expect
the commercial sector to win a campaign for charitable status to
be abolished in the case of organisations which are purely subcontractors. As part of this shift, volunteers will increasingly question
whether their act of charity is simply being used to enable government to cut costs and jobs.

Expect rapid growth of social enterprises: businesses where
much of their profit is used to improve the community as, for
example, in fair trade organisations. There are already 55,000
such enterprises in the UK, around 5 per cent of all businesses,
with a combined turnover of £27 billion a year.

Unable to deliver promises

The result of these developments is that governments will be unable to fulfil election promises. Most traditional functions of the state have drifted out of their control. Failure to deliver has contributed to disillusionment. Add to that the smell of corruption and the loss of confidence becomes acute. Even Westminster, regarded as the mother of all parliaments, has been seen as full of sleaze with evidence over many years of back-handers, secret favours and dishonesty. The UK may have the least corrupt democracy in the world, but the British people have lost confidence in it. An opinion poll showed the following attitudes:

Disbelieve politicians	90 per cent
Politicians tell lies to protect themselves	90 per cent
Ministers cannot be trusted	90 per cent

These results are almost identical to those in Russia, where 90 per cent of the people distrust members of parliament and 88 per cent distrust the government.

Countries with a reputation for political corruption

Rightly or wrongly, many countries have governments which their own people see as corrupt. It is part of a broader picture.

Bribery is often seen as just a local tariff payable to get things done. But poor people in these countries are the losers. Corruption means good projects are squeezed out in favour of bad ones. Honest officials give up. Bribes grow bigger. It becomes all but impossible for a company or a foreign government to do business without playing the corruption game. Scruples are soon swallowed. Germany is one of several nations in the EU where until recently bribes were tax deductible, while in contrast the US has always theoretically regarded bribery as an offence. Transparency International is an anti-corruption pressure group based in Berlin. There will be more such groups, together with new 'bribe-free zones' or 'islands of integrity' with public pledges by all who operate there not to accept or pay bribes.

The slow death of democracy

What is the point of voting when you cannot believe the words of a manifesto? What is the point of listening to a television interview with the president when you can't trust what he says? Voting is going out of fashion, young people are drifting away in droves. Less than half the electorate bothers to vote in some of the world's largest economies. A recent UK 'Big Brother' TV show polled more votes than the elected government.

Expect growing political agreement in most developed countries on issues such as health, education, social support, globalisation and foreign policy. Despite public appearances, most policiticans in mature, democratic countries agree on most things, which is why it is so rare for a newly elected government to reverse legislation that they opposed before they got into power.

When you add together the lack of ministerial power to make things happen (because of privitisation), and the high level of private agreement on most important issues, the result is a bored electorate.

Political debate in the media will be seen increasingly in future as irrelevant, insincere, posturing. Expect growing apathy about political parties, which will be replaced by passion for single issues. The exception will be nations struggling for political freedom and parts of the world experiencing radical change.

Crisis in current affairs media reporting

The truth that most politicians agree on most things in many nations is a secret which is uncomfortable for the media. It is impossible to create lively TV or radio interviews without injecting controversy and sharp debate. So programme makers are often tempted to invite participants into the studio who have highly coloured views, or try to create polarisation with aggressive interviews.

Media coverage of politics will continue to distort the truth in the rush for sensationalism. But this will not reverse the decline in audiences for political programmes.

Expect more countries to follow the example of Australia, where there is compulsory voting. This will mean more older people vote with consequences for ageing societies such as Japan, Italy and Germany. Expect electronic voting to become a low-cost and accepted method for referendums, with the same channel being used for instant opinion polls on a wide array of issues, influencing policy or even electing a government.

Tribalism in political leadership
When faith in ideology and parties dies, trust in the person is all that's left. Leaders rather than policies will dominate the future and new 'tribal elders' will emerge. Emotional attachment to a person and a group will be more powerful than electoral promises.

Hence Nelson Mandela, a man held in prison as a subversive for 27 years until 1990, became a national presidential figure in South Africa. He commanded the nation to change and it did. But where do you find another Mandela for the third millennium? Trust and respect are the pillars of tomorrow's politics. People like Mandela will continue to command the world stage, and will be rewarded with international honour. They will provide the future with global leadership based not on nationality, far less on party, nor even on office, but on international recognition among billions of people that here is someone (at last) who is worth following.

Death of political theory
The old left/right politics is dead. Old politics lumped together social justice and compassion with moral liberalism, and free markets with public morality and personal responsibility. But leftwing ideology finally died with the collapse of the Eastern bloc, while the right-wing, 'hands-off' government of the 1970s, 1980s and 1990s fell apart when confronted by the massive social challenges created by urbanisation. Right-wing rhetoric had little to say to those experiencing a taste of living hell on high crime, inner city estates, while left-wing state control had no power to create wealth.

Throughout Europe political parties have drifted right, particularly in the south and east. Spain, Portugal, Italy and Greece are countries in which the left has moved most sharply, together with countries such as Poland, Hungary, Estonia, the Czech Republic and others. The notable exceptions are France's Socialist party and Germany's Social Democrats. And both France and Germany are still in danger of being left behind by the harsh realities of globalisation.

Expect democracy to be questioned. American foreign policy has been driven by many factors, of which one is a passionate belief that democracy is good for nations. Expect this to be challenged when it becomes clear that in some nations, a free vote would result in immediate election of a radical Islamic government, far more hostile to US interests than the previous dictatorship. A counter-argument will be seen in examples of benign dictatorship, such as in the UAE. Democracy will continue to be viewed with some suspicion in many Arab nations as a flawed Western model that leads to moral decay and destruction of values which have been ordained by God. Despite this, we can expect some democratic progress in countries like Palestine, Lebanon and Egypt.

NEW POLITICS

Party politics has been replaced by single issues

Single issues will be the most important driving force in politics for the future.

OLD PARTY POLITICS	NEW ISSUES
World view	Narrow agenda
Systematic	Campaign
History	New causes
Tradition	Radical
Left/right	Sometimes irrational

EXAMPLES OF SINGLE ISSUES	
Environment	Europe/world
Animal rights	Britain
Abortion	US
Genetic revolution	Germany
Holocaust gold	US/Switzerland
Farm land rights	Brazil
Child labour	US/Europe

Single-issue politics

In a recent UK election it was highly significant that two new parties fielded between them hundreds of candidates – on single issues. One was the Referendum Party, promising a vote on Europe, and the other was the Pro-Life Party. Neither had a comprehensive manifesto – a plan for the nation as a whole. They were interested in one issue only. The trouble is that you can't run a nation for long on a cluster of single issues. If you do, you turn out to be rudderless, without any underlying purpose.

So what does 'single-issue' politics mean for voters? It means that manifestos in future are likely to be non-controversial lists of centre-of-the-road policies plus a cluster of other 'populist' issues such as the environment. Pragmatic politics means that governments are more likely to change policy or introduce one between elections, as a result of vigorous lobbying. Expect opinion polls to count more than parliamentary debate and more referendums on important issues.

Abortion will continue to be a big issue in the US

Abortion is an example of a growing single issue: pro-choice v pro-life. It is 40 years since the famous Roe v Wade case when the Supreme Court decreed that abortion was a constitutional right. Since then there have been a number of legal restrictions. The anti-abortion movement in the US is now bigger than the civil rights movement of the 1960s. Tens of thousands have been arrested, cautioned or imprisoned, while many pro-abortionists have been threatened, assaulted or murdered.

Single issues are more powerful than state law. Here is a great nation that allows abortion but where abortion has been almost outlawed in some states in practice. In one state, at the height of the protests it was hard to find a doctor willing to conduct abortions. Then the ban came on so-called partial-birth abortion – so single-issue groups can and do alter national law.

Single-issue groups are growing fast

Worldwide, Greenpeace has 3 million members in 32 countries and a budget of $146 million. In Britain, Friends of the Earth and Greenpeace have more members together than the Labour Party. Hundreds of companies now embrace environmental concerns.

Environment is top single issue for tomorrow

The environment will be the dominant single issue for tomorrow, feeding into post-millennial fears that the third millennium will be the last. Every now and then there is a major accident or climate-related event which attracts huge attention. The Union Carbide disaster killed 2,000 in India in 1984, and injured tens of thousands of others, after the release of clouds of highly toxic gas from a chemical plant.

Two years later Chernobyl spewed tons of radioactive gases and debris into the atmosphere, creating a huge radioactive no-go area in Ukraine and dumping so much radioactivity on western Europe that in 2006, 20 years later, 355 farms in Wales were still banned from sending sheep to market because of the risk to those eating them. Then there was the Exxon Valdez oil spill in Alaska, and others in Europe, together with global scares over BSE after cows in Britain were fed meat products infected with prions. Then there was the growing awareness of global warming.

A single issue can wreck your business

Real success in future will be far more difficult to define. It will mean demonstrating how your corporation makes a real difference for everyone: for shareholders of course, but also for customers, workers, the wider community, and in some small way, for the whole of humanity – for example, by protecting the environment.

The boards of just about every high-profile company can expect to meet single-issue activists at their annual shareholders' meetings. CEOs now need to know how to handle people hanging from ceilings, running naked down the aisles, shouting and asking awkward questions. Road builders, arms makers, water and oil companies are just some in the firing line, together with companies investing in operations with wasteful carbon emissions, child labour in India, animal experimentation for medical research, GM food – the list is almost endless.

In December 2002, Nestlé started legal action against the Ethiopian government to get compensation for assets seized in 1975. There was immediate outrage, among some consumers, with anger around the world that a wealthy food company was trying to extract money from poor or hungry Ethiopian subsistence farmers (most of the population).

Within 24 hours, the Nestlé board began to back down. By January, the board had negotiated a reduced settlement of just $1.5 million, of which every cent was immediately given back to the Ethiopian government for famine relief. But the damage to the brand was significant.

Nestlé was already on borrowed time in the minds of some consumers over previous accusations (almost certainly unjust) that the company was 'inappropriately' marketing bottled feeds for babies in the poorest nations. As someone with extensive experience of humanitarian aid in these countries, I consider such criticism misplaced, since the only people able to afford bottled milk are the middle class on high incomes, who are likely to follow instructions in safe preparation. However, this other campaign against Nestlé also damaged the brand. Thus we see that single issues are powerful and often relate to complex factors, and it can be very difficult for a company to regain consumer confidence, even when science is on their side.

Greenpeace and Shell – a sign of things to come

Another important example of wrong science leading to brand damage was seen in the row between Greenpeace and Shell. Dumping Brent Spar was always going to look bad – a large contaminated structure was to be sunk to the sea bed where it would gradually rust to pieces, releasing toxic waste. But Greenpeace got their facts wrong about the amount of oil and other contaminants on the rig. They ran a slick publicity operation and there was a vigorous consumer reaction, especially in Germany, with a widespread boycott of Shell products. British Prime Minister

John Major had previously said that the government would support sea dumping as safe, and a far more satisfactory means of dealing with the rig than land disposal. The government finally caved in and said they now wanted it disposed of on land. This single-issue group had become more powerful than the government.

Then Greenpeace realised their mistake. The amount of oil on board was less than feared. But the damage had been done and despite a public apology Shell was forced to continue with land disposal, even though most experts, and Greenpeace, now agreed that it was a worse solution for the environment. The dumping of the Brent Spar oil rig in the North Sea was therefore an important warning to every institution. It is an important case because big mistakes were made by both sides. Similar mistakes have been made by other corporations since. There was long-term damage to Shell, and great damage was done to the entire oil industry in image and increased disposal costs. There was also damage to Greenpeace, and costs to the environment and consumers.

It all showed the power of single-issue groups, small numbers of activists - and the key was control of the media. When it came to the raiding of Brent Spar, Greenpeace had a great advantage. TV news always gives priority to news stories with images and Greenpeace owned them all. They had cameras and satellite links on board the rig and did not allow other crews to land. They controlled the entire output.

The scenes are as spectacular as in any movie. Greenpeace chartered a helicopter to ferry supplies from a nearby vessel to the rig. Spectacular shots were taken of water jets from fire tenders actually hitting the helicopter as it hovered in mid-air hundreds of feet above. The craft shakes and whirls. Ten seconds of images like that seemed to brand Shell as the big bully and the activists as schoolboy heroes. And anyway, what did Shell have to hide? It looked dreadful and from that moment the battle was lost.

Corporate ethics is big business
Most chief executives of multinationals recognise that corporate and social responsibility is crucial to future business success.

Companies with a poor track-record in this area will be vulnerable to attack on a wide range of issues.

Corporate and social responsibility can take many forms. For example, fast-food companies will be in the firing line over the next few years over accusations that they are killing people, by promoting foods which contribute to diabetes. Expect these companies to respond by going further than the law demands. We will see new research into food addiction, new advertising campaigns about obesity and healthy eating, voluntary controls on marketing of junk food to children, improved food content labelling, new ranges of healthy eating alternatives, health warnings on some food products, and so on. All of these will be developed before governments and courts force action, just as we have seen in other areas such as GM food labelling. Food companies will also be likely to employ some of their strongest critics as advisers. This is a wise and effective strategy that has already been successfully used in other industries.

An example in food production is Nutreco, one of the world's leading suppliers of baby fish for fish farmers. Some years ago, a BBC documentary filmed disturbing scenes below fish farm cages, showing environmental damage. The share price fell 20 per cent in 24 hours. Nutreco had previously set itself an aim to lead the world in responsible, sustainable, environmentally friendly production of low-fat, healthy, farmed fish. To help them avoid similar criticism in future, they partnered with Friends of the Earth, to try to improve every area of operation.

Some time later, another similar documentary attacked fish farming practices in Brazil, which were also linked to the company. They immediately defended their reputation by demonstrating their active partnership with Friends of the Earth. As a result, the Brazilian story was quickly seen as a minor lapse of high standards by the world leader in ethical fish farming, and the story died.

Growing problems with 'Fair Trade'

Fair Trade products will gain market share by promising consumers that poor farmers will get a better return. Fair Trade will grow especially fast in the coffee industry on which 25 million families depend for income. Farmers typically receive 35 cents on $3 retail price, but prices have fallen, 600,000 jobs have been lost in South America alone and over 40 per cent of all global trade is in the hands of just four companies.

Fair Trade sounds a great idea, but is likely to be scrutinised in future. Food subsidies of any kind distort markets. Fair Trade creates an artificially high price for coffee beans, leading to over-production at a time when global reserves of coffee beans have been enough to last more than six months. Coffee prices were low because of overproduction. Demand has been falling. It will be argued by some in future that Fair Trade financing of the coffee industry would be better spent retraining coffee farmers to do something else.

Expect many more debates about how best to create a better world, but the trend is clear: every aspect of what corporations do will come under the closest scrutiny. Every large corporation can expect to be targeted by several hundred activist groups with a bewildering range of agendas.

Companies will continue to come and go, riding the wave of ethical fashions and fads with products designed to please the ethically sensitive, while some will rush to get close to activist groups to gain sympathy and support.

Ethical investment funds will continue to grow, prompting intense debates in future about definition, and regular scandals as 'ethical' companies are discovered to have broken unwritten rules. More than €1 trillion is now invested in European socially respon-sive investments – 15 per cent of all funds under management. In the US the proportion is around one dollar in ten invested – around $2.4 trillion.

Getting listed or unlisted as an 'ethical' company will be enough to see a CEO rewarded or sacked.

A single issue can strike fast and hard, suddenly threatening to overwhelm every other board priority. Every corporation should have a team watching out. Subscribe to newsletters. Join the relevant organisations, send members of the company to annual conferences. Listen to the gossip over coffee, and to comments on debates from the floor. Early warning is absolutely vital. Every large corporation should regularly give itself a single-issue 'health check'. The key to survival will be to seize and hold the 'moral high ground' in every way, with clear corporate values and well understood systems of checks, sanctions and public punishments.

McDonald's wins libel case but loses face

Look what happened to McDonald's. The world's biggest burger chain was attacked in pamphlets that made serious accusations. The authors were an almost penniless man and woman with strong views. The case became the longest libel case in British history. The trouble is that libel law prevents repeat of a libel – except in a court. And what is said in court can be printed indefinitely in a report of proceedings. So the case made matters far worse, even though McDonald's won. More recently rioters attacked McDonald's in India after it was revealed that 'vegetarian' French fries were contaminated with tiny amounts of beef products.

Holocaust gold

Over 50 years after the end of the Second World War, who would have thought that Nazi gold would have hit Switzerland so hard? After major rows and accusations of a cover-up, Swiss banks relented on traditions of absolute secrecy and published a list of several thousand dormant accounts from the war years, the majority of which were thought to relate to those who perished in the Holocaust. Unfortunately the same mistakes were made as by Shell. Instead of a swift decision to do what they were later forced to do anyway, the banks hesitated and seemed not to care. They collectively misjudged how acutely sensitive the issue was in the US, and began to react only when their own US offices began to warn of losing business over the 'scandal'.

Cause-related marketing

Single issues will be used powerfully by corporations to sell tomorrow's products. In a world where almost all products and services are becoming similar in price (falling) and quality (rising), one of the only ways to differentiate from the competition is with values.

Cause-related marketing means selling to people who believe in the cause more than the differences in the product.

An example has been Tesco's computer vouchers for schools in the UK – over £40 million worth of computers have been donated in return for vouchers given every time people spend more than £10 on food or other items. The scheme was a runaway success which sold itself largely through social pressure, with children recruiting parents who in turn recruited friends and work colleagues. Social networking is the best advertising you can have when your prices and products are identical to those of your competitors.

Among consumers, 86 per cent prefer companies that are helping the community and 81 per cent are more likely to buy products linked to causes they care about. Staff want to be proud of who they work for, and Tesco found staff loyalty increased as well as the quality of their recruits. Expect tens of thousands of new partnerships between businesses and charities to market products or services for mutual benefit.

Trade–environment disputes will grow

The World Trade Organisation is already being asked to sort out conflicts arising from different environmental standards between nations. Examples include the US–Venezuela row over high-sulphur oil exports. Another is the US dispute with India, Malaysia and Pakistan over the export of shrimp caught using 'environmentally harmful' fishing gear. The US has worried that Mexico's lax standards will mean companies in the US can relocate production there to cut down on environmental costs and then undercut US companies. There are already threats by some countries to slam extra import duties onto products made in countries with poor standards, to protect domestic producers.

The counter-argument is that green regulations make firms more competitive and creative, producing higher quality products for increasingly fussy markets. The theory is that these companies stay ahead, controlling pollution and degradation and winning new niche markets. In practice it is far more tempting for some industries to relocate where production is easy and cheap. Either way, environmental business is growing and is already valued at $1 trillion a year, a figure expected to rise dramatically by 2010 with carbon trading.

American mega-waste

The US heads the world league for waste and consumption
- 35 per cent of the world's cars for 4 per cent of the world population
- 19 per cent of the world's garbage – 3.5lbs in weight a day per person
- Almost three-quarters of a ton of rubbish per person a year
- 30 per cent of the rubbish is packaging

Every year that means:

- 15 billion disposal nappies
- 2 billion razors
- 1. 7 billion pens
- 100 billion kilograms of plastics
- 440 million kilograms of plastics is exported to Asia and land-filled there

In contrast, Europe is set to recover 90 per cent of its packaging waste in ten years. Expect many packagaing innovations to help the environment, including biodegradeable plastics, refillable plastic drink bottles, water-based inks, lower weight tins and reductions in volumes. Expect continued debate over what plastics are most environmentally friendly. Ordinary plastic stays inert in landfill while biodegradeable or incinerated plastic waste releases carbon into the atmosphere.

Traditional repair shops and fix-it industries have died, but are being replaced by an increasing number of waste exchanges and re-use centres. One of the problems is that local repair labour costs are very high compared with production costs, which are low because of mechanisation and cheap labour. This is an area where individuals will be encouraged to take positive action, at home and at work, with purchasing, consumption and disposal decisions.

ENVIRONMENTAL MEGA-ISSUES

'Carbon dioxide: they call it pollution; we call it life!' This was a recent TV slogan paid for by ExxonMobil, Ford and General Motors, aired by the Competitive Enterprise Institute. Expect such corporations to run far away from that kind of messaging in future, in response to consumer outrage. HSBC was the first bank to announce that it had become carbon neutral, joining the insurance company Swiss Re and Goldman Sachs. In 2006, Wal-Mart, Tesco, Sainsbury's and BP also announced major energy-conservation measures.

Global warming
Mega issues such as global warming and atmospheric pollution will bite hard. The future is about emotion, not science or graphs or tables. It does not matter what your own opinion is about the science related to the global warming debate. What will matter in the immediate future is the balance of public opinion, which is falling firmly on the side of those who consider global warming to be man-made and a global threat. Global warming will certainly be a major issue for the next half century. It is beyond debate that the level of carbon dioxide is rising rapidly in the global atmosphere. Many scientists think levels are higher than for a million years. Samples drilled more than 3.2 kilometeres into the ice of Antarctica show clear patterns of CO_2 and earth temperature changes (the latter indicated by different isotope levels of hydrogen in the ice itself). These correlate well with data from other sources for relatively recent events (e.g. last ice age), and provide a data set going back 450,000 years.

It reveals a worrying trend. World energy demands are growing at 2 per cent a year. By 2010 developing countries are expected to produce more greenhouse gases than developed countries – 55 per cent compared with 39 per cent in 1990. World energy consumption is set to double by 2040, assuming a 20 per cent increase in energy prices above 2006 levels. All this points to one thing: unsustainability. With only 4 per cent of the world's population, America produces 20 per cent of greenhouse gases. What happens when every developing nation wants an American lifestyle?

Little doubt about sea levels

Rising sea levels are a potential threat to most of the world's largest cities which were founded centuries ago around trading ports. Even if carbon dioxide levels remain at their 2006 level (impossible), many scientists think that the sea could continue to rise slowly for 1,000 years. However the ultimate catastrophe could happen over a few hundred years, with sea levels rising by up to 15 metres, as Greenland ice and part of Antarctica melt. The use of oil, gas and coal over the next 50 years is likely to be limited far more by concerns about carbon dioxide levels in the air more than by dwindling reserves. We already have technology to convert any form of carbon into any other. We have stocks of coal sufficient for 250 years at current levels of use, and every time oil prices rise, new oil reserves become commercially viable, such as the oily sands in Canada, stretching over a land area the size of Florida. Proven oil reserves are likely to continue to grow faster than consumption over the next 30 years.

There will continue to be huge debates over the exactness of the science of global warming, and continued scepticism, especially from parts of the US. Expect US policy to change rapidly following a series of climate-related events causing major losses on US soil, ranging from hurricanes to floods and huge forest fires, which alone cost the US over $1 billion a year. Fires have increased fourfold since 1986, partly because of longer, hotter, drier seasons. Once these kinds of events become linked in many minds with man-made emissions, political change will follow. The insurance argument will eventually win over the majority of those who still think that significant climate change is very unlikely, or is unlinked to human activity. Most people insure their lives for unlikely events such as a major fire at home, so that they have a means of survival in the event of disaster. However, it is difficult to have an insurance policy against a disaster from global warming, unless it consists of action taken now to mitigate the effects of an event that may turn out to be very unlikely. By the time everyone is totally sure what is really happening, it may be far too late to prevent 50–100 years of devastation with disruptive climatic events.

The Kyoto Protocol (or whatever replaces it) agreed in 2001 by over 190 nations – excluding the US – to limit global carbon emissions, will create huge international tensions by 2015. Expect every new flooding disaster or unusual drought to be blamed on global warming. Expect big problems with non-compliance by governments which fail to ratify global agreements, or to abide by them. Expect righteous anger from poorer nations when they find their own industrial revolutions are being held back by rich nations. Expect huge global markets in carbon, with rich nations failing to cut carbon emissions and only reaching targets by persuading (and funding) poor nations to reduce theirs. Expect major fraud with governments and large corporations misrepresenting carbon emissions. Around $30 billion of carbon was traded in 2006 – up from $10 billion in 2005. When carbon in gas or coal is burnt, most of this ancient substance remains in the atmosphere or is taken up by plants and trees which later die, releasing it back into the air. That is why planting trees is a very limited response to global warming. The only long-term solution is to extract carbon dioxide and put it back underground where it had been previously for millions of years.

It is already possible to capture 90 per cent of carbon dioxide from the chimneys of gas or coal power stations, and to pump the liquid gas into underground storage, for example replacing oil or gas already removed. While this can double the cost of generating electricity, the impact on consumers is likely to be less than 20 per cent in price rises, after taking distribution and other fixed charges into account. Such an increase will hardly be significant if phased in over more than ten years, compared with the mid-2000s huge price hikes in oil and gas.

Expect the US to eventually fall into line with global treaties, partly in a desire to reduce dependency on Middle East oil by developing alternative energy resources and by being more energy efficient.

The cost of stabilising carbon dioxide levels has been estimated by MunichRe to be 1 per cent of Global World Product. However, continuing without change could cost 10 per cent of GWP, with temperature increases of 5°C or more by 2100, resulting in radical shifts in weather patterns.

Top ten polluters – % global CO_2 emissions	
US	20.6
China	14.8
Russia	5.7
India	5.5
Japan	4.0
Germany	2.9
Brazil	2.5
Canada	2.1
UK	2.0
Italy	1.6

Extremist groups will take great exception to 'jet-set' travellers using more than their fair share of the earth's resources in 'selfish' travel for business purposes, where they think the same tasks could be carried out using the latest communication technologies. Expect airports and passengers to be targeted by activists. Expect many businesses to plant forests as part of their own 'carbon saving', and to offset carbon use by investing in alternative energy generation in different parts of the world. This will reduce other people's 'carbon use', creating a 'carbon credit' to offset against the company's activity.

Expect the world's first carbon-neutral airline, offsetting every ton of fuel used by investing into hydroelectric power and other alternative technologies. It will cost such an airline no more than $15 per short haul return flight and $45 for long haul.

Expect protests by industry at green tax on jobs, with an insistence that unless environmental controls are applied consistently worldwide, those countries with greater controls will simply see jobs moved out to countries where controls are weakest.

Power will always be directly proportional to a country's GDP when it comes to negotiations, so nations with big GDP will end up running the new global system. It could run very well on a few hundred global agreements.

Growing worries about sun, sand and beach holidays

The damaged ozone layer will continue to fuel tourist concerns about skin cancers such as malignant melanoma, the occurrence of which doubled in a decade. Sunlight will be blamed for an increasing number of other disorders, including cataracts and non-Hodgkin's lymphoma (a kind of cancer). Skin cosmetics will increasingly emphasise ultraviolet ray protection. Some sun screens are already so strong that with their use it is almost impossible to develop a 'normal tan'.

Expect brown, tanned skin to become less fashionable in some European countries, with a return to paleness as a sign of sophistication as it was in the nineteenth century, when a tan was a sign that you were an outdoor labourer. Beach holidays in hot parts of the world will become suspect in the eyes of increasing numbers of people.

Expect growth in culture holidays, exploration holidays, learning holidays, activity holidays, as more people take several short breaks a year in addition to a longer vacation. Risk, excitement and experience will open new tourist markets, especially for older people, including countries offering extremes of hot and cold ranging from the United Arab Emirates through to Greenland or Iceland, with a stronger emphasis on eco-holidays or sustainable tourism. The ultimate (non-eco-friendly) experience will be space tourism for $170,000 or weightless flights for $4,000. A healthy option for the same price will be a two-week holiday to India, Dubai or Thailand including a free coronary bypass or hip replacement plus convalescence. Health tourism will be a significant income generator by 2012, with up to 1 million health related visits a year to Thailand and 150,000 to India.

Loss of species

A quarter of all mammals face extinction by 2035. One in eight plant types are also threatened. Only 10 per cent of big fish in the ocean remain and most global fishing is under threat. Preserving biodiversity will be a growing priority, accelerated by awareness of global warming and loss of habitats. Almost half the world's land species are in Brazil and Indonesia. Expect special efforts to preserve the habitats of these countries.

Future generations will regard ocean fishing as strange an idea as feeding towns and villages on the meat of wild buffalo. Expect fish farming to become a global obsession with intense research to find ways to feed fish without using large amounts of other ocean fish and sea creatures, which themselves will then become an endangered resource.

The legacy of communism

Communist bloc countries became the worst polluters in the world and the cost is still rising. Azerbaijan is a small country with only 7.5 million people, yet by the beginning of 2002 over 4 million tons of extremely toxic waste had accumulated there. The Caspian Sea's unique bio-resources, including sturgeon fish, are all but destroyed – affecting four nations. During the 1980s, 15,000 tons of oil and oil products, 20,000 tons of mineral acids, 800 tons of dissolved iron and 500 tons of phenols were poured into the sea. Air pollution is terrible, along with water degradation, land erosion and salinisation. (See also water wars on pages 71–6.)

New power structures

The world will be hungry for non-carbon power, therefore expect booming investment in alternative generation from solar, wind, waves, tide, wood chippings and biofuel.

In the early 2000s research on renewables was less than 30 per cent of the billions spent on nuclear power research every year. Expect a huge growth in subsidies for wind farming, especially in windswept nations such as Britain where up to 20 per cent of energy could be generated this way. Future windmills will be smaller, quieter and everywhere. If the same levels of subsidy for nuclear energy were applied to wind, wave and solar sources, there would be rapid acceleration in development. Energy subsidies of various kinds will significantly distort energy generation markets for the next 30–50 years.

The US aims to have 1 million roofs covered by solar panels by 2010 but that will not be enough to reduce electricity demand significantly. Expect solar cell prices to fall rapidly with increased sales and to be a required feature of all new buildings in a number of countries.

Expect great debate over grand tidal schemes closing off the Wash and the Bristol Channel in the UK. The latter has the second largest tidal range in the world. Expect vast schemes to generate electricity in desert areas from solar panels, and new methods to carry it for large distances with far lower power loss. Expect energy generation to happen everywhere – even on the back of lorries.

Rubbish will be burned for power when it can't be recycled. A prime target is motor tyres. The US alone throws away 250 million a year. Heating produces a thick, smelly, black sludge from which other products can be made. But they can also be burned in a power station, as they are already in California.

Expect new materials to be developed that will be as revolutionary as plastics were in the mid-twentieth century. Plastics changed us all, whether nylon or polyester in clothes, plastic bags for shopping, food wrapping or the PVC dashboards of cars. Expect remarkable new fibres for clothing and fashion industries, and stronger, lighter products such as carbon fibre to be used more widely.

Expect more cars with aluminium bodies to beat rust. Expect cars with bodies of 30–60 per cent plastic, and other compounds, for example glass fibre. Expect car engines using ceramic technology for high efficiency, low fuel consumption and low engine wear.

Rethink on cars will accelerate

Severe restrictions on car use in major cities will become a way of life, leading to permanent controls in a bid to protect public health. At the same time expect efficiency of trains to be enhanced. Some of the latest high speed trains use more energy per passenger mile than cars unless they are travelling with a reasonably full load of passengers. Cars for short journeys will become unfashionable for a growing number. Already out-of-town shopping malls are falling from favour among town planners and governments in parts of Europe, while pedestrian precincts continue to sweep across town centres. Building more roads simply increases traffic. The nightmarish gridlock of cities such as Mexico City, Mumbai and Cairo will continue to raise questions about the future of cars.

In the longer term, restrictions on car usage are likely to affect shopping, rail travel and where people live. They will encourage local community life in some countries with a reversal of the trend to out-of-town superstores, and will discourage long-distance daily commuting in favour of living close to work in cities or towns, or teleworking.

Individuals can take steps to tackle their own contributions to these problems. For example, our own family home is within walking distance of schools, major shops and railway networks, while my wife and I work virtually. We aim to be carbon neutral, investing in new woodlands and alternative power generation to offset our own household emissions and travel.

Transcontinental smog

In the next two decades on current trends we can expect to see transcontinental smog: whole sections of the surface of the planet where the air on the ground is unhealthy to all and lethal to some. Smog kills by aggravating asthma, bronchitis and a host of other lung conditions and by directly increasing the risk of heart attacks through carbon monoxide exposure. In a city like Kolkata that could mean up to 25,000 extra deaths a year. Across a whole region or continent the results are unimaginable.

A recent hint of what is to come occurred in September 1997 when dense smog developed over 1 million square miles of South

East Asia. In Singapore the air quality fell to the point where breathing became the equivalent of smoking 20 cigarettes a day. President Suharto of Indonesia was forced to apologise for the forest burning – clearing land to grow food – which had been a large contributor, while Malaysia declared the severe haze a national disaster and schools were shut throughout Sarawak. The clearance itself was a product of land shortages and increasing population. Some estimates suggested that the fires released as much carbon dioxide as Europe produces in a whole year. Car exhausts were also a contributory factor.

The total population affected in some way was at least 300 million. If 50 million were severely affected, the increased deaths could have been higher than 1,000 every week, or at least 10,000 people. To this must be added the sick who survived. And that is just the beginning.

Between October and May a three-kilometre thick brown haze now covers much of South Asia and the north Indian Ocean. This is from urban emissions and forest fires, blocking sunlight.

We are gassing ourselves: human beings are profoundly altering the balance of gases in the atmosphere. At first, developing nations will continue to sacrifice air quality for economic growth. But within this generation air pollution in the worst affected countries is likely to become economically damaging, not least because of a loss of confidence among institutional investors from other nations. The pressure will be to clean up, to restore the image of 'civilised' urban life.

In July 1994 people were dying in London because of smog produced mainly from exhaust fumes. That summer I flew to Norway – and could not see the ground at any point, in clear skies at 35,000 feet. People were dying in Norway too. A week later I returned and my family drove to the most remote north-west tip of the British Isles to a Scottish island, where there are prevailing westerly winds, and where the air is usually very pure after travelling 3,000 miles over the Atlantic Ocean. The air was so polluted we could hardly breathe. It was the same across most of Europe.

The air in Mumbai and Kolkata is so foul on many days that it makes European smog look like the freshest mountain breeze. Consider this: if people in China own as many cars per 100 people by 2050 as we have in the West, there will be more cars in China alone by 2050 than there were on the whole earth in 2007. If they all ran on petrol, there would not be enough crude oil to keep them going, or enough wind or fresh air to disperse the massive cloud of pollutants.

Carbon taxes will cause international tension and conflict unless applied fairly – but that will be almost impossible. In order to be fair, carbon rations would have to be a fixed amount per person per year, perhaps sold on the open market as a tax on all carbon consumption, with subsidies for the poorest and most vulnerable. But that means villagers can no longer cut their own trees for fuel, and will condemn the poorest nations to a relatively carbon-free existence forever. Meanwhile the wealthiest nations will continue to ransack the earth's limited carbon supplies, and grab the largest slice of all the permits to pollute the atmosphere that every other nation also has to breathe. So while America burns fuel in its cars and air conditioning, Bangladesh may still drown in ever worsening floods. The loss of rain forests will add to the long-term effect, making future environmental corrections even more difficult.

Buildings will also be targeted

Around 50 per cent of earth-warming gas emissions in big cities are from homes. Expect homes in wealthy nations to become new energy target areas, with ultra-efficient boilers and better insulation – by law.

Expect new buildings to be designed with total life-time energy use in mind – construction, running costs and demolition and disposal. Expect geothermal heating to be in common use in many countries by 2020. This uses the principle of refrigeration to cool pipes under the ground in order to extract heat for radiators. Reversing the process cools a building while heating up ground pipes. Energy savings are typically 50 per cent of the cost of gas or electricity and 75 per cent of oil heating, even when the electricity needed for the heat pump is taken into account. The payback period can be less than ten years.

Weather predictions will be more accurate

If we can't control the atmosphere easily, at least we can try to predict its behaviour more effectively. Expect medium and long-range forecasts to increase steadily in accuracy. The limiting factor is not processing power or speed, but the lack of data sets for comparison. Accurate records of such things as sea temperature, air pressure and temperature have only been kept for a few decades, a mere blip in earth time. It will take another decade of earth-watching before we see major advances in forecasting. But at the same time, global warming should lead us to expect greater instability in weather patterns, and make predictions more difficult.

Discovery of low-cost clean fuels

The only clean fuel we know is hydrogen, because the only exhaust it produces is steam. Hydrogen buses are here already in cities such as Chicago and Vancouver, while Daimler-Benz and Ballard Power Systems are investing $300 million in fuel cell technology. But hydrogen is a low energy gas and has to be made by splitting water. The burning of fuels for anything other than heating is in any case extremely wasteful because so much is lost in heat production. The most efficient power source for cars would be the use of hydrogen to drive electric batteries. That sounds fine for the atmosphere, but it is not. After all, where does the hydrogen come from?

The answer is that in most situations hydrogen will be made by burning coal, gas or oil to generate electricity, which will then be used to convert water into hydrogen and oxygen. So most hydrogen vehicles will in effect be running on carbon, burnt many miles away.

Expect biofuel production to grow massively, stimulated by EU targets that by 2010 5.75 per cent of all road fuel should be from crops such as wheat or rapeseed – enough to require up to 10 per cent of the EU's wheat production. Some 30 per cent of US agricultural land could be needed to replace 10 per cent of transport fuel with biofuel. Expect the US and other nations to pursue their own rapid expansion of biofuel production. Expect growing concerns about the impact on prices of burning food products in cars or lorries. Second generation biofuels will be made from inedible by-products of crop production and will be a more sustainable solution. Biofuels will mean more income for farmers in many nations, linked to energy prices, placing further pressure on rain forests and other fragile ecosystems.

Nuclear power is a dead industry that will revive

Expect a huge (reluctant) rethink about nuclear power which is the only technology with enough capacity to produce unlimited energy with zero carbon emissions. Expect suggestions by 2010 that nuclear power could be used to trap carbon, removing it from the air. But feelings about nuclear power could change in a single day following another nuclear disaster like Chernobyl.

A graph of new nuclear power station starts show that after peaking in the late 1980s they then dropped to almost zero. What that means is that by 2030, on current trends, there will hardly be an active nuclear reactor left for industrial power generation. Expect to see another Chernobyl-type nuclear disaster sometime over the first three decades of the twenty-first century as all these stations age and become less reliable. Such an event will be likely to add strength to the anti-nuclear activist movement. Also expect to see growing concern about what to do with all the dangerous waste. One of the biggest nuclear-related industries in the decades to come will be disposal and dumping.

Nuclear hazards will worry third millennialists, who will be often reminded that plutonium is 30,000 times as dangerous as cyanide, with just one particle capable of causing cancer if it enters the lungs. Despite this, pressures to reduce carbon use will make nuclear energy increasingly attractive. Uranium accounts for only 2–3 per cent of the total cost of nuclear power, offering huge room for inflation of the raw material price, with minimal impact on energy costs. If the price is right it becomes viable to mine very low-grade ores such as granite, from which we will find supplies to last us millions of years. Expect a wave of new nuclear reactor contracts as existing nuclear powers copy the example of France, where 70 per cent of electricity is produced by fission reactions.

Expect several other nations to succeed in joining the nuclear club, despite concerns, particularly in the US, that such capabilities will pose a threat to other nations.

Cold fusion offers future generations the hope of almost unlimited power from sea water and lithium, with very little risk of radioactive leakage and waste compared with traditional nuclear energy production. The amount of lithium in a mobile phone battery would be enough to power an average home for two years, using a deuterium-tritium fusion reaction at very high temperatures. Expect many billions of dollars of research into cold fusion, after a decade of scientific muddle. It is likely that the first cold fusion reactor will be in operation by 2035 and the first commercial power plant could be working by 2050. The US, EU, Japan, China, Russia and South Korea are investing $5.5 billion to build the first prototype in France.

These experiments will renew the nuclear controversy in an increasingly energy-hungry world. Such technology remains speculative, but if even a fraction of the world's $1 trillion a year of military spending were directed to fast-tracking development, it will make radical new discoveries far more likely.

Co-generation of electricity

A huge, wasted by-product of electricity generation is heat, which is particularly inefficient when you consider that electricity itself is often used to generate heat. Expect to see many more small-scale generators, supplying heat to large buildings or housing estates as well as electricity, some of which will be surplus to need and sold to the national grid at prices which undercut big power stations.

Growing worries about electromagnetic fields and noise

Noise is a pollutant and anti-noise devices will be developed further. Anti-noise reproduces the exact opposite of every sound wave to wipe out sound. Expect anti-noise technology as standard inside cars and aircraft, and in homes near noisy sites.

Recycling a way of life

Every year more treaties on the environment are signed – there are over 100 to date, and they are generally effective. For example, CFC production has all but ceased following global agreement to protect the ozone layer. And recycling has become a way of life in many countries, so that many newspapers now boast that over 40 per cent of the paper they use for printing is recycled.

Expect recycling to become a specialised multibillion dollar industry assisted by subsidies and public goodwill. There will be a proliferation of waste sorting in many countries along with glass, plastic, cardboard, steel, aluminium and newsprint containers in car parks and shopping areas. Domestic refuse collection will become a new technology area with the packing and sorting of different waste types. Expect car-breaker's yards to become total recovery areas, with regulations in many countries demanding zero waste. Entire cars can be turned into granules of 18 different materials which are separated automatically.

Expect growth of reverse exports, using empty shipping containers from countries like India and China to send back waste for recycling. By 2006, more than 33 per cent of UK's recycled waste paper and plastics was being exported 8,000 miles to China – 200,000 tonnes of plastic rubbish, and 500,000 tonnes of paper and cardboard. With landfill disposal costs rising in the EU, exporting freight will be an increasingly profitable business. Expect other new kinds of recycled exports. Three million old cars could go each year to China in empty containers for local repair and resale.

Waste disposal companies will be popular with 'ethical' investment funds and will be profitable, mainly because of millions of free hours of labour provided by a willing population, who will clean, sort and carry billions of items every year, 'doing their bit' for the environment.

War and the environment

The trouble is that conflicts drive massive holes in all environmental programmes, as seen in the Kuwait and Iraq wars. Not only was there catastrophic environmental pollution through the bombing and burning of oil installations, but also continued environmental damage after the war ended.

THE GENETIC REVOLUTION

Another far-reaching issue is biotechnology. We are going to hear a lot more about genes in the future. We think of the digital revolution as highly significant but biotech is in many ways far more important. Digital technology may alter the way we live but biotech has the power to alter the very basis of life on earth. It is also a very efficient method of producing highly complex substances, whether biological compounds, medication or chemicals for manufacturing. As we have seen, health is one of the biggest areas of spending in developed countries, accounting for up to 20 per cent of GDP, and genetics will dominate health. In comparison nanotechnology will be disappointing in health care, except in surface coatings.

The genetic revolution could produce a rapid increase in life expectancy. As we have seen, leading biotech researchers believe we will be able to slow the biological clock. This has already been seen, for example, in nematode worms, who live twice as long when the DAF 2 gene is turned off. (For more on anti-ageing research see pages 111–12.)

Cut and splice

We now have the technology to take genes from any organism and put them into another – just to see what happens. Human genes have been added to mice, cows, sheep, rabbits, rats and fish, to name just a few. The Human Genome Project has already mapped in detail the entire human genetic code. The result will allow new tests for many of the 6,000 genetic diseases and thousands of others where genes are an important co-factor.

Individuals will find gene screening becomes a routine part of IVF embryo screening, life insurance and pension assessment, while some companies will try to screen the genes of certain job applicants. For example, there is a gene that makes it more likely that workers will develop lung disease if exposed to high levels of dust in the air. Far cheaper to test and eliminate carriers than to clean up the factory.

Low-cost machines already exist which are able to read in theory the entire genome of a human being in an hour, so it can be compared with similar patterns in other people in order to make predictions. In 1990, it was only possible to read 200 base pairs a day (base units of genetic code) but by 2005, machines were already reading 30 million base pairs a second using special florescent tags and laser beams to create unique bar codes for gene sequences.

A mouse has been born with 100 human genes (around 0.1 per cent of the human genome), while herds of humanised pigs have been created to provide humans with new hearts or other organs – probably unsafe due to the risks of transferring pig viruses to humans. Adult stem cells from bone marrow have already been used to create liver, kidney, brain and other cells. Similar work is being done using embryo stem cells – far more controversial. Expect adult stem cell technology to provide a miracle for those with diabetes. Replacement cartilage will produce perfect repairs in arthritis sufferers; scientists have already made perfect tiny human kidneys, by implanting primitive cells from 6–8 week old foetuses into mice. If they had used pigs, the result could have been a transplantable organ, but this would have raised many ethical questions.

Scorpion poison genes have been added to cabbages to kill caterpillars – but what might they do to people? Potatoes have been made with an insecticide gene from a soil microbe – immune to Colorado beetle. New kinds of maize and other crops are on sale, some producing fungicide or insecticide in their own sap. These 'green' crops need no sprays, but are they green inside? Then there are non-bruising tomatoes and bananas which will soon contain vaccines or other medical products.

Genetic prophecy
Ninety-nine per cent of all genes are the same in all people. That means all human differences are explained by the remainder.

Expect major efforts to match differences in these genes to illness, personality, intelligence and other factors.

Genes have already been linked to speech, memory, criminality, depression and obesity. For example, low Monoamine Oxidase A, activity on the X-chromosome is often found in people who are violent or anti-social; 33 per cent of all men have this gene. A study in New Zealand found that 44 per cent of all violent offences were committed by just 12 per cent of men in the country – all of whom had the gene as well as a history of abuse as a child.

Green products growing fast

Genetically modified crops are now becoming an accepted part of normal diet in the US, but expect consumer resistance to continue in the European Union.

Expect gene research to produce ultra-fast growing trees that cannot reproduce except by cuttings taken in a nursery. They will be one of many innovations to help meet some of the challenges of rising carbon dioxide. The ideal tree for growth and utility will have dark green, dense foliage on very short thin branches (less waste) and a tall straight trunk. Such forests will be very similar to fir forests today. No chance of any vegetation beneath – or wildlife.

Expect ultra-slow growing hedges and other plants that can be triggered into normal growth by the addition of special fertilisers when required, saving gardeners the hassle of trimming or pruning. Expect species recovery programmes in zoos for extinct animals, or for rare animals in captivity who will not breed. Original genes from all kinds of sources will be mixed where necessary with those from similar species to recover as much as possible of the original. Sources will include frozen tissue samples and cell cultures.

Also expect to see new smart drugs in widespread use by 2020, some produced by genetic engineering, that hold the promise of enhancing brain function, memory and processing speed. Such drugs are already in human trials and some studies show extraordinary improvements. Deprenyl is an example, not only possibly helping those with Alzheimer's disease but also extending the lifespan of rats by up to 40 per cent.

Expect to see abuse of such drugs by students working for exams and others under creative pressure, in much the same way as anabolic steroids are abused by athletes. Some reports suggest that anywhere between 3 per cent and 30 per cent of students in some US campuses are already taking Ritalin or Adderall in the hope of improving memory and exam performance. These medications are presecribed for Attention Deficit Disorder but are freely available in the same way as illegal drugs.

Expect the rapid adaptation of many kinds of wildlife to the megacity, including the emergence of new super-rats as large as small cats. However, these will be part of a process of natural selection, not the result of laboratory experiments. Designer animals are already here. Over half a million mutants were made in UK laboratories alone during 2005–06, each of which was a unique mix of two, three or more different species, for example transgenic sheep programmed to produce human substances in their milk. Next will be attempts to humanise cows to produce low-fat milk. The ultimate goal will be cows that produce human breast milk.

It all raises huge questions of safety and ethics – including issues of animal welfare. For example, one set of humanised pigs grew fast, with low-fat meat, but were blind, impotent and suffered from severe arthritis, so that they could hardly stand. Some people will refuse to eat humanised animals, others will be unhappy about culling them for organs. Genetic engineering poses profoundly challenging, unanswered questions.

Biotech industry blows up and settles down

Most smaller biotech companies will struggle to justify the huge investments, with false hopes raised by sensational headlines. Many will fold, merge or be taken over by traditional drug companies anxious to 'buy in' expertise, while others will survive only as subcontractors. Nevertheless, huge fortunes will reward companies that establish unique biotech products with a clear application to health, industry or food production. Expect some spectacular successes. Any optimism must be tempered by the fact that, as we have seen, new licensed drugs cost $1 billion to develop over 15 years to market, only 20 per cent of all drug trials result in marketable products, and gene therapy can have serious side effects resulting in lawsuits.

Human cloning

Animal cloning has been possible for a long time, first conducted in frogs in the 1950s. Mammal cloning is relatively recent. One method is artificial twinning: up to 128 identikit rabbits can be produced in one go this way, but not without risk. When the technique was tried on cows the calves had to be delivered by caesarean section because they grew to twice their normal size before birth.

Twinning is easy: just get a ball of cells shortly after an egg is fertilised and use a probe to separate them. If you do this early enough you find that each separated cell goes on to produce a complete new animal. Most mammals have been cloned this way. Scientists claimed (as they always do) that this would never work in humans. What nonsense: with 2,000 pairs of identical twins born every day worldwide it was clear that such cloning would have the potential to work extremely well in humans.

Dr Jerry Hall in Washington announced in 1993 that he too had succeeded in cloning human embryos by twinning. Then one leading expert on ethics in Britain said that cloning for spares could be quite a good idea, so long as the foetus was culled at an early enough stage. This amoral stance was just an example of what was to come.

More human clones

Then came Dolly: a cloned sheep made using a very different technique. Genes from an adult sheep cell were combined with an unfertilised sheep's egg. The result was the birth of a lamb that was an identical twin of the adult. Some scientists are saying they have already created viable cloned human embryos (in most cases for medical research). Births are only a matter of time, and may already have taken place, if current claims are to be believed.

Market for clones

There is certainly a big market. I have a constant stream of enquiries to my website from people asking me if they can be cloned even though I am strongly against it. 'Diane' told me that she wanted to clone her dad who was dying, offering her own womb as a surrogate: 'I intend to see that he goes on in this world.' She wanted to give birth to her own father's twin.

Another woman suffering from infertility wanted to use her own cells to make a baby rather than use donated sperm and eggs. A student wrote that 'it would be so neat' to be cloned. However, verified claims of birth of the first clones are likely to cause considerable unease among those who already feel that reproductive science is drifting out of control.

Cloning will be very popular among some groups with wealth: the ultimate in pedigree children. Supermodels could make a lot of money selling cells from their bodies to cloning merchants, who would offer childless couples the child of their dreams by creating a clone and then implanting it in a surrogate. In future humanised apes could be used as surrogates. Scientists are already able to sustain a foetus in late development inside a completely artificial womb, but hiring women in poor nations will cost less.

At a day-to-day level, cloning technology will mean that infertile couples can have a twin of the father or mother as their newborn baby, or that parents can 'recreate' a dead child, or that a clone can be created to assist in tissue donation for the existing child or adult. These will be the justifications used for pursuing the technology. However, there are enormous safety and psychological risks for the child. Even if the cloned child is healthy, what will be the emotional impact of growing up knowing that you are your mother's or father's twin? What about the pressures from a parent to 'relive' their own genetic potential – for example, to see how musical he or she might have been if given music lessons?

Designer babies

We already have the technology to make children to order, using the same technology as tried in animals. Physical and mental perfection is a dream for many. For those whose genes are already fixed, plastic surgery will continue to offer remarkable remoulding of faces, ears, necks, breasts, buttocks and thighs and will become increasingly common as a death-defying generation attempts to stop the ageing process.

Cloning raises interesting possibilities: women no longer need men and could produce an entirely female society. So, for example, a single woman, using her own egg and a skin cell, could give birth to her own twin, and in due course that twin could clone herself, with the process repeated through many totally female generations. Or we could create an entirely male society, once animals have been humanised sufficiently to carry humans in their wombs.

Cloning the dead will also be possible. Dolly was cloned using frozen cells, so any human could in theory be recovered from the grave as a baby so long as cells had been suitably frozen before death or shortly after. Living cells can be found in the human body undamaged for up to a week, so cell removal could be delayed for some time after death. Another way to clone the dead is from cells grown in culture rather than frozen. Such cultures can be maintained indefinitely. This means that a child dying of cancer could be 'recovered', allowing parents to give birth to an identical twin.

Of course the easiest way to alter the human race is the oldest method of all: mass sterilisation or genocide of the undesirable. Some 60,000 forced sterilisations of women with 'unwanted mental and physical characteristics' were carried out in Sweden from 1935 to 1976, with similar practices on a smaller scale in Denmark, Norway, Finland and Switzerland. Meanwhile 17 per cent of the entire world's population is already banned by law from having more than one child if the state decides that their genes are not worth reproducing – in China. Far less draconian but just as significant will be the widespread testing and destruction of embryos or foetuses because their parents decide that their genes are 'sub-optimal'. Such testing is already routine in IVF clinics.

So what does all this mean for the longer-term future? The third millennium will see human beings begin to take over life itself, redesigning plants, trees, vegetables, animals and even themselves. Every day new genes are discovered and more is understood about what each does. By 2015 we will have a very good idea about what will happen if a number of different types of genes are switched off and on. The twenty-first century will be known as the age of the gene.

Genes are the ultimate in miniaturisation. A conventional laboratory to make insulin would occupy a vast area and cost several billion to construct, needing huge numbers of staff. Yet that entire production unit can be compressed into not just the size of a house, not just one room, not merely a single flask or test-tube, but into the cytoplasm of a single living cell.

Once a single bacterium receives the human gene for insulin, it carries on dividing and growing forever, eating food and making insulin. Insulin production becomes as simple as brewing beer, except that we are using bacteria instead of yeast and the product is insulin instead of alcohol. Every complex chemical product you can think of will be made by gene technology in brewing vats. Medicines, vaccines, precursors of new plastics, new fuels – whatever. More complex substances can be made in genetically engineered insects or in the milk of mammals such as cows and sheep.

Limb and organ regeneration

Expect progress in regeneration of fingers, hands, feet, arms and legs by 2035. There are well documented cases of children regrowing finger tips after amputation. The Pentagon has been quietly funding research into regeneration for years, hoping to find new ways to help amputees. Salamanders are able to regrow entire legs using stem cells in the stump which are activated as in children by trauma. Scientists are searching for the right chemical triggers to stimulate the process, without at the same time risking a cancerous overgrowth.

Whole new organs could in theory be made inside humanoid bodies with heart, lungs, liver and kidneys, or inside the bodies of growing animals of suitable size. Teeth and kidneys have already been grown from one species inside the body of another. In future we will have the capability to make human beings which are growing but technically dead because they have no brain, possibly no arms or legs, created solely as organ factories. Expect many ethical questions about gene technology to be dominated by the 'yuk' factor, which will determine not whether something is right (which for many people will be too confusing to think about) but merely whether it is acceptable to the majority.

Biocomputers

Biotech will be used in new generations of intelligent machines and computer chips will be routinely connected to living tissue. Many successful experiments have already grown brain cells onto the surface of chips, and chips have been successful fused with the brains of paralysed adult humans so they can control machines by thought. People with nerve damage will have computer-enhanced muscle control, or improved sight or hearing.

Humonkeys

It will not be long before humonkeys have been made. Perhaps such embryos already exist. The technology is proven. Hybrids are easy to create. Take geep for example, a combination of sheep and goat, made by rolling together two balls of cells from two different embryos shortly after fertilisation.

But how many human genes does an animal have to have to gain human rights? A lawyer friend of mine says that the critical factor would be a creature with more than 50 per cent human genes, but that is incorrect. We differ genetically from monkeys by less than 2 per cent and from amoeba by around 14 per cent. So if you are adding 1 per cent of human genes to a monkey cell from which a clone will be made you had better watch out. A mere 0.3 per cent of human genes put into a monkey could be more than enough to give the monkey speech.

Can monkeys go to heaven?

Theologians, philosophers and lawyers need to think now what their reaction will be when such a hybrid is displayed to the world, as it most surely will be. Is it a monster to be destroyed? Does it have a human right to life? Can it be eaten? Is it morally

responsible before a court of law? Can it be tried for murder?
Is it allowed to marry and procreate with 'normal humans' or
to mate with other animals? Is it in need of salvation? Does it
have a soul?

And long before the headline proclaiming its existence reaches
us we will find religious leaders are being confronted by new forces,
which will be added to by the animal rights movement as it seeks to
blur the ethical distinction between animals and humans. It could
all produce a crisis of faith for many, brought up on the traditional
teaching that humans have been created 'in God's image'. So what
is that image? Are monkeys 98 per cent of the image of God? Is
all life a manifestation of the image of God to some degree or
another?

These questions may hit us far sooner than we think. Historically a key trend can be seen when it comes to biotech: unlike
the digital revolution, where industry experts hype the next steps
and where most people have some understanding of the speed
of progress, biotech is often deliberately downplayed by those
who know most. The atmosphere is commonly one of secrecy and
flat denial, for one reason: fear. Computers raise no great moral
challenge and do not threaten the safety of life on earth. Biotech
does. Few health and safety issues are raised by computer production and no ethical issues, yet such things happen every day in
biotech.

Computer developers are unhindered in their work. They
can enjoy the intellectual challenge of pushing technology to
the limits without worrying about prosecution or being slammed
in the media. Biotech specialists are quite different. Many are
acutely sensitive to the delicate nature of their work. They fear
uninformed public reaction and shun the limelight. They keep
quiet about experiments and sometimes (in my experience) do
not even publish at all. Ethical committees tend to be dominated
by those in the industry who are biased towards less regulation
rather than more.

Germ warfare

We now have the technology to create highly dangerous human viruses for research into disease or for use in war. By 2015 we could have the capability to create viruses which selectively target specific racial groups. This high-tech ethnic cleansing technology will cause international outrage but will be difficult to stop. The poor man's ethnic cleansing machine could be a child vaccination programme, which among other things contains a virus with an outside coating similar to that of human sperm. The result would be antibody formation against sperm, and infertility in a future generation of men. Expect intense efforts to reduce or stop global biotech warfare research, as part of a wider fear about weapons of mass destruction falling into the hands of militant extremist groups.

Islam takes a stand

Four hundred Muslim intellectuals gathered recently at Jakarta. In a joint statement they declared that revolutionary changes in science and technology had 'reduced man to a material being that is spiritually bankrupt, morally unbound'.

This anti-science feeling is general and widespread. Of British adults, 83 per cent say that modern science creates as many problems as it solves. Yet 81 per cent also think we are fortunate to live in an age when scientific development is proceeding at such a pace. The logical consequence of the first finding is that spending on science does not improve quality of life any more than it damages it. What, then, is the point of previously much-worshipped scientific progress? This is a fundamental shift from mid to late twentieth century optimism, to the first signs of a third millennial rejection of the logical and rational.

Thus scientists are increasingly a race apart, drawn into their own world by the eccentric belief that science means benefit to people. Many scientists are baffled, upset and perplexed by what they see as the negative irrationality of so many ignorant and prejudiced people who would want to wreck their work, given half a chance.

Scientists working in biotech, reproduction or other areas of life sciences already find themselves increasingly on the defensive, retreating into the comfort of professional forums and conferences, bastions of intellectual openness and inquiry. This is why so few research scientists today are comfortable with ethical committees controlled by lay people who 'just don't understand'. The issue of using live animals in medical research is an example where public discussion has become difficult, with scientists in fear of their own safety.

Who owns a species?

The world will soon have to face more big questions arising from biotech. Is it right to allow a company to own an entire species? Is it right to create a species which by its genes is guaranteed to suffer? Both questions have been raised by the creation of the oncomouse, designed to develop fatal cancer 90 days after birth. The oncomouse was created in America for the testing of cancer treatments and is commercially owned, protected by patent.

Patents on human genes

Is it right for companies to own human genes? A man in the US developed cancer and gave cells for research. The genes were used to develop a diagnostic test and the process was patented. He was furious. 'I own my own genes,' he said. He challenged the company and fought them all the way to the Supreme Court. He lost his case. Humans no longer have the right to own their own genes in the US.

We urgently need gene technology to feed the world and prevent disease – but we do need to ask what kind of world we are creating, now we have the ability to alter the very basis of life itself.

ANOTHER 'BIG IDEA'

Clusters of single issues do not make a political creed. The vacuum in politics will remain. Ever since communism collapsed there has been a void. Communism defined everything. So long as the

Eastern bloc remained, the rest of the political framework made sense. But where are idealism and energy in political life today? And in the depths of this empty chasm we will see new things emerge.

Lesson from communism

Karl Marx was born in Prussia in 1818 and died in London in 1883. He wrote *The Communist Manifesto* in 1847, and it was published in 1848. Marx took ideas and applied them in a programme for the whole of humankind. He was a product of his time: a protester against the Industrial Revolution, which placed so much wealth and power in the hands of so few, enslaving millions in primitive working conditions.

Communism was originally driven by a cluster of single issues, such as over-industrialisation, worker control, equality of wealth. Yet the communist revolution only began more than 50 years later. Lenin was born in 1870 and formulated his own version of Marxist thinking in the early years of the twentieth century, publishing *What is to be Done?* in 1902. The 'Big Idea' came after the death of the original thinker.

Tomorrow's 'Big Idea'

Expect to see another 'Big Idea' emerge (or several conflicting ones), radically different from any large-scale political system seen in the twentieth century. This new 'ism' will feed on the stored-up energy and desire for change created by four twentieth-century revolutions: Information, Communication, Automation and Globalisation. The longer the delay in its coming, the longer and deeper the vacuum will have become and the greater the speed with which it is likely to grip the earth. The four twentieth-century revolutions themselves will guarantee that when the new 'Big Idea' arrives, it will impact on politics and government action at tremendous speed. Expect that a Big Idea may grow out of Islamic or Christian activism but be separate from mainstream traditions.

What will be this new 'Big Idea'?

Listen to the voices of single-issue activists today and you begin to get an idea of some of the elements that will be swept up in the 'Big Idea'. It is likely to be:

◆ driven out of a set of writings
◆ backed by a charismatic personality or personalities
◆ able to catch the popular mood
◆ deeply satisfying to millions who have felt lacking in direction
◆ the trigger of intense passion
◆ capable of mobilising communities, nations and armies
◆ the spirit of the new age in the third millennium
◆ radically different from the old left/right
◆ a mass movement hard to analyse or describe
◆ constantly adapting and reinterpreting
◆ rapidly changing
◆ long lasting in its effects
◆ highly confusing to old 'logic' politicians.

What happens if you roll post-modernism, new-age intuition and organised religion together – all of which are growing globally? You get the beginnings of a new world order. Global government for a global village. In this ever-shrinking global village where sovereign states are weakened by global forces, it is unthinkable that traditional governments will survive.

. . . .
CHALLENGES TO MANAGEMENT
. . . .

Ready for reaction against twentieth-century values

◆ How ready are you for a significant third millennial shift in market 'culture', in the way people think and behave – for example the possibility that sun-soaked holidays may go out of fashion?

Loss of government power

- ◆ Are you as well 'in' with the EU in Brussels as you have always been with New York, Washington, Bonn, London or Paris? Does your company influence EU policy formation or similar regional trading blocs elsewhere?
- ◆ Are you integrated into other networks such as the World Trade Organisation or United Nations?

Influence of non-profit organisations

- ◆ Are you ready for non-profit organisations to sweep beneath you with lower prices, no shareholder dividends to find and with voluntary sector subsidies, including tax advantages?
- ◆ Are you prepared for the whole concept of 'reasonable profit' to become high profile, with large profits increasingly labelled as anti-social?
- ◆ Does your company have an adequate community action programme to help offset some of these pressures?

Bribery and corruption

- ◆ What are the official and unofficial lines regarding the paying of bribes or backhanders to get things moving in countries where such practices are considered normal?
- ◆ Do all staff adhere to your policy?
- ◆ Does the policy or practice need review in the light of the rapidly changing climate of public opinion in wealthy nations?
- ◆ Are you prepared for current practice to be mercilessly exposed by competitors or others in the global media?

Single-issue activism

- ◆ Do you have an effective way of monitoring single issues relating to your work?
- ◆ What early warning system do you have in place?
- ◆ Do you have positional statements worked out which can be released at very short notice on a wide range of single-issue time-bombs, any of which could attract overwhelmingly negative public attention at very short notice?
- ◆ Do you have a think-tank which applies up-and-coming activist issues to current corporate activity?

- Do you have a rapid-response media unit, able to make an instant, confident, well-considered response to a breaking news story, within 10–20 minutes, 24 hours a day, representing the whole company in an authoritative way?
- Have you ever carried out a 'practice run' responding to a major story?
- When did you last do so?

Single issues into corporate policies

- Have single issues been adequately reflected in corporate policy, e.g. energy use, waste recycling, environmental degradation, smoking, ageism, racism, sexual harassment, ethical investment, genetic screening, animal rights?

PERSONAL CHALLENGES

Single issues

- What single issues are most important to you?
- What steps can you take as an individual to pursue that agenda at home or work, e.g. care for the environment?
- What steps can you take to recycle waste?
- What steps can you take to make your lifestyle less car-dependent?

Genetic revolution

- If your insurance company insists on gene screening, are you sure that you want the information for yourself?
- How will the knowledge affect your attitude to life?
- Do you want to eat genetically modified food?
- If not, are you looking out for labels – where they exist?

CHAPTER 6

Ethical

A new morality

We have seen a world that is increasingly Fast, Urban, Tribal, Universal and Radical – but what does all this do to people? Is this really the kind of world we want to live in? And how do we decide what is right and wrong? As we have seen, whenever we think about future trends we are forced to consider these 'softer' issues again in the light of them.

THE FINAL FACE OF THE FUTURE IS ETHICAL

The final face of the future therefore is ethical: to do with who we are and what we want to be, how we should behave, our values and beliefs. In some ways this face is the most important. It is central to our being. It is the answer to many concerns about the future raised in earlier chapters. It is the balance to all that has gone before. Our values carry us through times of tremendous change when the whole world appears to be endlessly spinning. They provide context and meaning.

Our values are the bedrock of an urbanised society, providing answers to the problems of social decay, relationship breakdown and addiction. These same values can turn the vicious tribalism of civil war and other conflicts into forces for good, for stability, for belonging. Values provide the framework for constructive globalis-ation, for new political thinking and for new scientific horizons. Values are the basis for all individual life and for all community. Without personal values we become robotic, instinctive creatures with no sense of meaning, purpose, direction or morality. Without

common values social interaction, community life, communication and commercial activity become all but impossible. Values
define us, they provide the framework by which society operates.
Personal and community values often differ from corporate or
globalised values, which are often driven by a far narrower agenda
such as return on capital or corporate survival. Common values
are likely to be derived from belief about our place in the universe,
our origin and destiny, from philosophical or religious roots. And
these values are often forged through defining moments.

Defining moments

Defining moments are points of no return in history: 'Never again'.
They happen when communities or nations react to a trauma.
Their effect lasts a generation. They define the ethical values of
that generation. With the increasing sophistication of communications and greater access to traumatic news events, there will be
more and more defining moments. Our new ethical code will be
based on lessons learned from them.

The Second World War was a defining moment. Never again
must there be a world war. Never again must we see a nuclear
weapon exploded in anger. Never again must we see millions of
people herded into death camps. It led to the birth of the European
Union, as a grand scheme to make a European war less likely.

The Vietnam War was also a defining moment. Around 50,000
US citizens were killed. A generation later the shadow of Vietnam
still hangs over every American foreign policy decision.

The terrorist attacks on the Pentagon and World Trade Center
twin towers on 11 September 2001 was another defining moment,
not just for America, but for many other nations. A defining
moment was the global unity in the UN about the desirability of
disarming Saddam Hussein's Iraq, and the profound disagree-
ment about how and when it should be done. Yet another was the
collapse of Enron and the epidemic of corporate scandals, leading
to a complete rethink about corporate governance, corporate social
responsibility, share options, excessive remuneration packages,
conflicts of interest, transparency, trust and so on. Another was
SARS, the emergence of bird flu and other mutant viruses as global

threats. A further example was hurricane Katrina and the destruction of New Orleans – blamed by many on global warming.

Laws define ethics

The passing of a law can also become a 'defining moment' and define ethics, as well as being an expression of them. For a world which has largely rejected absolutes, laws are the way we make sense of the grey area in between. Yet the legal system itself, in some nations, is a mess – particularly in the US.

Compliance is dead except as a defensive strategy

The cost of complying with regulations has rocketed for larger companies following Enron and other scandals with a vast number of new regulations including Sarbanes-Oxley and Basel II. However, compliance will be useless in future except as a defensive strategy to keep directors out of prison. Compliance will not protect your job or your brand from attack, in a world where public mood changes yet again in response to the latest scandal.

For example, bribery used to be perfectly within the law in some EU nations – with bribes set against tax as a legitimate business expense. The more you bribed, the more the government rewarded you. But in today's world, that kind of past government support is no defence. It is no good appearing in a CNN interview and pleading that although you personally handed over multi-million dollar bribes in Asia or Africa to get a deal, it was legal, tax-deductible and therefore morally right. It would be wise not to argue on live TV that anti-bribery laws should be revoked. But if executives say they support anti-bribery legislation, they risk being judged by their own values for their own past actions.

This means we have to go far beyond mere compliance, seeing it as the barest minimum and an unsafe guide for future conduct, based as it is on past legislation, which in turn is a response to old history. We have to anticipate how public mood could change and build business on foundational values which are likely to be more enduring, setting a standard for an entire industry to follow and in this way strengthening values associated with the brand. Thus

going beyond compliance is a strategy that will be closely linked
to cause-related marketing. Differentiate yourself on values when
price and quality converge (page 212).

US legal suits gone mad

Expect a crisis in the US legal system. Comprehensive reforms will
be under way by 2010. Every aspect of US life involves lawyers in a
way which amuses and shocks those in other nations. The number
of lawsuits has tripled in 30 years. Laws cost money, as do civil
actions. The US will price itself out of the world market in key
industries without radical changes.

Take employment law. Why bother to base a business in the
US if it means risking expensive litigation? Already five out of six
corporate executives say that fear of lawsuits increasingly affects
their decisions. Group cases bring big rewards for law firms. When
Publix, an employee-owned supermarket chain, settled a sex-
discrimination class action on behalf of 140,000 employees for
$81.5 million, the legal firm made $18 million.

Expect more mediation and arbitration, price wars, competition from non-lawyers for some services, judges rather than
juries setting damages and new limits on civil actions. However,
consumer activism will make it likely that other nations will move
closer to the US system while the US carves out reforms.

Single issues and ethics go hand in hand

Single issues define the problem, but ethics tell you what position
to take. Expect more fierce debates and soul-searching over such
issues as arms sales, as attempts are made to define exactly what
arms are. Do you include machine tools used to make arms, for
example? A globalised company can find itself with several conflicting positions on such an issue: shareholder values, public perceptions in manufacturing and buying nations and the opinions of
company employees. There may also be a variety of government
attitudes, even within the same decade – ranging from approval, to
turning a blind eye to outright opposition and public prosecution.

Political correctness and thought control

Political correctness will grow in power in the next three decades
as single-issue groups attempt to control the words we use. It is
hard to express certain ideas if many words are banned. 'Mentally
challenged' instead of 'mentally handicapped'. 'Senior citizens'
instead of the elderly or retired. 'Visually impaired' instead of
blind. There will be increasing conflicts between those campaigning against discrimination, who want everyone to be seen as the
same, and other activists who want to draw maximum attention
and sympathy to particular groups for fundraising purposes.

Countless charities today are faced with a stark choice: be
politically correct and broke or sensationally incorrect and full of
funds. So a cancer charity, to be politically correct, should refer
to 'people with cancer', rather than to 'cancer sufferers', because
the latter implies that all people with cancer suffer. Yet suffering is
what triggers sympathy, and more money from research.

Defending civil liberties

In many countries which pride themselves on human rights and
civil liberties, people today can have their homes broken into by the
police or secret service, their telephone tapped and bedroom or
office bugged, simply because a politician or senior policeman says it
should be done. No warrant is needed in many countries: the police
can hold you for weeks or months without warrant or explanation,
possibly using interrogation methods that many would describe as
torture. You can be arrested for joining a peaceful demonstration.
If you are silent on arrest a jury may be invited to conclude that you
had something to hide. You have no right to information the government holds about you. Britain, the US and many other nations may
have a benign democracy, but in a country with a malignant dictator
laws like these are likely to be thoroughly oppressive.

Expect to see civil liberties on the agenda of activist groups in
most nations of the world, especially as online wireless technology
becomes even more powerful in offering ways to track people.
Human rights will continue to be a major issue, especially in the
negotiation of trade agreements with developing countries. There
will be many agonies of conscience over whether a government

should buy or sell in major contracts with 'odious' regimes – and debates on how such things should be determined.

Expect the US to challenge countries like China over human rights but for this to continue to fall on deaf ears. China's government believes the greatest human right is to be able to eat food rather than starve. It believes it is being successful in giving its citizens a reasonable standard of living, and as the country evolves it is becoming more and more open to the rest of the world.

Human rights and human responsibilities

British consumers now spend more on electrical goods and services than on cigarettes and alcohol – more than £30 billion, increasing by more than 10 per cent a year. Expect to hear much more about human responsibilities, with responsibilities and rights becoming equal pillars of global codes of ethics. The Universal Declaration of Human Rights was a product of the Second World War, and was set out in 1948. Expect a similar Declaration of Human Responsibilities. The InterAction Council, a group of international statesmen committed to global responsibility, said recently: 'In a world transformed by globalisation, common ethical standards for living together have become an imperative, not only for individual behaviour but also for corporations, political authorities and nations.'

A new motivation

While many households with children struggle to survive, with both parents out at work and adults labouring almost until the day they die, growing numbers in many other countries have become so well off that they no longer need to work to eat and expect more than money for the work they do. Of 30–40 year olds in the UK, 90 per cent want to leave conventional business jobs, 90 per cent are looking for higher purpose at work, and 59 per cent see no meaningful purpose in their work or their organisation. Similar patterns are being seen in many other wealthy nations. This adds up to a motivational crisis which will damage every business that fails to address it. What is the point of a strategy if no one cares?

In many developed nations, work–life balance is now the number one or number two career priority. This is a huge shift in attitudes from the 1980s. An example was the decision by one of America's highest-flying women executives to quit her rumoured $2 million a year job as president and CEO of Pepsi to concentrate on being a mother – at the age of 43. Three years earlier the UK head of Coca-Cola had done the same. Fifty year olds are taking generous early retirement packages, and are taking on modestly rewarded charitable work. Many 40-year-old high fliers have made enough to stop working, if they slim down consumption and live in a smaller house. Downward mobility is increasingly common and will become more so. Fewer hours, less ambition, more personal rewards and new priorities, as seen in the boom of community volunteering. Expect a growing number of companies to promise a 'better work–life balance' as part of their job attractions in a bid to win the war for talent. A huge challenge will be delivering on the promise.

Reaction against speed and constant change

Speed and constant change will give added value to things that are unchanging and therefore by definition old. Antiques, listed buildings, preservation orders. Bits of towns will become islands of eternity to be maintained the same for ever, surrounded by whirlwinds of concrete new developments that are forever being pulled down. Ancient trees – or even those 50 years old – will acquire ever-increasing respect, together with unspoiled moorlands and woods. Old houses, more and more unsuited to an ultra-smart age of wired, intelligent, low-energy buildings, will continue to be popular, for those who can afford to run them and the cost of converting them to fit third millennial building regulations for heat loss and carbon-use reduction.

Building a better world – crisis of purpose

Building a better world will be a dominant theme in future: corporate citizenship and the need for workers to feel they are doing something worthwhile will attract huge attention. Many people are realising that there is more to life than selling. There is more to life than managing. There is more to life than working. In fact there is more to life than life itself. What will I leave when I die? How will my children remember me when I've gone? I was taking a seminar of senior executives of a major financial institution recently. There was a manager there from New York. 'I'm torn right now,' he said. 'I need to be at home with my 14-year-old son who's about to fail his math.'

He described how he argued with his son over work.

'You'll never get on if you don't learn your math.'

'Why should I?'

'You won't be successful.'

'Don't care.'

'You won't be able to get a great job like I have.'

'You can stuff the job. Look what it's done to Mum and to me. I don't want a job like that. I'd rather sweep the streets.'

The father was shocked, not only by his son's negative attitude to school, but by all the stored-up resentment his son felt over the times when Dad had left for work early, come home late, or been travelling yet again. This was a voice of a post-millennialist reacting against pre-millennial values, the belief that more means better and progress means money, and money means happiness. But it may not. Hardship carries misery, but so can wealth. Expect huge growth in research on human happiness and radical questions about values when the results confirm the truth. International research shows that happiness is strongly linked to some or all of the following: mid-range income, good friends, stable marriage or partnership, strong faith or spirituality, being an extrovert, liking your job, living in a stable democracy.

Relationships are all you have left

Agony columns are full of advice about how to have happy relationships. In a fractured, increasingly disordered and fast-moving world, long-term relationships are going to matter more. One sign of success for tomorrow will be to be living happily with the same person for a long time. It shows either that you made a great choice with your partner, or that you were a highly desirable mate to be able to attract such a remarkable partner, or that you are a great partner yourself. What's so smart about a string of failed marriages, shacked-up arrangements or temporary flings?

There is a fundamental human need for security, for some things at the root of our being that do not change. Most humans cannot cope with complete and continuous changes in all areas of their lives without becoming at risk of emotional disorder and inefficiency, as more and more resources are mopped up coping with everyday life. Change is a major cause of stress: whether moving house, job, having a child or getting married or divorced. Statistics show that married employees are healthier and often more successful, and so are their children. This kind of data will go on accumulating, bringing new social conventions.

Expect to see a whole new relationship industry move out of the agony columns and marriage guidance centres and into government- and company-sponsored support and advice schemes. A workforce with happy, stable relationships helps government and employers through increased productivity and lower social support costs.

The growth of volunteering

Expect further growth of volunteering in developed countries as more people discover new ways to make a difference and find personal purpose – 60 per cent of US citizens work for nothing, giving an average of 200 hours a year of their time. If each hour was costed at the average wage, the value of this gift would be the same as 4.5 per cent of GDP or 12 per cent of the Federal Budget. But if you include informal volunteering – for example, shopping for a sick neighbour – the percentages rise even higher. Similar statistics can be found in most EU countries and in many other parts of the world. We are hard-wired to be community citizens and you'll find a similar spirit in most people in the very poorest African villages or wealthiest Swiss towns.

The growth of large-scale philanthropy

Expect rapid growth in the number of high-net-worth individuals who make major financial gifts to create a better future. Not only are the numbers of super-wealthy growing rapidly in almost every nation, but so is their social sensitivity.

In 2006, the Bill Gates Foundation was almost doubled in size to over $80 billion with a $37 billion gift from a global investor, Warren Buffet. The foundation in that moment became as large as Disney or Honda in the traditions of Carnegie and Rockefeller. Expect many others to be encouraged by their examples. Much of this new effort will be directed at helping those in the poorest nations, particularly in Sub-Saharan Africa. Expect great challenges as these foundations attempt (and often fail) to spend vast amounts of new money wisely, without waste, avoiding corruption, directing resources to smaller groups who can have the greatest impact at lowest cost. Expect rapid growth of intermediaries: medium to large non-profit organisations which create clusters of small community-based organisations, which are presented to large donors. Expect a new emphasis on efficiency, outcomes, cost-benefit, measureable impact, as business disciplines begin to change philanthropy.

The level of humanitarian assistance to some emerging nations will be sufficient to cause a rise in the value of their currencies, creating difficulties for local businesses which depend on exports. The greater the aid, the harder it will be for some of these businesses to sell. This is yet another reason why we can expect huge investment in sustainable local businesses through micro-loan schemes and other social enterprise initiatives, aimed at sustainable community transformation.

THE STRUGGLE FOR BELIEFS

In the light of all we have seen, it is no surprise to find in the early stages of this new millennium an intense, growing hunger for spirituality. In the 1960s the great debate was between those who believed in God and those who were atheists. Atheism has all but died in many secularised Western countries. Now the great debate is not over whether you believe, but what or who you believe in and whether it has changed your life. In the midst of moral confusion, expect a growing hunger for certainty, conviction, ultimate values and authority. In an age of scepticism and cynicism, expect a growing interest in people whose lives seem to demonstrate deep sincerity, integrity, conviction, and whole-hearted commitment to a cause. That is why there has been a rise in fundamentalism of all kinds, a growth in the numbers of passionately devoted adherents to various religions. Part of this mass discovery of faiths has been the beginning of a new, third millennial morality.

Faith in anything, anyone. Faith that causes a peripheral member of the British royal family to crouch under a plastic pyramid because she believes it is a source of power. Faith that causes ordinary men and women to hug trees in local parks. Faith that causes intelligent people to study full-page spreads of personal advice based on the position of the stars. There is a small section of the Western world that will not make an important decision if Mars is wrongly aligned with Jupiter, whether it's to buy a house, sell shares or accept a new job. Faith is everywhere.

There has been a wholesale rejection of the scientific, logical, rational model of the world that reduces all existence to fixed, predetermined and mechanical systems. Thus doctors are having to struggle with a new generation of patients with serious illnesses who throw modern medicines away and opt instead for alternatives which many doctors regard as unproven, untested and with little or no scientific basis. The medicines they reject in favour of ancient remedies have often been through years of rigorous field tests in different countries with the cumulative experience of thousands of patient years.

More than 17 million people in Britain alone now use alternative medicines or therapies, aromatherapy and homeopathy being the most popular. So some third millennial patients have more confidence, when it comes to health, in the alternative lifestyle than in the scientifically proven. Expect laws to tighten in many nations, requiring companies to verify claims made for improvements in health. This will intensify a culture clash between those who feel that scientific methodology is not a valid test of 'whole person medicine', and those who insist on 'objective' scientific data. But even the most hardened physician accepts that faith in the doctor or the treatment is vital to success.

Studies show that if a doctor believes that the tablets he

prescribes are genuine painkillers, many patients will experience relief, even if the tablets contain no active ingredients. This 'placebo' effect is very powerful.

Growth of Islam and Christianity

The great world religions are continuing to grow rapidly. While the world population grows at 1.4 per cent a year, Islam has been growing at 2.2 per cent and has 1.3 billion adherents, representing 21 per cent of the world population. Christianity has also been spreading at 1.4 per cent a year, with 2 billion adherents and 32.5 per cent of the world population. Explosive growth is being seen in Africa, Asia and Latin America, with a rediscovery in the richest nations and a reassertion of the validity of the Christian faith at an intellectual level. Protestant churches are growing 3.5 per cent a year worldwide – pentecostal churches fastest of all.

Expect Christianity to grow fast in all former communist countries as well as in China, where 70 million have found faith since the 1950s despite severe persecution. In South Korea there is at least one church congregation with more than 1 million members. In Argentina over the past decade churches have sprung from nothing to number many thousands of people, and the same has been happening across most of Latin America. Africa has seen extraordinary growth in church attendance, which is now affecting politicians and governments. This renewal of spiritual energy will have a long-term impact which is already beginning, although we are in the very earliest stages. The global uprising of life-changing faith, which provokes passion and provides purpose, should not be underestimated. Faith will be a major force in shaping the values, emotions, policies and lifestyle choices of the future.

Expect divisions within each world religion between radicals who remain rooted in traditional teachings based on, for example, the Bible or the Koran, and those who feel that they have almost divine authority to accept or abandon whatever writings they like in the creation of their own personal spiritual journey, to interpret these writings in a highly idiosyncratic way.

This orthodox–liberal divide will deepen over issues like homosexual marriage, abortion, euthanasia and embryonic stem cell research. While liberal churches will argue that they are more attractive and culturally relevant in the US and Europe, expect most church growth there and in the rest of the world among Christian communities that adhere to traditional teachings and express strong spirituality. Just as we have seen radical Islamic movements, expect similar neo-puritan movements among younger Christians, campaigning aggressively against such things as alcohol and drug abuse, materialism, greed, abortion, promiscuity, adultery, same-sex unions, pornography and social justice.

Even in Britain, a country where public displays of religious fervour have tended to be frowned on, politicians in the last two elections have sought to outdo each other in public Christianness. Many made a point of announcing that they go to church and that their faith has led them directly to the party they now support. In the 1980s it would have earned them no favours to use such language, but now many politicians sense an electoral advantage through being seen to be sincerely Christian, in a world increasingly dominated by sleaze. This public identification with traditional Christian faith is very significant in an age when so many had written off the impact of the Church.

Politicians are populists and are experts at detecting shifts in public mood. They clearly sensed that the mood of the nation was changing, from collective scepticism about faith to a fresh hunger for it and genuine respect for those who had it.

The nation certainly has been shifting. Between 1994 and 2005 an estimated 1 million British adults, including myself, attended a 12-evening course (and most of them a residential weekend) introducing them to the basics of the Christian faith. These Alpha courses swept the country after being piloted in a large Anglican church in central London: Holy Trinity Brompton. Over the same period it was not uncommon to see up to 70,000 people gather in the open air in London to pray for the nation, walking through the streets with colourful banners as part of the March for Jesus. This London-led phenomenon quickly spread, with simultaneous annual marches happening in dozens of cities. On a single day around 12 million people marched and prayed together in over 100 nations across every time zone.

Then there are annual week-long residential Christian conferences, now attended in Britain by well over 250,000 people, who
spend millions each year to hear the best teachers and experience a
dynamic across the denominations that they can never find in their
own places of worship. All this is surprising to people who drive
past redundant church buildings, or wander into vast cavernous
churches containing just a tiny handful of the elderly. There is
still a demographic bulge, which means that while attendance is
growing strongly in the younger age groups it is not completely
offsetting a loss through death of a much older generation. But
something is changing.

Religious politics

Over the next decade expect to see growing political movements
powered by religion, for example Hindu fundamentalism in India
and Buddhist fundamentalism in Sri Lanka and farther east. It has
already been happening for a long time in the Middle East with
Islam. In 1980, Islam's fifteenth century heralded the Iranian revolution, Afghan religious leaders declared war on Russian infidels,
and religious extremists killed Anwar Sadat, president of Egypt.
The Islamic political movement will continue to grow in depth and
strength. Many Islamic activists have a powerful and understand-
able desire to be ruled by governments which follow the Koran's
rulings and standards. Theocracy has greater moral validity than
democracy to many people. Democracy can be seen as merely
the collective will of the apostate and immoral majority. Expect
therefore a strong political or governmental dimension to Islamic
activism, in contrast to Christian activism, which will tend to focus
on particular moral issues rather than on trying to impose an entire
way of life on a reluctant majority, with new forms of government.

In the 1970s and 1980s there were posters everywhere in Britain
with messages such as 'No to Conservatives, Labour or Liberals,
yes to Socialist Workers Party' – the SWP was and is on the extreme
left. Today those posters are more likely to say 'No to the rest, yes
to Islam'.

In the meantime, Arab states continue to live in uneasy tension.
While the extremes of moral code and dress in some countries

are being challenged and replaced by a more moderate form of fundamentalism, Islamic politics will become more assertive and structured in thinking about global issues.

Expect huge efforts to promote greater understanding between Islamic nations and those with a Judaeo-Christian heritage. Expect similar efforts to try to obtain a lasting settlement between Israel and the Palestinians, in a wider search for global stability, following repeated episodes of extreme violence, and retaliation on both sides.

Expect continued debate over the so-called 'clash of civilisations', often dominated by ill-informed and arrogant voices. The 'clash' will often be represented as a one-dimensional conflict between Islamic and Judaeo-Christian cultures, but in many areas the followers of these world religions will discover they have more in common with each other than with secular humanists, especially over ethical issues.

Christian politics

Christians are also becoming politically aggressive, not only through single-issue campaigns over issues such as abortion and euthanasia, but through organising the beginnings of new parties such as the Christian Democratic Party. The Catholic church continues to encourage action – for example over abortion.

Expect to see further contrasts, for example in the battle over schools in the US – where school prayers are banned, but where Christian schools will go on growing, and where more than 2 million children are now educated at home, usually for religious reasons, to protect them from secular and potentially disruptive influences. Expect to see America divided by new faith–government partnerships, using the Church as a delivery mechanism for drug rehabilitation and a host of other social programmes funded by the state.

Whether you are a follower of Jesus as I am, or of Mohammed, or of Buddha or the patterns in the stars, whether you are a devout Jew, believe in Karma or reincarnation, or some other life-force, or in nothing at all, spirituality will be a central issue shaping values, politics and people movements, a dominant influence for the next 100 years.

CENSORSHIP

Censorship and the media

Islam is highly insistent that what is holy should be respected, as seen in angry global protests following publication of offensive cartoons in Denmark. Christianity has been more docile in the past 50 years but is becoming less so. Hence the largest ever protest against any film when in August 1988 *The Last Temptation Of Christ* was released at Universal City, California. The protests were dismissed in a statement: 'No one sect or coalition has the power to set boundaries around each person's freedom to explore religious and philosophical questions.' Yet the same company had earlier decided not to film Salman Rushdie's *Satanic Verses*. This kind of double standard will not be sustainable, and elements in the Christian community can be expected to adopt a harder line in future.

The media always tend to push out the boundaries and hence are first in line for flak. So animal rights activists attacked Disney in 1990, demanding that 'anti-wolf' suggestions be removed from *White Anger*. Disney was also forced to print a disclaimer that 'there is no documented case in North America of a healthy wolf or pack of wolves attacking a human'. Even the cartoon *Beauty and the Beast* attracted similar pro-wolf protests. More recently, southern Baptists initiated a boycott of Disney over benefits offered to gay partners and for allowing their parks to be used for 'Gay Days'.

Expect plenty more big fights between religious groups (especially Christian ones in the US) and the media. For a variety of reasons, there is a huge gulf between those in the entertainment industry and the general public when it comes to religion. While 78 per cent of the US public pray at least once a week and more than 40 per cent attend weekly services, a survey of 104 of the most influential leaders of creative TV in the US found that 93 per cent seldom or never attended a church service and 45 per cent claimed no religious affiliation whatsoever.

Even more striking, many of those who shape popular culture have personally rejected the church. The same survey found that while 93 per cent said they had received a 'religious upbringing', only 7 per cent were currently 'regular participants' in church or synagogue services. Thus the media culture and conscience clash will continue, not as a deliberate conspiracy against belief but as an inevitable expression of this huge gap in world-view.

Censorship and the Net
With pornography and gambling together accounting for between 10 and 30 per cent of all online trade, regulation will be a key target. Yet the web also helps guarantee freedom.

Censorship and link to undesirable behaviour
A huge battle will be waged over media freedom in the next two decades. The liberal trend towards total relaxation of controls will be more than offset by a conservative trend towards nannying the public. Both extremes will leave the majority of the public bemused: they will want changes to reduce access by children to adult-rated material, yet greater freedoms for consenting adults. The digital age will enable both requests to be fulfilled – in theory. In practice, every control will be subverted by adults and older teenagers who are lazy, or irresponsible. Controls will also be undermined by lightning advances in the web world which will ensure that for several years to come any child who is sufficiently knowledgeable can access just about any film or other media he or she wishes. Expect the censorship issue to grow in importance with ever greater worries about the effects of over-exposure on a rising generation. Then will come a revolt, spearheaded by the Islamic community and Christian alliances, seeking global agreement as far as possible.

Such a religious movement will be opposed by predominantly secular groups with claims that media output is pure fantasy for the most part, and incapable of altering behaviour. More importantly, the claim will continue to be made that actions such as rape or violence are entirely unrelated to media output. The counterclaim will grow stronger by the month, that the media has a mild influence on almost everyone, a significant influence on a few and a major effect on a small but all-important minority, who go on to commit major crimes.

Television has only been with us to any degree since the 1950s and relatively uncensored TV for less than a generation. Video recorders have been the property of the masses for even less time. Society has yet to come to terms with these media channels and it will take until 2015 or longer for the verdict to come, but when it does it may spring with a vengeance, with powerful government backing in several continents. There could be huge economic pressures on broadcasters, forced by advertisers who are themselves under pressure from consumers and ethical investors.

In the meantime expect to hear more voices like that of Janet Daly writing in the *Daily Telegraph*. She wrote that even if the link were unproven, 'it is wrong to base a species of entertainment on terror and the inflicting of pain. That is all that needs to be said and that should be enough.'

Right in the middle of a puritan swing, expect to see strong liberal voices arguing for yet more relaxation, talking about a return to the Dark Ages. The process of 'cleaning up' has already begun as seen in the US ban in 2006 of online payments for gambling sites. In a single week an entire US industry sector closed down, wiping billions off share prices of online betting companies.

Our world will become increasingly one of extremes

Elections will be won and lost on issues like these. We all want a market economy, but at the same time think that there should be justice, fairness and equality of opportunity in a compassionate world where health and education are available to all. But there's more to life than these things alone. We could have all these – as most people to a large degree already do in many nations – yet find we are in some kind of living hell, with dark forces (some would say market forces) ripping the heart out of community life and millions of miserable people

Media influence is undeniable. The whole advertising industry is based on the fact that media messages change what people do. Expect a growing number of cases where there are widely publicised links between a gruesome slaying and obsession with a certain film or TV character. Expect the call for controls to grow louder, and also a rise in frustration levels as people discover that in a globalised world, international agreement is needed to regulate satellite channels in particular, as well as web TV.

Media ownership

Expect increasing protests and government worries over the centralised control of globalised media empires able to pump out vast amounts of propaganda on particular issues when needed. People like Rupert Murdoch will come in for a lot of criticism as their highly successful empires control more and more traditional media channels.

However, the protesters will have to contend with the argument that the increasing glut of channels, together with the web, also dilutes power. Indeed, politicians and advertisers alike will have to work harder than ever in tomorrow's world to catch a nation's attention in a way which would have been comparatively easy in the 1990s.

Battles over software will be at the centre of the future media wars, with decoder boxes at the heart. Which decoder do you have? Whose software are you using? Which cable network serves your home?

A NEW WORLD RELIGION?

Expect to see all major world religions continue to reinvent themselves, as their traditional teachings are reinterpreted in a very different age and culture from any ever seen before. The roots of the Christian faith have remained virtually unchanged over 2,000 years but expressions, understanding and practice have varied greatly. For example, in Christianity expect to see new mixtures of the contemporary (attempts at ultra-cultural relevance, youth churches and other experiments) with the traditional and mystical. Tradition fuses our present experience with the living spiritual echoes of worshippers over centuries. Symbolism will become very fashionable as a means to express depths beyond the trivia of words. Life-changing faith will spread, connecting to emotion, adapting to culture, and then altering it significantly.

A totally globalised world will create a 'market' or a vacuum for a new world religion, which will feed into the aspirations of the third millennium. We could well see a world-recognised prophet emerge over the next few decades with charisma, dynamism and teachings which capture the global imagination. The biggest issue will be truth: is there such a thing? While the great religions such as Judaism, Christianity and Islam are rooted in historical events and proclaim timeless truth about an unchanging God, offering exclusive understanding of him, new-age beliefs in the late twentieth century have borrowed heavily from some aspects of Hinduism, which emphasises a more general approach to truth, and a fluid ethical framework without absolutes.

A new world religion is unlikely to be just more of the same; in other words it will not be just a mish-mash of beliefs centred on a conviction that there is no such thing as absolute truth.

In a constantly changing world, certainty about ultimate issues such as personal destiny becomes increasingly important. That is the appeal of fundamentalism. Expect therefore that a new world religion will be marked by dogmatic teaching and a claim of exclusivity and superiority to all previously understood truths about God. Expect the leading prophet of such religion to offer 'the final revelation', the missing pieces of understanding of perfect knowledge that humankind has not before been ready to receive. Such a prophet will promise that humankind is 'coming of age' and is only now able to receive the truth. The claim will be that all the great religions pointed in part but did not provide the complete picture. Such a prophet could sweep millions of adherents of other religions, including Christianity, into a new religious movement. And it could all happen quite rapidly.

A NEW WORLD ORDER

With so many problems in the world, will we see a new world order? Is there a way of rolling together the authority of more than two hundred governments and thousands of sub-national governments worldwide? The British Empire was built on the belief that world government could bring huge benefits to humankind, before it dissolved into a Commonwealth of 51 states. In one sense a new world order is growing by default, as we have seen, for example, over the proliferation of environmental treaties, and the global struggle against terrorism. Yet institutional rule is weak and weakening.

More international treaties will create global control

The more international treaties there are, the more an informal global government emerges. Expect more agreements like Kyoto (global warming), START (Strategic Arms Reduction Treaties), the Chemical Weapons Convention and the Open Skies Treaty. Similar agreements on a wide range of issues will attract more than 170 nations as signatories. The United Nations was founded to 'save succeeding generations from the scourge of war' and 'to reaffirm faith in fundamental human rights, in the dignity and value of the human person'.

The real trouble is that, as we saw over the Iraqi conflict, UN member nations are unclear what they want the UN to do and how it should perform those roles. Peacekeeping has become politically and practically dangerous. The emphasis has switched to building economic security. The UN council is unlikely to embrace another Iraq or Somalia or Bosnia with great enthusiasm, but countries which stop in-fighting will be offered plenty of peace-building incentives. The UN will help with elections, the judiciary, education, health, government infrastructure, agriculture and trade.

One of the roles the UN performs best is the preparation of the world's weakest economies for foreign and internal investment. The great problem is that the nations in the General Assembly have widely differing opinions and agendas. Each is clear about what it wants but there is no agreement.

Expect the fall-out from the Iraq war to be profound, with huge efforts made to try to reintegrate the US into a consensual approach to world affairs. Expect the US to pursue dialogue while retaining right to independent action on all matters of national interest: a stance which will provoke growing anger and resentment around the world. But the trend is clear: global governance will be essential to our peaceful and prosperous future. The unprecedented spirit of collaboration that has emerged since the collapse of communism will deepen despite crises and setbacks. A key and increasingly urgent global challenge will be finding a solution to the Israeli/Palestinian issues of security, justice and peace. This will be important in reducing a major focus of intense anger among many millions of people.

Code of conduct

Despite differing positions on many issues, there is growing agreement on an international code of conduct. Indeed, international trade is impossible without it. World trade requires basic principles: integrity, honesty, obligations, mutual respect.

International courts

You cannot trade unless there is trust that both parties will honour the agreement. There are rules to the game, and those who play are expected to keep to them.

Voluntary codes of practice and self-regulation will not be enough. International laws will be needed. While individual nations may reform their own legal systems, another level will be created. The beginnings are already here: for example, the trial for war crimes of national leaders in one country by a court composed of other countries' representatives.

Expect to see a growing number of countries sign up to an international court, able to hear cases which are almost impossible for any single country to deal with. At present attempts to create global law for a global village are stopped before they have even started in many cases by extradition procedures, which are usually activated only if both countries accept that a crime has been committed, and respect each other's legal systems.

Regional law courts are well established, in the EU for example. Expect supra-regional courts to be dealing with a wide variety of international crime cases by 2015. History shows that law and order is imposed most rapidly where there is a lack of it. Therefore these new powers will be agreed by nations as a matter of urgent necessity, when faced with their own impotence.

Cyberspace is a country needing government of its own

One interesting area will be laws governing the Internet and cyberspace. It is already becoming obvious through disputes over the naming of sites that nations are losing control to a new nation, to a new territory altogether. As we have seen, whole communities are developing a complete trading environment and cyberspace is almost tax free.

Until early 1998, no one in the world could get a name approved (i.e. an address on the web) without a US agency authorising it. Endless rows broke out as companies in different parts of the world with the same name fought to use their name in the cyber-village. Which company should win? The first to register? But is that unfair when a tiny company has won global cyber-rights to a name that is also that of a multinational known the world over? Should the US always decide? Clearly it was nonsense to give so much power to one nation, but what would replace it? From where should cyberspace be run?

At present, cyberspace is run by a benevolent but ineffective dictatorship, created mainly by US agencies. This cannot and will not last, nor will any other benevolent dictatorship of non-elected, unrepresentative authority. Expect calls for democracy in cyberspace with electronic votes for every cyber-citizen (e-mail user) who registers to vote. Then we will see elected cyber-government, with legislative powers backed by a moral imperative. Of course those powers will operate only inside the cyber-world, but they will offer a more effective means to tackle email spam, fraud, extreme pornography and web-linked child abuse.

GLOBAL GOVERNMENT

In summary then, expect to see various expressions of global governance emerge and co-align into the first stages of a new world order over the next few decades, with components derived from all the above. The beginnings will be hardly noticeable, but the technology of tomorrow could give it remarkable strength. Globalised structures to regulate a globalised world – although at every stage construction will be slowed by tribalism and other radical forces.

Expect periods of intense negotiation to define global ethics in more detail, whether attempts to create a total global ban on human cloning, a response to international terrorism or ethnic genocide, limits on global monopolies, or world agreements on slavery, child labour, work practices and other issues of human rights and responsibilities. Many issues will be polarised between emerging and developed nations. All these debates will be increasingly influenced by a post-millennial rethink in wealthier nations, by a generation no longer impressed by speed, urbanisation, material wealth and globalisation. A generation which itself is becoming radical, ethical and spiritually aware.

CHALLENGES TO MANAGEMENT

Where do your ethics come from?

- What are the key ethical issues facing your company in the next decade?
- Where do your corporate ethics come from? Shareholder views? The board? The chairman? Each region or department? Informal chats with colleagues at conferences?
- Do you have an ethical forum, committee or think tank?
- How do you decide when company ethics need to change with the times, for example over corporate governance?

How well protected are you against civil litigation?

- Class-action suits are expensive to deal with and can tie up a major corporation for five years or more, with a damaging effect on company valuation and stock prices.
- How well protected are you against group actions?
- How sensitised is your legal department to which angry groups might take your company on in the third millennium?

Political correctness

- Who decides corporate policy regarding political correctness, e.g. the use of language, sexist terms such as 'chairman', or are these things decided chaotically and inconsistently at hundreds of different levels?
- Are you culturally sensitised to where it really matters and where it does not?
- Have you resolved the globalisation conflicts where a global approach may be disastrous in, say, Saudi Arabia on the one hand and the US on the other?

Motivation

- How able are you to motivate staff who are not so interested in more money?
- How are you going to retain the best who don't need you and want to work under their own terms, perhaps contracting to you part-time or more flexibly, maybe for less cash?
- Is your personnel policy geared up for this growing social revolution?
- Have you fallen into the trap of encouraging a culture where people who are at work from 7 am till 10 pm are seen as 'better' than those working fewer hours?
- How can you improve morale and job satisfaction, helping staff to feel that in some small way they are helping to build a better world?
- How can you help create a feeling of family, of belonging?
- What about the balance between work, leisure and family in your own life – are you a model worth following?

Reaction against constant change

- Are you ready for a world where constant change is seen as far less attractive than stability and constancy?
- What will that do to your corporate culture?
- How can you help people find security in things that do not change, to help them cope with changes that do have to be made?

Respect for relationships

- How friendly is your company to men and women who have just got married, or have young children, or who are fighting to save their marriages, or who have sick and dependent relatives at home?
- Is your corporate culture likely to increase marital happiness and child well-being – or contribute to break-up and distress?
- Does your company policy reflect the importance of happy home life in obtaining the greatest productivity from employees?

Spirituality
- ◆ Is your company sensitised to changing cultural influences in many nations as a result of a revival of commitment to religion?

. . . .
PERSONAL CHALLENGES
. . . .

Ethical challenges touch sensitive areas in our personal lives. Here are some important questions that many senior executives are asking, as they grapple with life in an increasingly fast, urbanised, tribal, globalised, radical and chaotic world.

Giving your values high priority
- ◆ How are you going to thrive in a world which is fast, urban, tribal, universal and radical?
- ◆ How do you want your future to be different from the past?
- ◆ How much time have you given to working out what motivates you, what your own values are?
- ◆ What holds your life together? Is that reflected in the workplace or is there a danger of leaving your values behind?
- ◆ How motivated are you by your current work situation?
- ◆ Do you work for an organisation which reflects your own values?
- ◆ If not, how important is that to you?
- ◆ Do you need to look for another job?
- ◆ When are your personal values more important than promotion, e.g. time with family, less mobility, honesty and integrity?

Upwards or downwards mobility?
- ◆ Is your priority for the next five years upwards or downwards mobility, or to stay about the same?
- ◆ Have you considered creative opportunities to work in different ways – for example with job sharing?

Consistency
- ◆ Is your own management style consistent with your values?
- ◆ Is your lifestyle consistent with your own values?

Stability
- In a world which is constantly changing, which parts of your own life are going to stay the same?

Relationships
- Is there more to life than work for you?
- Is that reflected in how you live?
- How balanced are the various areas of your time and energy?
- How will your children remember you when you have gone?
- How are you preparing them for the future?
- Are you happy in your relationships?
- What can you do to improve the situation?

Purpose
- What is the purpose and meaning of your life?
- How are you helping to build a better world?
- Do you have a sense of direction other than merely pushing doors, seizing opportunities and enjoying what life offers?
- What do you want to achieve?
- What are your personal aims and are they realistic, achievable, measurable?
- How will you recognise your own success?

Spirituality
- What does faith mean to you?
- How important is spirituality to you?
- Is this an area you want to invest in?
- When work and money have gone, what will you have left?
- Are you giving yourself enough personal space?
- Do you have a sense of personal destiny?
- Are you spending time with people who have a spirituality you respect?

Afterword

Turning the cube – Optimist or Pessimist?

So, then, these are the six faces of the future. As I lecture about the future around the world people often ask me if I am an optimist or a pessimist. Surely, they say, the future contains so many disturbing challenges that it must worry you. The truth is that I am excited about the future and pleased to be alive at this time in history. The potential of technology is intoxicating, while the moral and environmental challenges we face are considerable. The choices are for good or for evil: to fulfil our own God-given destiny or to abandon the great design for living, the road to chaos and destruction.

It's impossible to keep all six faces of the future in view at once, and some are more important than others. But all are vital to keep in view from time to time. Some are related as pairs and seen together: Fast and Urban, Radical and Ethical. Tribal and Universal are opposites and hard to view at the same time.

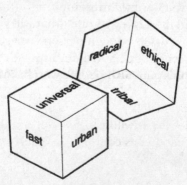

The interesting thing about the cube is that it creates two different worlds. The world most executives live in most of the time is fast, urban and universal. A rapidly changing, globalised village. However, there is another side, a world which is tribal, radical and very ethical. It may involve fewer people, but how many tribal, radical and ethical people do you need to change a society?

When I pose that question to high flyers from all over the world they almost always come back with a similar answer: very few. You don't need many radical activists in a population to change its values, to alter government policy, to make a difference to how corporations behave. Most CEOs, chairmen, board members and senior managers would say that probably less than 2 per cent of the population with tribal, radical and ethical outlooks could be enough to affect a society profoundly.

We can argue about the exact percentage, but one thing is clear: while it is right for organisations to focus mainly on the obvious and immediate challenges of a fast, urban and universal world, they also need to keep turning the cube – not tossing it at random, but from one side to the other.

As someone who shares a common desire to build a better and more sustainable kind of world, to challenge values, to provoke justice, fairness and a compassionate use of technology, for the benefit of the whole of humanity, I find it very encouraging that the doors of influence are so open. I enjoy the fast, urban and universal world but am disturbed by its challenges. Never before in human history have we needed ethics as much today to see us through. Either we take hold of the future or the future will take hold of us.

. . . .
TEN CONCLUSIONS FOR MANAGEMENT
. . . .

1 Prepare for the unexpected
The future will deliver us wild cards which could win us the game or wipe us out. That means contingency plans and flexibility.

2 Faster reaction times

Everything needs to be geared to rapid response from top to bottom. If you think things are changing fast, get ready for double and treble the present speed of change.

3 Flatter structures

Pyramids can't cope with post-millennial life. Either get flatter or get smaller. Build associations, franchises, partnerships, co-operative alliances. Decentralise and empower.

4 Teams and partners

Third millennial life is too specialised to have everything done in-house. Teams and partners keep everything alive.

5 The global village

Globalisation has only just begun. The millennial generation is growing up in a global village that we have only seen the foundations of. A key challenge will be to shrink management lines geographically using technology. Those who can't cope with virtual communications just won't survive. Be a responsible global citizen.

6 Cultural Sensitivity

Globalisation will mean more cultural sensitivity not less. The oldest mistake is to think that other people think like you because they speak the same language.

7 Investing in technology

Information tech, biotech – use it, control it, make it happen. Select people who like technology, who are excited by it, who have the creativity to adapt around these new tools.

8 Creating family

In this fractured and dislocated world people still spend more time working for you than doing any other single activity, so take care of them. Make them feel special. Make them family, with a sense of identity, value and belonging.

9 Purpose and meaning

Help your team find ways to feel that they are building a better world. Who wants to spend their entire lives doing something that adds no value to anyone, has no purpose and no meaning?

10 Leadership will be everything

No amount of committees, strategies or parallel plans will help one jot without dynamic, visionary leadership. So how do you know if you are a leader? How do you spot leaders under you and over you? Ask one simple question: are people following you? Who are they following?

Leaders don't lead by position, they lead by inspiring trust and confidence. Leading through fear of punishment invariably results in disaster, with resentment and rebellion sowing the seeds of destruction. Leading through dynamic vision and motivation invariably results in energy and progress.

. . . .
TEN CONCLUSIONS FOR INDIVIDUALS
. . . .

1 Prepare for the unexpected

Your whole world is going to be changed – now is the time to prepare. You have already begun that process by reading this book and working through some of the action points. You can help shape and build a better world.

2 Plan to react faster

Some of the greatest opportunities can flash by in a moment. That means thinking things through now, and discussing possibilities with others – for example your partner. Remember: take hold of the future, or the future will take hold of you.

3 Invest in technology

One of the best investments you can make is in powerful personal technology. Get familiar with what networks can do for you and keep watching – the digital society is growing faster than you think.

4 Keep well informed

Those who stay ahead of the future will be exceptionally well informed. So how do you manage this without adding to information overload? Read a weekly summary such as *The Economist* together with a couple of quality daily newspapers. Make sure that you regularly skim-read a couple of popular computer magazines.

5 Stretch your horizon

Take opportunities for executive training. Just the experience of meeting others will stimulate fresh thinking, as will the presentations. Consider your longer-term future.

6 Think laterally

Most people are blind to their own potential. Employers in future are going to need some very unusual combinations of skills and backgrounds. So keep an open mind about the sort of jobs you could go for. Keep building on what you have but keep broadening too. The next step up could involve a sideways move.

7 Make time for people

In ten or twenty years' time the world will have rushed by and all you will be left with are memories, money and relationships. Relationships give you people to share memories with or to enjoy what you have. At the end of life, relationships are all you have left. Invest in people.

8 Be who you are

With so many conflicting pressures and events, be who you are. Don't let the system clone you into conformity. Stick by what you believe and what you know to be true. People will respect you for it. Take time to reflect. Explore your own spirituality and faith.

9 Enjoy today

You are the most important person affecting your future. Life can only be lived once. Be kind to yourself. Enjoy each day. Seize the moment before it fades. Today is the day of opportunity.

10 Celebrate the past

Celebrate the past, with its highs and lows, the good and bad times, the triumphs and disasters. It has all shaped the present, made you what you are, and your past will help you understand your future.

Take hold of your future – or the future will take hold of you.

Appendix

Measuring your FUTURE

So how can you measure up your organisation against the Six Faces of the Future? How can you assess your own strengths and weaknesses in tomorrow's world? I am grateful to David Stanley's imaginative help in developing this simple 'Star Treatment' method of Futuring your organisation. The six faces of the cube are, as we have seen earlier in this book, weighted in different ways according to time, place and industry. But if we squash the cube flat and make a circle we can begin to make a Future-Chart as a measuring device.

The technique is simple and fast: mark on each of the six lines how strong you think your organisation is in the six key areas: FAST, URBAN, TRIBAL, UNIVERSAL, RADICAL and ETHICAL. When the points are joined up you get a unique shape. Every industry has its own preferable shape – for example, an online bank is strongest shaped as a sword, an ethical investment fund is strongest as a butterfly.

When you and your team have FUTURED your own organisation – do the same for your competitors. The final stage is to re-FUTURE your organisation as you would like it to be in five years' time. This can then help locate areas where the most change is needed and enable a focused analysis of key areas for transition. Of course, this is an empirical 'feel' and a more comprehensive FUTURE audit is a major task, based on a comprehensive survey, using a calibrated series of formal questions and answers to identify where the organisation is at each element on the chart.

See typical industry profiles below – used as worked examples. Of course every executive in every company will have their own view as to the FUTURE rating of their organisation, but the discussions generated are very valuable in identifying strengths and weaknesses.

THE BASIC GRID

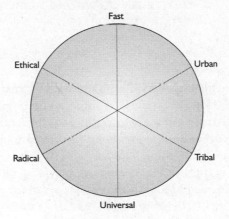

The typical and successful e-bank is strong on Fast and on Universal, but weak almost everywhere else because the other faces are less important, and energy directed there may adversely affect the core business.

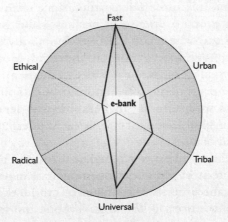

In contrast, an ethical investment fund is usually based in one country – partly because ethics vary so much with culture. So it scores high for Tribal, and also for Urban as it benefits from factors such as the ageing population. Of course it also rates high on Radical and Ethical, but not on Fast because ethical funds are usually by their nature cautious, reflective, safe and secure in approach.

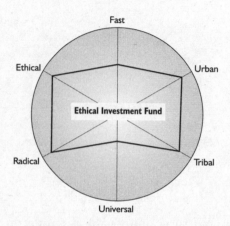

The coffee wholesaler is in a mixed position typically with a range of complex issues to face. Coffee drinking scores high under Urban as a social institution, dependent on demographics and fashion. It is also a Tribal drink, since it is usually shared in a family or group of friends or business colleagues. Coffee is a global business – the second largest commodity traded in the world after oil – so scores high on Universal. However, coffee scores low (usually) on Radical, since activists are successfully damaging the image of the coffee industry as exploiting the poor. It also scores low on Ethical, since the industry seems unable to form a clear ethical framework for what it does, adding to the Radical vulnerability.

Although the initial process is informal and can be carried out rapidly in the context of a workshop, a rigorous methodology can be applied to the process. The first step is to identify the vision-holders and influencers in the organisations and to bring them together.

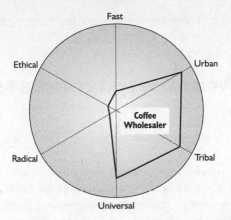

FUTURE VISION

◆ Describe where you want to be using the FUTURE framework.
◆ Create your ideal star shape – recognising that you can't be best at everything.
◆ Compare with star shapes of competitors.
◆ Workshop with key decision-makers to identify five key factors for the company's future success, coming out of each of the six faces. Out of these 30 issues, select 10 as the most important and split into two: high and medium impact.

CURRENT STATE

◆ Analysing surveys of opinion-shapers and other target groups to see how well the company shapes up to the challenges as identified. e.g. How good are we at encouraging flexible home-working?
◆ Combining these with other data gathered from various sources to help establish key target areas for action, which can then feed into an effective change-management process.
◆ Sharing the results of the FUTURE process and the emerging new vision, plus the need for action.
◆ Following through with measurables and strategic planning/ action.
◆ A result should be that the FUTURE shape of the organisation changes.

Acknowledgements

I am indebted to the many thousands of senior executives from over 50 nations and every business sector who have shaped this fourth edition by their participation in presentations on the Six Faces of the Future around the world. Their personal insights during discussions in seminars, workshops and conferences, and over lunches and many dinners, have been crucial in better understanding the way in which their own industries and nations are heading. I am also grateful to those in many emerging nations who have taught me so much about changes in their countries, in connection with the work of the AIDS agency ACET.

I am particularly grateful to Professor Prabhu Guptara, at Wolfsberg UBS, whose unfailing encouragement led directly to the publication of this book. I am also grateful to a large number of other people for their perspectives and comments. Thanks to Jonathan Rice, Shirley Bray, Martin Roder, Penny Williams and Elizabeth Dixon who all played vital roles in research, checking text and editing.

I am also indebted to a host of great thinkers, debaters, speakers and writers whose work over the years has permeated my own thinking and influenced my evolving view of the world, consciously or unconsciously. I owe a lot to such people as Nicholas Negroponte, Charles Handy, Lynda Gratton, John Naisbitt, Peter Cochrane, Kenichi Ochmae, C.K. Prahalad, Fons Trompenaars, David Smith and the team of the Global Future Forum. David Stanley also made a very useful contribution to the method for futuring an organisation described in the Appendix.

I am also grateful to many others who have encouraged, shaped and influenced my life: Sheila my wife and best friend for more than 30 years, my parents and many fellow travellers along the way such as Steve Clifford and Gerald Coates.

Statistics and other important data are from published government and other official sources, as well as from those working at the cutting edge of future research into areas that will change our world.

Index